My Never Ending Journey of Life

Lance Garbutt

GOWOR
INTERNATIONAL PUBLISHING

My Never Ending Journey of Life © Lance Garbutt 2015

www.neverendingjourneyoflife.com.au

The moral rights of Lance Garbutt to be identified as the author of this work have been asserted in accordance with the Copyright Act 1968.

First published in Australia 2015 by Gowor International Publishing

www.goworinternationalpublishing.com

ISBN 978-0-9925258-9-7

Any opinions expressed in this work are exclusively those of the author and are not necessarily the views held or endorsed by Lance Garbutt.

All rights reserved. No part of this publication may be reproduced or transmitted by any means, electronic, photocopying or otherwise, without prior written permission of the author.

Disclaimer

All the information, techniques, skills and concepts contained within this publication are of the nature of general comment only, and are not in any way recommended as individual advice. The intent is to offer a variety of information to provide a wider range of choices now and in the future, recognising that we all have widely diverse circumstances and viewpoints. Should any reader choose to make use of the information herein, this is their decision, and the author and publisher/s do not assume any responsibilities whatsoever under any conditions or circumstances. The author does not take responsibility for the business, financial, personal or other success, results or fulfilment upon the readers' decision to use this information. It is recommended that the reader obtain their own independent advice.

I dedicate this book to my mother and father, my past self and who I have become in the past few years. I would also like to dedicate this book to anyone who has been through similar experiences and is looking for a great new start in life.

A Personal Note From The Publisher . . .

Hi there!

As the Founder of Gowor International Publishing, my publishing house, I make it part of my practice to offer a personal review for my authors about their book. The reason I do this is so that you, as the reader, can glean a further understanding into why this book is about to become a valuable part of your life.

Lance is one of the most inspiring, strong and big-hearted people I have met. I remember our first conversation very clearly. Lance opened up and shared the story about where he has come from and how he made an incredible and courageous decision to change his life and make the most of being alive. His commitment and dedication to doing exactly that ever since he made that decision – the turning point – has already touched the lives of many, many people through living his enormous, diverse and exciting bucket list life.

Lance sees life as it really is: a great adventure. He takes every opportunity to see or do something new to keep his soul alive and thriving and his heart fulfilled, and now he is passing that infectious spirit on to other people through this very book (which of course is an item on his bucket list). Lance gives his life it all more than most people I know. He holds nothing back. He goes after what he dreams. And he cares that other people do the same. His presence has touched my life in a meaningful way and I will always remember Lance as I forge forwards on my own never-ending journey of life.

May the life-loving spirit of Lance touch your life as you read this book and go about living the life that you have dreamed of!

With inspiration,
Emily Gowor
Founder of Gowor International Publishing

Contents

Chapter 1: Life: A Journey of Progression 9
Chapter 2: Proud Achievements 18
Chapter 3: Life's Memories and Experiences in Someone Else's Shoes .. 20
Chapter 4: Random Acts of Kindness (Good Deeds) 22
Chapter 5: Circle of Influences – People to Meet In Life 25
Chapter 6: Workout Challenges 27
Chapter 7: Money and Finance and Things I Want to Buy 29
Chapter 8: Running, Walking, Swimming and Bike Riding Events 31
Chapter 9: National Parks and National Beauty Worldwide 46
Chapter 10: Rainforests, Mountain Ranges, Craters and Deserts 51
Chapter 11: Board Games, Backyard Games, Puzzles and Toys 54
Chapter 12: My Home Lifestyle Dreams 57
Chapter 14: Theme Parks and Renowned Rides Wordwide 58
Chapter 15: Zoos Worldwide 60
Chapter 16: Health, Beauty Therapy and Body Imaging 66
Chapter 17: Comedians of the World 68
Chapter 18: Memorials of the World and Days of Remembrance "Lest We Forget" 71
Chapter 19: Festival Events Wordwide 73
Chapter 20: Music Festival Events 76
Chapter 21: Live Bands and Singer Performances 79
Chapter 22: Top DJs of the World 81
Chapter 23: Photo Opportunities 83
Chapter 24: Career Achievements 85
Chapter 25: Live Sporting Events 86
Chapter 26: Expos and Family Events 89
Chapter 27: Historic Houses, Cottages, Buildings and Museums 90

Chapter 28: Caving Experiences 98
Chapter 29: Art Galleries and Famous Artworks 100
Chapter 30: Mountain Peak Challenges 102
Chapter 31: Animal Encounters.. 104
Chapter 32: Social Media 116
Chapter 33: Play Musical Instruments... 117
Chapter 34: Food Challenges, Baking and Making Food, Restaurants and Desired Tastes.. 119
Chapter 35: Camping and the Outdoors... 123
Chapter 36: Find, Search, Seek and Discover 124
Chapter 37: Astrology and the Stars.. 125
Chapter 38: Bridges/Dams and Famous Roads of the World 129
Chapter 39: Australia's Big Statues.. 133
Chapter 40: Visit the Seven Continents... 136
Chapter 41: Visit All States/Territories and External Territories of Australia 137
Chapter 42: Visit All States of America 156
Chapter 43: Countries of the World To Visit.. 158
Chapter 44: List of Sports To Participate In Around the World............ 162
Chapter 45: Video Games.. 165
Chapter 46: Visit Famous Beaches, Lakes, Rivers and Waterfalls 179
Chapter 47: Books Collection and Goals 184
Chapter 48: Express Yourself, Creativity, Learning Skills and Education 186
Chapter 49: Charities.. 189
Chapter 50: Dancing Lifestyle 190
Chapter 51: Martial Art Skills.. 192
Chapter 52: Aircraft Flying Experiences.. 193
Chapter 53: Dress Up Experiences 197
Chapter 54: Driving Experiences 199
Chapter 55: Visit the Seas and Oceans of the World........................... 201
Chapter 56: Drink Tasting 203

Chapter 57: Markets and Gardens 204
Chapter 58: Hotels, Motels and Boatels 207
Chapter 59: Castles, Palaces, Towers, Ancient Ruins and Abbeys 210
Chapter 60: Scenic Tours 215
Chapter 61: Spiritual Guidance 216
Chapter 62: Churches, Cemeteries, Cathedrals, Tombs, Temples and Ghost Tours 217
Chapter 63: Movies List 221
Chapter 64: Water Adventures 232
Chapter 65: Flying Adventures 235
Chapter 66: Sand Adventures 237
Chapter 67: Land Adventures 238
Chapter 68: Snow and Ice Adventures 244
Chapter 69: Space Adventures 246
Chapter 70: Train Adventures 247
Chapter 71: Iconic Landmarks of the World 249
Chapter 72: Live Entertainment 253
Chapter 73: Personal Lifestyle and Iidiotic Stuff! 255
Chapter 74: Clocks and Lighthouses 259
Chapter 75: Elevators and Steps 262
My Inspirational Accomplishments 264
Follow Me On My Journey 271
Acknowledgments 272
About the Author 273
Your Bucket List 274

Chapter 1:
Life: A Journey of Progression

"In the end, it's not the years in your life that count. It's the life in your years."

Abraham Lincoln

Firstly, I would like to introduce myself. My name is Lance Garbutt and this is the story of my life, the challenges I have gone through and the lifestyle I now live. I am 29 years old, living the life of a bucket lister and enjoying every moment of it. I wish to share my journey as I have developed into a stronger person and living a life many people dream of. This is my journey that never stops: an endless journey of discovering what I'm capable of in my lifetime and doing everything possible to give everything a go in life. Enjoy life because you never know what day will be your last.

It's my intention that you can use this book as a source of inspiration for your own bucket list. You can find ideas for living a bucket list lifestyle through every section of the book. Our lives are meant to be lived – enjoy every moment. You can have fun; no matter if it's something small or big off your list, enjoy doing it. With so many ideas to be found in one place, you, as the reader, can join in and carry the book wherever you go, ticking off your own personal lists with the opportunity of using the ideas I have come up with and making them your own. Tick off the square boxes in the book of everything you have completed in your lifetime! It's never too early or late to live a dream-filled bucket list lifestyle, so why not start today? Enjoy life and encourage others to do the same.

I aim to help others realise their potential in life and how they can create their own dreams, travel the world and run the race they always wanted to – anything they put their mind to, they can achieve. I want my readers to enjoy their lives. I can tell you now my weekends are packed full of bucket list ideas, and I achieve them every weekend. I want others to have an amazing life and help them realise enjoyment in life is at their doorstep. You don't have to spend a lot of money and you don't need to travel too far to achieve something you always wanted to do. Many things you may have already done in life but there is so much more. I know from experience the world is full of possibilities; my bucket list keeps growing and I can't wait to inspire others to read it and join in the fun this world has to offer. I would love so much, and it would make my dreams come true, if I had people walking up to me and thanking me for changing their life for the better or a person asking me for an autograph because I have impacted their life incredibly. Life is amazing and my aim is to help others realise that the world holds many opportunities to develop themselves.

My inspiration to live a bucket list lifestyle came after a few months of saving money. With the changes in my lifestyle and all the money I saved from bad habits, I wondered what possibilities the world could offer to help me enjoy my life. Virtually most of my life I was a video gamer and not paying attention to the outside world. It gave me the opportunity to sit down and pull apart ideas and brainstorm things. While many others were out there enjoying and sharing their life stories with their grandkids and family members, I thought to myself, I want to be the same. I don't want to be that grandfather or family member that tells stories only about video games. When the time comes and my eulogy is read, all it says is "This man was a great man – all he did in life was play video games". I want to be that man they say enjoyed his life, lived for every moment, inspired many people and helped a lot of people in need. He was a man with a mission in life and knew exactly what he wanted in his life. His message has been read all over the world and he is leaving a great legacy for his family name.

Make your dreams become a reality. Only you can believe in yourself and take any dream you desire to the next level. Don't let any ideas drift away and go to waste; so many people waste their time living day-by-day with boring lives and, at the end of the day, take all their ideas and knowledge with them to the graveyard. Unfortunately, this is the truth. If more people realised their potential, anything in this world is possible and anyone could be successful. Embrace your future and push yourself to limits you never knew you had inside yourself.

I can barely remember a lot of my childhood, but seemingly enough. Many of us choose to remember the negative impacts in our lives rather than the positive ones. I have come to realise this as I have gotten older. One thing I do remember of my childhood, however, is suffering from severe eczema. It was a painful experience – itching like there was no tomorrow. Eczema is a skin condition that makes the skin inflamed and irritated. It got so severe that I was covered all over my body from my face to my feet. Not only did I suffer the pain of the skin irritation, but people at primary school looked at me differently, as in "what is wrong with him?" But luckily, eventually Mum found a great doctor to help me get over this part of my life by introducing me to a cream called "Aristocort." I still have it every now and then, but no longer over my entire body. The dreaded dentist is a thing we remember as kids that lasts with us a lifetime and some of us have fears of going due to a bad experience when we were young. As kids, a lot of us remember painful things like stitches and hurting ourselves while playing in the back yard. But from these simple experiences we develop life lessons and try to avoid doing these things that caused such pain in the first place, or try to be brave and face the fears head on.

Developing through my teenage years, I struggled to think where I would like to be in my life and who I would like to become. I never had any idea, so I just continued with pushing my way through high school and earning my HSC. I was getting some decent results, learning every day, having 100% attendance throughout my senior years of high school; it helped with studying for my HSC.

I never knew what I would like to do until one of my teachers suggested retail as they saw my talents while working in the school canteen and how I handled customer service. My skills developed from a young age while helping Dad at markets and visiting garage sales. So, along came a work experience opportunity where I was offered to work for a retail outlet. They were impressed with my work efforts and soon offered me a position for permanent part time. My skills developed and a new trainee manager position opened. I went for the position – a lot of training and the longest speech in front of high management that I have ever done – but it helped me to be able to talk to people even more and I got accepted for the role. A few years later, I advanced in my career and became night department manager.

I enjoyed this work very much, and the people I worked with made impacts in my life as well. However, many nights dancing late and long hours in management, along with a robbery, impacted greatly on my health. A lot of stress on my body took its toll and I developed acute stress disorder, which developed into depression. It shook my body up with the realization of how my life would be changed from that day forward trying to get back into work. I was upset every time I was there I was and unable to work. I had to have time off work. I had three weeks off and went back to work, but I couldn't do it anymore. The stress and fear of something like this happening again was too strong for me as I was still young. It impacted on my mind a great deal and I needed time out for myself to readjust my own life, so I sent in my resignation for the position. It was a great job, but things come along in your life telling you somehow it's time to move on even if it's under bad circumstances. After developing depression, I was under medication from the doctors for over a year. During this time, I turned to video games and drinking large amounts of soft drinks, and eating takeaways while curling up in my own world and forgetting about everyone around me. I wish I knew the things that I do now back then; I would have enjoyed my life more. But, I never had that drive for life as much as I do now. Back then it was all about career, now it's about life itself.

Life has its ups and downs, but no matter how many problems we have in our lives there is always someone in the world going through worse situations and dealing with impacts that have changed their lives. After going through my own personal problems, a year was long enough out of work. One day when I was playing a video game, one of my brothers came over to my house and said to me, "How you going, bro?" I turned around and told him I was going well, I have all this money in the game I was playing. He replied, "Wow, bro, you got a lot of money for the game, but how much do you have in real life?" It woke me up out of my situation and the next day I was organising to do some courses in hospitality. A month later, I found a job at a local hotel giving me the opportunity to start my hospitality work career doing bartending and bistro waiter. I developed some life lessons in the industry and worked there for two years before moving on. I needed a change.

I then started my career within door-to-door sales. Yeah, it's annoying for many to have people knocking on their doors and trying to sell things, but the door-to-door sales I was doing was business-to-business. I quickly became a leader, running my own team and developing my skills in life of leadership, development and personal challenges.

I worked for three months with a warehouse transport company when I was offered a full-time position. I became permanent full time in June 2011, and I have been there ever since. When commencing this job I was 200kg. Just before becoming permanent, my father found out he was a diabetic. A few of my brothers had high blood pressure and a few years earlier Mum went through a bad time in life with bowel cancer.

After finally realising and looking into what could happen in my future, I needed a change from drinking 30 to 40 litres of soft drinks a week. It was time for me to see my local GP. I had my blood pressure tested and all medical check-ups from blood sugar levels, cholesterol, vitamin levels to even the basic check-ups. I needed to find out as much as I possibly could to what shape my body was in from years of bad habits. All the blood test results were good, but my blood pressure was 162/132. I came home and tipped out all the soft drink; I was determined to make a change in my life.

I suffered from massive headaches for three weeks after giving up the soft drinks. Nowadays my blood pressure is a lot better, down to 120/72, as I push my body to achieve a healthier lifestyle. I changed my diet also along the way and added vegetables, from not touching any until age 27. There was a big change for the better.

I came to a realisation of just how bad the soft drinks were, making my blood pressure so high. I personally didn't want to be one of the people taking high blood pressure tablets every day of their life just to maintain the right levels. I knew soft drinks were bad for a person, but refused a lot of my life to change my bad habits. The exact moment I heard the news of my blood pressure was the day I went home and tipped out all the soft drinks in the fridge and then never touched them again. Also, a few months after, I tidied up my diet lifestyle a bit. However, the main cause was soft drink: rechecking after one month showed massive drops in blood pressure. My lifestyle was changed gradually: first I got rid of soft drinks, then adapted to eating vegetbles and reducing the amount of food intake, then adapting to walking, jogging and soon after running. You don't have to be the fittest person in the world, you don't even need to come first, as long as you're out there enjoying the time and jokes with other runners and having fun. Remember, if you're getting upset over coming last, you're still doing more than the people sitting on the couch at home.

My mother battled through a tough time, going through third stage bowel cancer consisting of six months of chemotherapy and six weeks of radiotherapy. My mum knew she had it and needed to rest and go through the chemo and radiotherapy. She had to maintain her sleep to keep fighting the cancer battle. She stayed off work for 10 months and was determined to get back to her working career. Today Mum is a very strong, persistent lady and a fighter and I am proud to see she got though it all. It was a tough time for myself, as at that stage of my life, I was going through severe depression. With family help, I got to see Mum often and it brought our family closer together while Mum was battling the bowel cancer. Cancer is a huge impact in many people's lives. If you sit in a classroom with 30 people and ask how many people are battling cancer, or if they know someone that has gone through or died from cancer, almost the entire class will put up their hand. It's a massive impact in today's society.

My father's diabetes began due to having been bogged down earning money for his six kids, working long hours to provide a good standard of living for his family, losing a nursery business and going into depression due to financial loss. Many things can contribute in impacting how diabetes begins in someone's life. He could have avoided ending up with type 2 diabetes by doing more exercise and changing his eating patterns; he also could have changed his work to be better for his health and lifestyle, though less financially rewarding. Diabetes is a huge part of the world today and hopefully one day they will find a cure. If I didn't change my eating patterns and get rid of the soft drink from my life, I was headed down the same path as my father. I have done a whole lifestyle change and not only do I work through the week, I also enjoy my weekends and the lifestyle I love to live.

My brothers dealt with high blood pressure for some time. It doesn't have to be set in stone that you will need to be on medication for your lifetime. Dealing with blood pressure is something only oneself can maintain. Impacts leading to my brothers going through it were caused by family history, stressful jobs, and living and maintaining career-driven lifestyles to support their families. They could have changed the way they lived their lives and spare time and not stressed out about their working roles. Life is meant to be enjoyed and, yes, we all need to work to make a living. But going to work to be yelled and screamed at won't help anyone's health, it will only make your blood boil.

One of my first holiday experiences away from the comfort of my family was a trip to Coffs Harbour. I had many great experiences, from the Cartoon Bunker Expo, jet skis at Coffs Harbour Beach, and even a trip to the Pet Porpoise Pool where I had a unique animal encounter of being kissed by a dolphin and also a seal. A great hotel experience while I was there was a very relaxing hot stone massage and facial pampering package. You've got to spoil yourself every once in a while and enjoy life the way you want to. I even had the chance to be part of the show where I was called up to feed a fish to the dolphin as it did flips into the air to catch the fish off a stick. Looking back at photos during this time makes me wonder why I didn't do anything about my health sooner. I was 200kg back in 2008, and virtually stayed that way for a few years after; it was only the awakening news that I actually had to change my lifestyle. Why is it we always wait for bad news of any kind before we change our lives? Why not change your bad habits today and enjoy life, live with no regrets and never dwell on your past?

Many challenges have been met while pushing myself to lose weight. Many emotions have occurred such as strength, pain, anger, upset, struggle and many different emotions are felt while conquering what we feel is out of reach. The great challenge for many people is weight loss. I personally have had a large weight loss from 200kg down to 140kg, staying around 140kg for a while now. Don't be set back if you're not going any lower because you could be building muscle which weighs more than fat in the end. Weight loss is a goal for many and all the feelings that you've suffered with because you were overweight won't vanish overnight with a new body. As you learn your own worth through diet, exercise and perseverance, your attitude may take a turn for the better. In losing weight you're not only losing kilograms, but emotional baggage as well. People like to see you succeed in losing your weight, help cheer you along; not all people are jealous of what you are achieving for yourself. Yes, sometimes you cry and it's hard work to lose the weight, pushing your body out of its comfort zone, but when the body gets used to doing something, it maintains it more strongly. There are various stages of exercise of pushing our bodies, but only oneself can determine what our bodies can handle. To start exercise we commonly start from walking to jogging and then, as our legs and body get used to it, we adapt and become runners – baby steps make us stronger in every step we face in our lives.

Along the way I came to the conclusion my life didn't involve many accomplishments other than sitting playing video games, drinking soft drinks and going to work. So, I started a bucket list lifestyle with one of my biggest goals being to conquer an ultramarathon, marathon and half-marathon, which I completed on 4 January 2014 – 12 hours, 55 kms. I never really planned on being able to run that far as all I had accomplished before this run was a 5 km run. I wanted to test my abilities and strength of my mindset to see what my body was capable of achieving without limits by pushing the barriers and knocking down what the runners call "the wall", continuing and fighting to the finish, and achieving a highly recognised bucket list item that many people listen to and go "wow."

Some other major bucket list goals that I aim to achieve I know will be a massive challenge for myself. But I've learned anything you put your mind to can be achieved, you just need to push yourself, one foot in front of the other. No matter how big or small, or how fast or slow, when you get there you will learn things about yourself you had never known before. The challenge I speak of is to aim to complete every run in New South Wales Wide, then later Australian Wide.

When I first started, I was aiming to complete an ultra-marathon, not sure if I could do it. But all along the way I had people tapping me on the back and cheering me on: "Come on, big man, you can do it, don't give up on me, just one more lap, mate, one more lap." Half the time I was tempted to just drop and give up, but when someone challenges me and says I bet you can't do the 50 kms, I have to prove them wrong. I rarely back down from challenges and take what they say in. It only drives me to succeed more and achieve the finish line to tick a large accomplishment in my life. When they said, "Come on, it's only short laps, you can do it," I kept running the short runs to the end of the night. It was a massive achievement and life-time goal to tick off my bucket list and I was so happy, I got a nice trophy for the cabinet to be proud of. From a night of not knowing anyone in the event to smiling my way through to the finish line with the supporters chanting my name and cheering me on, to the little kids giving me high fives for support by the end of the night, everyone who participated and watched me run knew my name. It's a rare thing in any event, let alone a massive event like this: coming from a small run, like pub to pub or city to surf, to stepping up to the ultra was a big difference for me, but I'm glad I did it. One thing that made my night was one of the lead runners saying to me, "Mate, just keep going; seeing you and smiling makes me keep going strong."

I never was a runner, but I realised you don't need to be the fastest person in the event to be noticed; to hold your head high and run, walk and jog your way to the finish line and have millions of people watch and cheer you on is an amazing feeling that I recommend others experience in their lifetime. Not many people in life can say they have completed a marathon, let alone an ultramarathon. People sometimes laugh when I tell them I have a bucket list, but then they listen to my inspirational stories about any experience in life is a life experience worth giving a go. I'm not the richest of people, but I just want to enjoy my life as much as I can. A lot of things in life involve a lot of cost, but I see my life experience differently. From museums, historic houses, travel experiences, to many other crazy ideas on my list – like visiting every country. I am not sure I will conquer all my list, but I am determined to give it a go.

I started the list in January 2012, thinking to myself there has to be more to life than this computer screen we all stare at on a day-to-day basis. Therefore, I told myself I have to enjoy my life and tick something off my bucket list every weekend. From there onwards I have currently completed 1531 from the 9012 on my list. There comes a time in a person's life when you need to walk away from all the drama and people who create it. Surround yourself with people who make you laugh and get rid of all the negativity in your life, because life is too short to draw off the negative things. Enjoy and be happy to the best of your ability; remember, falling down is a part of life, but getting back up is living.

Your strength is found when you tackle the seemingly impossible things in life; surround yourself with a circle of positive people and anyone can go far in their lives. One of the first things I completed on my bucket list was to climb the Sydney Harbour Bridge, which my fiancé got me as a present for Valentine's Day 2012. From that point I thought to myself, "I had fun doing that, what else are people doing in their lives that's fun?" It made me smile when I saw a documentary of 100 things to do before you die about Sebastian Terry, a fellow bucket lister. I followed him, then found another guy off YouTube, Travis Bell. These two inspirational people in my life helped me realise there is more outside our day-to-day lives than work, home, eat, sleep, repeat every day. I was determined to become the same inspirational type of person and help others in their quest to enjoy life's wonders.

Travis Bell helped me achieve skills in myself I never knew existed. He helped me realise what I want to achieve in my life, like really wish to achieve, to change my mindset on how I conquer every goal on my bucket list. For example, "buy a new car." Okay, what colour is it?, how much will you pay?, what does it look like?, what company is it from?, how many seats does it have?, what add-on options do you have in your dream car? In other words, he helped me realise the more detail you put into a single goal will help you achieve it faster, and dreaming about a goal helps you achieve that goal the way you want it to be in your life. He also helped me to conquer fears such as public speaking, going outside comfort zones and just doing it and don't let others judge your life. It's your life; you need to live it the way you want it to be lived and don't let anyone stop you, not even family or friends.

I was very happy to meet Sebastian Terry in person, one of the people I was hoping to meet in life. He helped me realise writing down a list of things I want to achieve helps to tick things off my list. I also learned from him that public speaking not only attracts audience attention, but it is fun also – from attempting world records to getting the crowd involved and telling their stories. We strive to enjoy our lives, but sometimes we need to step back and look at the bigger picture. Help others out: charities, volunteer work, anything to help others, random acts of kindness. Not everything in life should be all about ourselves; we should try and help other people in need also. Life is a puzzle: everything you learn in life connects together and makes you the person you become and develops the knowledge you have to pass down and onwards to others. You don't need to be top of the class to be recognised in life. You develop your skills throughout your lifetime and each thing we learn changes the way our destiny is headed.

My list consists of 9012 items, and counting; I add to it on a continuous basis. It is categorised below for your viewing. It's a huge achievement for me to come this far in my life and I'm enjoying every moment of it. I hope others enjoy their life also.

Chapter 2: Proud Achievements

"In order to succeed, we must first believe that we can."

Nikos Kazantzakis

When we experience proud achievements in our lives, we strive to obtain recognition from others. We want our lives to mean something – we don't just want to exist for the sake of living, wasting our lives away until the day we die. I, for one, strive to be the greatest person that I can be and am proud to say I will give everything a go in my life that I possibly can and achieve and help others realise and work towards their own proud achievements in life. Follow your heart and realise life is really worth living and offers so much potential for each and every one of us to make a difference and make our journeys and stories in life extraordinary to anyone we tell.

- ☐☐ Act in a play
- ☐☐ Attain my CSP status
- ☐☐ Be a guest speaker
- ☐☐ Be a member of the audience in a TV show
- ☐☐ Be an extra in a movie
- ☐☐ Be asked to autograph my picture for someone
- ☐☐ Be in a television ad
- ☑☐ Be in the newspaper
- ☐☐ Be interviewed by a talk-show host
- ☐☐ Be interviewed for TV
- ☐☐ Be invited to speak overseas
- ☐☐ Be listed on a patent
- ☐☐ Be on the front page of a newspaper or magazine
- ☐☐ Be on live television
- ☐☐ Be part of a talk-show audience
- ☐☐ Be sponsored by an organisation
- ☐☐ Be the first in the world to do something
- ☐☐ Circumnavigate the globe
- ☐☐ Complete 25% of my bucket list
- ☐☐ Complete 50% of my bucket list
- ☐☐ Complete 75% of my bucket list
- ☐☐ Complete 100% of my bucket list
- ☐☐ Compete in the Australian Masters games
- ☐☐ Compete in an Olympic sport
- ☐☐ Do a "once in a lifetime" thing twice
- ☐☐ Do a motivational seminar for a stadium of people

- ☐☐ Do a presentation in front of a school classroom
- ☐☐ Drive around Australia
- ☑☐ Earn a medal
- ☑☐ Earn a trophy
- ☑☐ Experience LIFE to the fullest
- ☐☐ Feature in a Bollywood movie
- ☐☐ Get a letter from the King/ Queen for turning 100 years old
- ☐☐ Get in the Guinness Book of World Records
- ☐☐ Have a book done as an audio book
- ☑☐ Have a professional photo shoot by a newspaper or magazine
- ☐☐ Have my own banner
- ☑☐ Have my own business cards
- ☑☐ Have my own coffee mug design
- ☑☐ Have my own keyring design
- ☑☐ Have my own notepad design
- ☑☐ Have my own pen design
- ☐☐ Have my picture on a billboard
- ☐☐ Have my picture on a calendar
- ☐☐ Have my picture on a flyer
- ☐☐ Hold an Olympic medal
- ☐☐ Make a comic strip
- ☐☐ Make a documentary movie
- ☑☐ Make a New Year's resolution and complete it by the end of the year
- ☐☐ Make a short movie
- ☐☐ Be a movie star for a day
- ☐☐ Receive a knighthood from the Queen/ King of England
- ☐☐ Represent Australia, my home country, at something
- ☐☐ Set foot on all seven continents
- ☑☐ Start my own business
- ☐☐ Visit every country on earth
- ☐☐ Win a prize from Boys Town Lotteries
- ☐☐ Win a prize from Endeavour Lotteries
- ☐☐ Win money from the cash cow on sunrise
- ☑☐ Win something from a radio station
- ☐☐ Win the Australian of the Year award
- ☐☐ Win the Father of the Year award
- ☐☐ Win the lottery
- ☐☐ Witness something truly majestic
- ☐☐ Write a screenplay

Chapter 3:
Life's Memories and Experiences in Someone Else's Shoes

"You are never too old to set another goal or to dream a new dream."

C. S. Lewis

Life offers many memories that can and will never be replaced. These moments in our lives mean something truly special to our hearts and our families: the first time we obtain passports, the moment we reach significant milestones of the ones we love, or a birthday milestone. These memories help us realise as we get older and time passes by we are not alone and people around us truly care and are there beside us when special moments in our life happen: becoming a parent for the first time, a really great day to look forward to in life; finding family history, about where we came from, who our ancestry are and who they were, and what they did in their lives to impact the way we have become – who we are today floating down by generations.

From time to time we need to think about others and how they live their own lives. We just live our own and not worry that there are people out there that deal with troubles in their lives. If we are put into their position, how would we react to day-to-day problems? Would we freak out? Would we adjust? Would we give up hope? The answer is, never give in to problems in life because life will guide us in the right direction and we will always make the best of any outcome, good or bad. Look at the bright side of life rather than the downside and hold our heads high and strive to make good memories worth living.

- ☐☐ Be independent
- ☑☐ Become a Godparent
- ☐☐ Become a parent
- ☑☐ Celebrate five-year anniversary (from the date we first meet)
- ☐☐ Celebrate 10-year anniversary (from the date we first meet)
- ☐☐ Celebrate 15-year anniversary (from the date we first meet)
- ☐☐ Celebrate 20-year anniversary (from the date we first meet)

- ☐☐ Celebrate 25-year anniversary (from the date we first meet)
- ☐☐ Celebrate 30-year anniversary (from the date we first meet)
- ☐☐ Celebrate 40-year anniversary (from the date we first meet)
- ☐☐ Celebrate 50-year anniversary (from the date we first meet)
- ☐☐ Celebrate my 100th birthday
- ☑☐ Create a bucket list
- ☑☐ Create my family tree
- ☐☐ Do something really brave
- ☐☐ Dress as an old man and see how people are treating the elderly in your city
- ☑☐ Get engaged
- ☑☐ Experience a sunrise
- ☑☐ Experience a sunset
- ☑☐ Get a passport
- ☐☐ Grow old with someone
- ☑☐ Grow up with a family pet
- ☐☐ Have a child
- ☑☐ Have a conversation with a stranger on an aeroplane
- ☐☐ Have a conversation with someone at least 100 years old
- ☐☐ Have at least one grandchild
- ☐☐ Hold my child right after it's born
- ☑☐ Inspire someone
- ☐☐ Leave a legacy
- ☐☐ Marry my special girl
- ☑☐ Find meaning of family name and frame it
- ☐☐ Pass my knowledge of life on to future generations
- ☐☐ Pass something down/start a family heirloom
- ☐☐ Read my child the children's classics
- ☐☐ Realise on my death bed that I have lived my life and have no regrets; and all my mistakes are nothing to be regretful about
- ☐☐ Retire
- ☐☐ See my children succeed
- ☐☐ Spend a day in the life of a homeless person to see how life is when everything isn't given to you
- ☑☐ Teach a child how to do something
- ☑☐ Teach a child to tie their shoes
- ☐☐ Walk in the shoes of a blind person and have a guide dog to see how they live their lives
- ☐☐ Witness a birth

Chapter 4: Random Acts of Kindness (Good Deeds)

"Be kind whenever possible. It is always possible."

Dalai Lama

In today's society, a lot of the time we simply forget to help out others in times of need; it's always a good thing when you look at life in another way and realise others are in a worse-off position than you are. It makes you feel really good about yourself when you perform a good deed and help others in their times of need. It helps you realise greed isn't the key to a good life; helping others helps you become a more loving, caring person and brings out your inner beautiful personality. It could be anything from donations, to giving things that mean something to you, to helping a random stranger in trouble and needing somebody to help them solve a problem.

- ☑☐ Bake something for a neighbour
- ☐☐ Be a best man
- ☑☐ Be the designated driver for friends
- ☐☐ Buy a homeless person lunch
- ☐☐ Buy a present to give to a children's charity
- ☑☐ Buy an unexpected gift for someone
- ☑☐ Buy cakes or fruit for your colleagues
- ☐☐ Buy everyone in the bar a drink
- ☑☐ Cut someone's hair
- ☑☐ Do a chore that you don't normally do
- ☑☐ Do some community service
- ☑☐ Do something good or something nice for an old person
- ☐☐ Do volunteer work in a third world country
- ☑☐ Donate your old things to charity
- ☐☐ Entertain the elderly at a nursing home
- ☑☐ Forgive someone for what they've done
- ☑☐ Get back in contact with someone you've lost touch with
- ☑☐ Give a (sincere) compliment
- ☑☐ Give blood

- ☐☐ Give food to a homeless person and take time to talk with them
- ☑☐ Give someone a hug
- ☐☐ Give unwanted toys to a children's hospital
- ☑☐ Give up your seat to someone
- ☑☐ Give your unwanted clothes to a homeless shelter
- ☑☐ Have a conversation with a stranger
- ☑☐ Help a complete stranger for the good
- ☐☐ Help an endangered or injured animal
- ☑☐ Help change a tyre
- ☐☐ Help grant someone's last wish
- ☐☐ Help in a natural disaster recovery project
- ☑☐ Help other shoppers
- ☑☐ Help out someone in need
- ☑☐ Help someone conquer a phobia
- ☑☐ Help someone who's lost
- ☑☐ Help someone whose car is broken down
- ☐☐ Help with a science fair project
- ☑☐ Hold a door open for someone
- ☑☐ Hold up a "free hug" sign and hug someone
- ☑☐ Invite your neighbour round for a drink and a chat
- ☑☐ Leave a 100% tip
- ☑☐ Let one car in on every journey
- ☑☐ Let someone have your parking spot
- ☑☐ Let someone in front of you in the queue
- ☑☐ Make someone laugh
- ☑☐ Make someone new feel welcome
- ☑☐ Offer to help with someone's shopping
- ☑☐ Offer to mow your neighbour's lawn
- ☑☐ Offer your change to someone struggling to find the right amount
- ☑☐ Pass on a book you've enjoyed
- ☑☐ Pay for someone in the queue behind you
- ☑☐ Pay for the person behind you at a toll/drive through
- ☑☐ Pick up litter as you walk
- ☑☐ Put change into someone's expired meter
- ☑☐ Read a story with a child
- ☑☐ Say "Bless you" when someone sneezes
- ☑☐ Say sorry (you know who to)
- ☐☐ Send a letter to a random address and see if they write back
- ☑☐ Send compliments to the chef
- ☐☐ Send out holiday cards for Christmas
- ☑☐ Send someone a letter the old way in a mailbox
- ☐☐ Serve food at a soup kitchen
- ☐☐ Serve on a jury
- ☑☐ Share your umbrella
- ☑☐ Sign a petition
- ☑☐ Spend a day giving high fives to everyone you see
- ☑☐ Take time to really listen to someone
- ☐☐ Teach English to someone from a foreign country
- ☑☐ Tell someone if you notice they're doing a good job
- ☑☐ Tell someone they mean a lot to you

- ☑☐ Treat a loved one to breakfast in bed
- ☑☐ Visit a sick friend, relative or neighbour
- ☑☐ Visit someone who may be lonely
- ☐☐ Volunteer at an orphanage
- ☐☐ Volunteer your time for a charity
- ☐☐ Walk an old lady across the street
- ☐☐ Witness a crime and fill out a police report

Chapter 5: Circle of Influences – People to Meet In Life

"Surround yourself with only people who are going to lift you higher."

Oprah Winfrey

The people that influence our lives determine who we become and who we strive to be, and we learn from them as they inspire us to be a greater person than who we already are. They impact our lives to make us realise more potential in ourselves and learn new and amazing things that guide our way, making us a stronger person and finding how others have changed their lives and how they got to the position they're in today.

Public figures make an impact through public speaking and motivational seminars, and help us to discover our inner potential to be able to bring our own confidence from within. Others impact our lives like sports teams, money makers, inspirational people, globally known icons and strong empowered people who have changed their lives for the better.

- ☑☐ Attend a Sebastian Terry bucket list seminar
- ☑☐ Attend a Travis Bell bucket list seminar
- ☑☐ Contact someone with same name
- ☐☐ Meet a billionaire
- ☐☐ Meet a famous DJ close up
- ☐☐ Meet a famous model
- ☑☐ Meet a famous singer/band
- ☐☐ Meet a member of the royal family
- ☐☐ Meet a millionaire
- ☑☐ Meet a monk
- ☐☐ Meet a sports star
- ☐☐ Meet a sports team and have them autograph a jersey
- ☐☐ Meet Adam Sandler
- ☐☐ Meet an actor
- ☐☐ Meet an actual samurai
- ☐☐ Meet an astronaut
- ☑☐ Meet an author
- ☐☐ Meet an Olympian
- ☐☐ Meet Cadel Evans
- ☐☐ Meet Craig Lowndes
- ☐☐ Meet Dynamo, see his magic tricks
- ☐☐ Meet Ellen DeGeneres
- ☐☐ Meet Hamish and Andy

- ☐☐ Meet Jason Edwards, National Geographic photographer
- ☐☐ Meet Kelly Slater
- ☐☐ Meet Oprah Winfrey
- ☑☐ Meet Pat Farmer, ultramarathon athlete
- ☐☐ Meet real gypsies
- ☐☐ Meet Rob Schneider
- ☐☐ Meet Sir Richard Branson
- ☐☐ Meet someone born on the same day as myself – 19th June 1985
- ☐☐ Meet the Commando
- ☐☐ Meet the Dalai Lama
- ☐☐ Meet the Pope
- ☐☐ Meet the Sunrise crew
- ☐☐ Meet the Today Show crew
- ☐☐ Meet Tony Robbins
- ☑☐ Shake a soldier's hand
- ☐☐ Visit a death row inmate
- ☑☐ Visit Dad's family

Chapter 6: Workout Challenges

"Failure will never overtake me if my determination to succeed is strong enough."

Og Mandino

We strive to push our bodies to their total extremes. We empower ourselves and aim to conquer goals we set for ourselves – monthly challenges or even a weekly challenge – just to change the way we see our lifestyles and change into someone better in life and become a stronger person than the person we were yesterday. We make our bodies, mind and even our inner strength stronger. We push ourselves to succeed, to make our lives better, to become the people we want to be. Challenges are really hard to begin with, but over time anything is possible. We just need to believe in ourselves to achieve our future dreams and passion for our lifestyles.

- ☐☐ 24-hour treadmill challenge! (run to raise money for Alzheimer's Australia)
- ☐☐ 30-day ab and squat challenge
- ☐☐ 30-day ab challenge
- ☐☐ 30-day arm challenge
- ☐☐ 30-day beach body challenge
- ☐☐ 30-day crunch challenge
- ☐☐ 30-day dumbbell challenge
- ☐☐ 30-day extreme squat challenge
- ☐☐ 30-day full body workout
- ☐☐ 30-day lunges challenge
- ☐☐ 30-day plank challenge
- ☐☐ 30-day push-up challenge
- ☐☐ 30-day sit-up challenge
- ☐☐ 30-day squat challenge
- ☐☐ 30-day tricep dips challenge
- ☐☐ Be able to do the "scorpion" yoga pose
- ☐☐ Be able to lift my own body weight on my arms
- ☑☐ Be able to lift my own body weight on my legs
- ☐☐ Be in a body building contest
- ☐☐ Challenge a world champion
- ☐☐ Climb to the top of a rope and ring the bell
- ☐☐ Do one push-up each day to make 365 counts by the year end
- ☐☐ Do 100 consecutive push-ups
- ☐☐ Do 50 consecutive push-ups
- ☐☐ Do boot camp program for a week

- ☐☐ Do some sort of physical exercise for 20 minutes, every day, for a year
- ☐☐ Experience a Pilates class
- ☐☐ Experience a yoga class
- ☐☐ Have six-pack abs
- ☐☐ Learn to meditate
- ☐☐ Meditate with a monk
- ☐☐ Learn Tai Chi
- ☐☐ Take a Spin class
- ☐☐ Take a survival class
- ☐☐ Do the Commando Tough Beasting event
- ☐☐ Do the Commando Tough Evasion event
- ☐☐ Do the Commando Tough Gunslinger event
- ☐☐ Do the Commando Tough Signature Session
- ☑☐ Touch my toes
- ☐☐ Try Pilates on a stand-up paddle board
- ☐☐ Try yoga on a stand-up paddle board

Chapter 7:
Money and Finance and Things I Want to Buy

*"It is not how much we have, but how much
we enjoy, that makes happiness."*

Charles Spurgeon

Buying things we want or like gives us joy and content, but do we really need everything we buy – like the silly clock that you saw and now gathers dust in a corner of a room, or the pair of shoes you bought six years ago and have only worn once? We spend a lot of our time wasting money when in reality we should be saving it. Yes, it's nice to have a treat once in a while, but stop for one minute and think of those that don't have one – like the old man sitting on the bench with holes in his shoes, or the young girl who is wet and hungry. These things we should think of too; instead of buying yourself the $300 bag, how about spending $40 on a pair of shoes for the old man, or $30 for a raincoat for the young girl and a sandwich to stop her from being hungry? We all have money in one way or another, but think of the people that don't. Give them something to smile about and that they will use, instead of buying another pair of shoes that will sit in the box for six years.

- ☐☐ Achieve absolute debt freedom
- ☐☐ Become a billionaire
- ☐☐ Become a millionaire
- ☐☐ Bet $1000 on red or black on roulette and not care if I lose
- ☑☐ Bet on the winning horse
- ☐☐ Burn money
- ☑☐ Buy/sell something on eBay
- ☐☐ Buy 100 scratchie cards
- ☑☐ Buy a 30kg adjustable weighted vest
- ☐☐ Buy a big tool chest and fill it full of tools
- ☐☐ Buy a cabinet for all my medals and trophies in life
- ☐☐ Buy a customised sealing wax set
- ☑☐ Buy a GoPro camera - adventure cam/waterproof
- ☐☐ Buy a gold bullion
- ☐☐ Buy a gold Rolex
- ☑☐ Buy a hiker's backpack
- ☐☐ Buy a house

- ☑☐ Buy a laptop
- ☑☐ Buy a lotto ticket with the numbers off a fortune cookie
- ☐☐ Buy a mountain bike
- ☐☐ Buy a pair of Google Glass hi tech glasses software
- ☐☐ Buy a pinball machine
- ☐☐ Buy a private island
- ☐☐ Buy a race horse
- ☐☐ Buy a road bicycle
- ☑☐ Buy a scratchie map and scratch places I visit
- ☐☐ Buy a telescope
- ☑☐ Buy a video camera
- ☑☐ Buy a web camera
- ☑☐ Buy a wide-angle lense for my camera
- ☐☐ Buy a world globe
- ☑☐ Buy an infomercial item
- ☐☐ Buy an iPod
- ☐☐ Buy an original newspaper from the past
- ☐☐ Buy and wear a "Keep Calm" shirt
- ☑☐ Buy land in Scotland and become a lord
- ☑☐ Buy my fiancée 50 red roses for Valentine's Day
- ☐☐ Buy some eclipse safety glasses
- ☑☐ Buy some hookah conquest shoes
- ☐☐ Collect a coin from every country I visit
- ☐☐ Do the 52-week money savings project
- ☐☐ Gamble in Las Vegas
- ☐☐ Glue money to the floor and watch as people try to pick it up
- ☐☐ Go out and buy a real Christmas tree
- ☑☐ Have shares in a company
- ☐☐ Have your own skyscraper or tower built
- ☐☐ Hire an island of your very own for a week
- ☐☐ Invest in commodities, such as gold and silver
- ☐☐ Invest in real estate
- ☐☐ Own a grand piano
- ☑☐ Own a nice camera
- ☐☐ Own a polaroid camera
- ☐☐ Own a signed team jersey
- ☐☐ Own a theme park
- ☐☐ Own a zoo/aquarium
- ☐☐ Own multiple investment properties all over the world
- ☐☐ Own my own business building
- ☑☐ Pay off car loan
- ☑☐ Pay off credit card debt

Chapter 8: Running, Walking, Swimming and Bike Riding Events

"One finds limits by pushing them."

Herbert Simon

Be inspired by others, appreciate others, learn from others, but know that competing against them is a waste of your time. You are in competition with one person and one person alone, and that is yourself. You are competing to be the best you can be. Aim to break your own personal records and never look back. Know how hard it seems if you're in first place or in last place. It does not matter; stay strong and just strive to be a better you than days before – even if you're in last place people will still clap and cheer you on. You are doing it for yourself, which is always most rewarding and honourable for your personal health. My personal aim is to strive to complete every race around the country I live in, the beautiful country of Australia, and also take on various countries around the world – to see the beauty of the world while I run across as many countries as I possibly can in my lifetime.

- ☐☐ 100km Del Passatore (Italy)
- ☐☐ 100km, three-day multi-stage trail - Trail fest
- ☐☐ 12 hr. Dusk Till Dawn Mountain Bike Endurance Race
- ☐☐ 3 Points Challenge and Ocean Swim
- ☐☐ 3 Waters Marathon - Bunbury, 50km, April
- ☐☐ 6000D La Plagne (France)
- ☑☐ 7 Bridges Walk
- ☐☐ 7 Peaks Run
- ☐☐ 96 km the Kokoda Challenge, Gold Coast
- ☐☐ A walk through the brilliantly hued cliffs in Rouissillon, France
- ☐☐ Abel Tasman Coastal Classic - New Zealand
- ☐☐ Aboriginal Heritage walk
- ☐☐ Adelaide Marathon - Adelaide, 42.2km, August
- ☐☐ Adrenathon in the Glenworth Valley
- ☑☐ Akuna Bay
- ☐☐ Alice Springs Running Festival
- ☐☐ Alzheimer's Australia Memory Walk and Jog, 7.5km, Leichardt Oval

- ☐☐ America Bay walking track
- ☐☐ Amsterdam Marathon (Netherlands)
- ☐☐ Angkor Wat International Half-Marathon (Cambodia)
- ☐☐ Antarctic Ice Marathon
- ☐☐ Apeldoorn Marathon (Netherlands)
- ☐☐ Armadale Half Marathon
- ☐☐ Arthurs Seat Challenge, Victoria
- ☐☐ Asics Bridges Fun Run - Langley Park, Perth, 10km, April
- ☐☐ Athelstone Easter Mob Bun Run - Athelstone Primary School, 10km, April
- ☐☐ Athens Authentic Marathon
- ☐☐ Athens Marathon (Greece)
- ☐☐ Athlete's Foot Greenbelt Half Marathon - Athelstone, 21.1km, May
- ☐☐ Auckland Marathon
- ☐☐ Austin Marathon (Texas)
- ☐☐ Australia Day Fun Run at Coffs Harbour - 10km
- ☐☐ Australian Outback Marathon
- ☐☐ Avenue of the Giants Marathon (California)
- ☐☐ Avondale School Fun Run in Cooranbong, NSW
- ☐☐ Awesome '80s Run
- ☐☐ Bagan Temple Marathon
- ☐☐ Bairne walking track
- ☐☐ Balmain Fun Run
- ☐☐ Balmoral Burn - June Massive Hill
- ☐☐ Banff-Jasper Relay (Alberta)
- ☐☐ Bankstown Half Marathon - Lake Gillawarna, Bankstown, 21.1km, September
- ☐☐ Bankstown Heart of the Lake Fun Runs, May
- ☐☐ Barbados Marathon (Barbados)
- ☐☐ Barcelona Marathon (Spain)
- ☐☐ Bare Creek Trail Run
- ☐☐ Baroko Marathon (Czech Republic)
- ☐☐ Barossa Marathon - Tanunda, Barossa Valley, 42.2km, May
- ☐☐ Bathurst Half Marathon - Bathurst, 21.1km, May
- ☐☐ Baw Baw Trail Run Festival
- ☐☐ Bay Adventure Summer Run - Halifax Reserve, Shoal Bay, 12km, February
- ☐☐ Be Number One on Race Numbers Bib
- ☑☐ Beach Walk for Brain Cancer - Shelly Beach to Curl Curl Beach
- ☐☐ Behobia-San Sebastian (Spain)
- ☐☐ Beijing Marathon (China)
- ☐☐ Bendigo Half Marathon - Rosalind Park, Bendigo, 21.1km, January
- ☐☐ Bennette Ridge Track
- ☑☐ Bents Basin
- ☐☐ Berghofers Pass
- ☐☐ Berlin 25K (Germany)
- ☐☐ Berlin Marathon (Germany)
- ☑☐ Bicentennial Park Walk
- ☐☐ Big Coast Run, Kamai Botany Bay National Park, Kurnell
- ☐☐ Big Forest Run
- ☐☐ Big Nasty Mud Run
- ☐☐ Big Red Run - 250km Multi Day Run - Simpson Desert, NT
- ☐☐ Big Rock Run
- ☐☐ Big Sur International Marathon (California)

- ☐☐ Big Trail Run, St. Ives Showground, St. Ives
- ☐☐ Bike Ride 100km
- ☐☐ Bike Ride 10km
- ☐☐ Bike Ride 20km
- ☐☐ Bike Ride 30km
- ☐☐ Bike Ride 40km
- ☐☐ Bike Ride 5 km
- ☐☐ Bike Ride 50km
- ☐☐ Bike Ride 60km
- ☐☐ Bike Ride 70km
- ☐☐ Bike Ride 80km
- ☐☐ Bike Ride 90km
- ☐☐ Bilpin Bush Run
- ☐☐ Birrawanna Walking Track
- ☐☐ Blue Pool Walking Track
- ☐☐ Bluff Lookout - Glenbrook
- ☐☐ Boar Head Rock
- ☐☐ Bobbin Head Cycle Classic
- ☐☐ Bogong to Hotham Rooftop Run - Mt Bogong, 64km, Janurart
- ☑☐ Bondi to Bronte Walk
- ☐☐ Boogie Marathon (North Carolina)
- ☐☐ Boston Marathon (Massachusetts)
- ☐☐ Boulder Backroads Marathon (Colorado)
- ☐☐ Brave Heart Battle (Germany)
- ☐☐ Brazilian Butterfly Queen of the Lake - Albert Park Lake, Albert Park, 10km, February
- ☑☐ Brick Pit Ring Walk
- ☑☐ Bridge Run
- ☐☐ Brisbane Marathon Festival
- ☐☐ Broome Marathon - Cable Beach, Broome, 42.2km, July
- ☐☐ Brussels 20K (Belgium)
- ☐☐ Budapest Marathon (Hungary)
- ☐☐ Buffalo Zombie Mud Run
- ☐☐ Bunbury Australia Day Fun Run - Leschenault Inlet, Bunbury, 10km, January
- ☐☐ Bunbury Marathon - Bunbury, 50km, April
- ☐☐ Burke and Wills Trek
- ☐☐ Burra Koran Flat
- ☐☐ California International Marathon (California)
- ☐☐ Camden Haven King of the Mountain in Laurieton, NSW
- ☑☐ Campfire Creek Track
- ☐☐ Canberra Marathon - Canberra, 42.2km, April
- ☐☐ Cape Otway
- ☐☐ Cayman Islands Marathon (Cayman Islands)
- ☐☐ CellCom Green Bay Marathon (Wisconsin)
- ☑☐ Centennial Park Walk
- ☐☐ Centrepoint Tower Fun Run Up the Staircase
- ☐☐ Central Coast Half Marathon - Memorial Park, The Entrance, 21.1km, November
- ☐☐ Centre Walking Track
- ☑☐ Charles Darwin Walk Wentworth Falls
- ☐☐ Chicago Marathon
- ☐☐ Cinque Mulini (Italy)
- ☑☐ City to Surf Sydney, (Australia), 14km, August
- ☐☐ City to Surf, Perth
- ☐☐ City2Sea
- ☐☐ Coast 2 Kosci 240 km Marathon
- ☐☐ Coast to Coast Marathon (Italy)
- ☐☐ Coast Walk 100km - Palm Beach to Bundeena
- ☐☐ Coastal Classic - Otford, 29km, September

- ☐☐ Color Me Rad 5k Australia
- ☑☐ Color Run Sydney - Centennial Park, Sydney, 5km, February
- ☐☐ Colour Me Active - Newnham UTAS Campus, Newnham, 4.8km, February
- ☐☐ Colour Me Rad - Sydney Motorsport Park, Ferrers Rd, Eastern Creek, 5km, February
- ☐☐ Columbia Gorge Marathon
- ☐☐ Compete in 100 half-marathons in my lifetime
- ☐☐ Compete in 100 marathons in my lifetime
- ☐☐ Compete in 100 ultramarathons in my lifetime
- ☐☐ Compete in 25 half-marathons in my lifetime
- ☐☐ Compete in 25 marathons in my lifetime
- ☐☐ Compete in 25 ultramarathons in my lifetime
- ☐☐ Compete in 50 half-marathons in my lifetime
- ☐☐ Compete in 50 marathons in my lifetime
- ☐☐ Compete in 50 ultramarathons in my lifetime
- ☐☐ Compete in 75 half-marathons in my lifetime
- ☐☐ Compete in 75 marathons in my lifetime
- ☐☐ Compete in 75 ultramarathons in my lifetime
- ☐☐ Compete in a triathlon
- ☑☐ Complete 100km
- ☑☐ Complete 10km
- ☑☐ Complete 15km
- ☑☐ Complete 20km
- ☑☐ Complete 30km
- ☑☐ Complete 40km
- ☑☐ Complete 5km
- ☑☐ Complete 50km
- ☑☐ Complete 60km
- ☑☐ Complete 70km
- ☑☐ Complete 80km
- ☑☐ Complete 90km
- ☐☐ Complete a marathon in all seven continents of the world
- ☐☐ Complete a Spartan Beast Race
- ☐☐ Complete a Spartan Sprint Race
- ☐☐ Complete a Spartan Super Race
- ☐☐ Complete Hell and Back
- ☐☐ Complete the Ironman Triathlon
- ☐☐ Complete the Norseman Extreme Triathlon
- ☐☐ Comrades Marathon 89K (South Africa)
- ☑☐ Conservation Hut Walk
- ☐☐ Cooks River Fun Run - Strathfield, NSW, June
- ☐☐ Copenhagen Marathon (Denmark)
- ☐☐ Cortina Dobbiaco Run (Italy)
- ☐☐ Cracovia Marathon (Poland)
- ☐☐ Create my own running group
- ☐☐ Cremorne Point to Mosman Bay Walk
- ☑☐ Cromer Northern Trail Walk
- ☑☐ Cross a waterfall on stones
- ☐☐ Cuba Trail Marathon (Cuba)
- ☐☐ Cupid's Undies Run Melbourne - Watermark Docklands, 1.5km, February
- ☐☐ Cupid's Undies Run Sydney - Sydney, 1.5km, February
- ☐☐ Cursa Bombers 10K (Spain)
- ☐☐ Cyprus Four-Day Challenge (Cyprus)

- ☐☐ Dallas White Rock Marathon (Texas)
- ☐☐ Dam tot Damloop (Netherlands)
- ☐☐ Dantes Glen
- ☐☐ Darden Elles Pass
- ☐☐ Dendy Park Urban Run - Dendy Park, Brighton East, 2km, February
- ☐☐ Detroit Marathon (Michigan)
- ☐☐ Dingo Dash
- ☐☐ Do 50km a month for a year for a total of 600km
- ☐☐ Dubbo Running Festival - Taronga Western Plains Zoo, 21.1km, September
- ☐☐ Easter Island Marathon
- ☐☐ Eat Brain Run Sydney 5km Obstacle Course
- ☐☐ Ecco Östersund Marathon (Sweden)
- ☑☐ Echo Point
- ☐☐ Ecomaratona dei Marsi (Italy)
- ☐☐ Egmond Half-Marathon (Netherlands)
- ☐☐ Eindhoven Marathon (Netherlands)
- ☑☐ Electric Run Australia
- ☐☐ Elvina Track
- ☐☐ Emerald Nuts Midnight Run - Central Park, NYC
- ☑☐ Empire Pass
- ☐☐ Enduro Bike Ride
- ☐☐ Enschede Marathon (Netherlands)
- ☐☐ Enter a bike race
- ☐☐ Etape Bornholm (Denmark)
- ☐☐ Eureka Climb - Steps Run
- ☐☐ Euroka Clearing
- ☐☐ Euroka Creek
- ☐☐ Evans Lookout to Beauchamp Falls
- ☐☐ Everest Marathon, Nepal
- ☐☐ Fiji Flood 500km Fun Run
- ☐☐ Fjällmaran Mountain Marathon (Sweden)
- ☑☐ Fletchers Lookout
- ☐☐ Flinders Island Running Festival - Flinders Island, 50km, September
- ☐☐ Florabella Pass
- ☐☐ Florence Marathon (Italy)
- ☐☐ Flying Pig Marathon (Ohio)
- ☐☐ Foot of Africa Marathon, (South Africa)
- ☐☐ Foreshore5 - Newcastle, 5km, March
- ☐☐ Fortis City-Pier-City Loop (Netherlands)
- ☐☐ Freedom Trail Run - Byron Bay Hinterland, November
- ☐☐ Freedom Trail Run - Nightcap National Park, Byron Bay, 40km, October
- ☐☐ French Riviera Marathon (France)
- ☐☐ Fuber Steps
- ☐☐ Fun Run Pink Melbourne - Albert Park Lake, 5km, January
- ☑☐ Fun Run Pink Parramatta -Parramatta Park, 5km, March
- ☐☐ Fun Run Wollongong - Wollongong Harbour, Wollongong, 5.4km, March
- ☐☐ Geraldton Marathon - Geraldton Yacht Club, 42.2km, July
- ☑☐ Giant Stairways
- ☐☐ Gibberagong Walking Track
- ☐☐ Gladiator Rock'n Run
- ☐☐ Glenbrook Crossing

- ☐☐ Gloria Jeans Fun Run: Forster, NSW - 5K
- ☐☐ Glow Run Australia
- ☐☐ God's Country Marathon (Pennslyvania)
- ☐☐ Gold Coast Airport Marathon (Australia)
- ☐☐ Gold Coast Bulletin Fun Run: 21km, Skilled Park, Robina, April
- ☐☐ Gothenburg Half-Marathon (Sweden)
- ☑☐ Governor Phillip Lookout Walk
- ☐☐ Grand Canyon Walk Blue Mountains
- ☐☐ Granollers Half-Marathon (Spain)
- ☐☐ Great Alpine Walk
- ☐☐ Great Ethiopian Run 10K (Ethiopia)
- ☐☐ Great Manchester Run
- ☐☐ Great Nosh Footrace
- ☐☐ Great Pyramid Race and Country Fair in Gordonvale, Qld
- ☐☐ Great Ocean Road Marathon
- ☑☐ Great River Walk
- ☐☐ Great Wall of China Marathon (China)
- ☐☐ H C Andersen Marathon (Denmark)
- ☐☐ Hamburg Marathon (Germany)
- ☐☐ Hardrock Hundred Endurance Run
- ☐☐ Hardys McLaren Vale Half Marathon - Hardys Tintara Winery, McLaren Vale, 21.1km, October
- ☐☐ Hatfield & McCoy Reunion Marathon (West Virginia)
- ☐☐ HBF Run for a Reason
- ☐☐ Head to Head Walk Run - Crescent Head Beach, 20km, August
- ☐☐ Health.com.au Sandy Point
- ☐☐ Health.com.au Spring into Shape
- ☐☐ Helsinki Marathon (Finland)
- ☐☐ Herald Sun/City Link Run for the Kids - Melbourne
- ☐☐ Hike along the unrestored section of the Great Wall of China
- ☐☐ Hike the Appalachian Trail
- ☐☐ Hike the Inca Trail to Machu Picchu – Cuzco, Peru
- ☐☐ Hike to the bottom of the Grand Canyon
- ☐☐ Hike to the summit of Diamond Head Volcano for most amazing views of Waikiki - Oahu, Hawaii
- ☐☐ Hill to Harbour - Newcastle Harbour, 21.1km, April
- ☐☐ Himalayan 100-mile Stage Race (India)
- ☐☐ Himalayan Kingdom Marathon (India)
- ☑☐ Historic Lennox Bridge Walk
- ☐☐ Honolulu Marathon (Hawaii)
- ☐☐ Hood to Coast Relay (Oregon)
- ☐☐ Hot Chocolate 15km Run
- ☐☐ Houston Marathon
- ☐☐ Humpy's Marathon in Anchorage
- ☐☐ Illawarra Fly Treetop Walk
- ☐☐ Illumi Run
- ☐☐ In Flanders Marathon (Belgium)
- ☐☐ Inca Trail Marathon (Peru)
- ☐☐ International Lake Garda Marathon (Italy)

- ☐☐ Irvine Lake Mud Run
- ☐☐ Istanbul Eurasia Marathon (Turkey)
- ☐☐ Jabulani Challenge, April, Kuringai National Park
- ☐☐ Jacaranda Fun Run
- ☐☐ Jack Evans Track
- ☑☐ Jamison Lookout
- ☑☐ Jellybean Pool
- ☐☐ Jerusalem Bay Track (to Jerusalem Bay and back)
- ☐☐ Joburg City Marathon (South Africa)
- ☑☐ Join a running group
- ☐☐ Jungfrau Marathon (Switzerland)
- ☐☐ Kakadu & the Nitmiluk Dreaming Trail
- ☐☐ Kanchenjunga Ultramarathon (Nepal)
- ☐☐ Katoomba to Jenolan Caves - 42km
- ☐☐ Keep It Real 50km Mountain Bike Endurance Race
- ☐☐ Kilimanjaro Marathon, Tanzania
- ☐☐ Knapsack Lap Race Six Hours - Glenbrook, January
- ☐☐ Knysna Forest Marathon (South Africa)
- ☐☐ Kosciuszko Run and Half Marathon 22km - February
- ☐☐ Krispy Kreme Challenge Fun Run
- ☐☐ Kununurra Half-Marathon - Kununurra, 21.1km, June
- ☐☐ La Champenoise (France)
- ☐☐ La Ronde Cérétane (France)
- ☐☐ La Ronde des Foies Gras (France)
- ☐☐ La Trans'Aq (France)
- ☐☐ La Transbaie (France)
- ☐☐ Laguna Phuket International Marathon (Thailand)
- ☐☐ Lake Tahoe Marathon (California)
- ☑☐ Lane Cove National Park
- ☐☐ Larapinta Trail Trek
- ☐☐ Las Vegas Marathon (Nevada)
- ☐☐ Launceston Ten - Town Hall, St. John St, Launceston, 10km, June
- ☐☐ Lawson's Long Alley
- ☐☐ Le Grand Raid de la Réunion (Réunion)
- ☐☐ Leadville Trail 100 - Colorado
- ☐☐ Les 20K de Paris (France)
- ☐☐ Les crêtes du Pays Basque (France)
- ☐☐ Les Fouleés de la Soie (China)
- ☐☐ Lidingöloppet (Sweden)
- ☐☐ Life Support Beachside Dash
- ☐☐ Lindfield Rotary Fun Run
- ☐☐ Lisbon Half-Marathon (Portugal)
- ☐☐ Lithgow King of the Mountain Race 4.2km
- ☐☐ Ljubljana Marathon (Slovenia)
- ☐☐ Lockers Loop
- ☐☐ London Marathon
- ☐☐ Los Angeles Marathon (California)
- ☐☐ Loskop Marathon 50K (South Africa)
- ☑☐ Lyrebird Dell
- ☐☐ M7 Blacktown Running Festival - Marathon
- ☐☐ Madrid Marathon (Spain)
- ☐☐ Magdala Creek
- ☐☐ Maitland River Run - Maitland, 12km, May

- ☐☐ Malta Marathon Challenge (Malta)
- ☑☐ Manly - Spit Bridge Olympian Pathway
- ☐☐ Manly Fun Run
- ☑☐ Manly Scenic Walkway
- ☐☐ Marathon de Sables (Morocco)
- ☐☐ Marathon du Cognac (France)
- ☐☐ Marathon du Medoc, France
- ☐☐ Mardi Gras Marathon (Louisiana)
- ☐☐ Mardi Gras Rainbow Run: Sydney 6km
- ☐☐ Marikenloop (Netherlands)
- ☐☐ Marine Corps Marathon (Virginia)
- ☐☐ Maroubra Fun Run
- ☐☐ Marrakech International Marathon (Morocco)
- ☐☐ Marseilles-Cassis (France)
- ☐☐ Marvejols-Mende (France)
- ☐☐ Maui Marathon (Hawaii)
- ☐☐ MBank Lodz Marathon (Poland)
- ☐☐ Melbourne Marathon Festival
- ☐☐ Merimbula Fun Run - Merimbula, 10km, May
- ☐☐ Mesa Falls Marathon—Ashton, Idaho
- ☐☐ Mezza di Monza (Italy)
- ☐☐ Miami Half-Marathon
- ☐☐ Middle East Peace Run
- ☐☐ Midnattsloppet (Sweden)
- ☐☐ Midnight Sun Marathon (Norway)
- ☑☐ Mini Mosman Fun Run 5km
- ☐☐ Monaco Marathon (Monaco)
- ☐☐ Mongolia S2S Marathon
- ☐☐ Montreal Oasis Marathon (Montreal)
- ☐☐ Mother's Day Classic - Adelaide - Peace Park, 7.2km, May
- ☐☐ Mother's Day Classic – Canberra, Commonwealth Park, 10km, May
- ☐☐ Mother's Day Classic - Darwin - East Point Reserve, Fannie Bay, 8km, May
- ☐☐ Mother's Day Classic - Hobart - Domain Athletics Centre, Upper Domain Road, Hobart, 8km, May
- ☐☐ Mother's Day Classic - Parramatta - Parramatta Park, 8km, May
- ☐☐ Mother's Day Classic - Perth - Langley Park, 8km, May
- ☐☐ Mother's Day Classic - Sydney - Sydney Domain, 8km, May
- ☐☐ Mount Desert Island Marathon
- ☐☐ Mount Fuji Marathon
- ☐☐ Mount Ku-ring-gai Track to Berowra Station
- ☐☐ Mountain bike down Death Road in Bolivia
- ☐☐ Mous Dash – Brisbane Sky Run
- ☐☐ MS Colour Dash Canberra - Black Mountain Peninsula, Acton, 5km, January
- ☐☐ MS Colour Dash Hobart - Royal Hobart Showgrounds, Hobart, 5km, January
- ☐☐ MS Colour Dash Melbourne - Docklands, Melbourne, 5km, January
- ☐☐ MS Colour Dash Sydney 5km Darling Harbour, Sydney, January
- ☐☐ MS Fun Run and Walk 5km Sydney, June

- ☐☐ Mt Solitary Ultra near Katoomba - 45km Trail Run, April
- ☐☐ Mt Ainslie Run Up and Power Walk In Canberra
- ☐☐ Mud Run
- ☐☐ Mud, Sweat and Beers - Obstacle Course - Wagga Wagga 10km, March
- ☐☐ Muddrella Obstacle Course
- ☐☐ Muddy Boots 10k
- ☐☐ Mudgee Running Festival
- ☐☐ Mutawintji Gorge Walk
- ☑☐ Narrabeen All Nighter in Sydney, NSW
- ☐☐ Narrowneck Night Run in Katoomba, New South Wales
- ☐☐ National Capital Marathon (Ottawa)
- ☐☐ Neat's Glen
- ☐☐ Nemo 33, the world's deepest swimming pool
- ☐☐ Neon Run Adelaide - Botanic Gardens, Adelaide, 5km, April
- ☐☐ Neon Run Melbourne - Albert Park Lake, 5km, February
- ☑☐ Neon Run Sydney Botanical Gardens
- ☐☐ New England's Covered Bridges Half-Marathon
- ☐☐ New Year's Resolution Fun Run - Harold Stevens Athletic track, Coburg, 12km, January
- ☐☐ New York City Marathon
- ☐☐ Newcastle Running Festival - Newcastle, 21.1km, April
- ☐☐ Nice Half-Marathon (France)
- ☐☐ Nordea Riga Marathon (Latvia)
- ☐☐ North Central Trail Marathon (Maryland)
- ☐☐ North Face Ultra Trail du Tour du Mont-Blanc (France)
- ☑☐ North Head
- ☐☐ North Pole Marathon
- ☐☐ Northern Argus Clare Valley Half Marathon - Clare Valley, 21.1km, April
- ☐☐ Northwest Passage Marathon—Arctic Canada
- ☑☐ Nurses Walk
- ☐☐ Oaks Cycle way
- ☑☐ Oatley Park Fun Run - Oatley West, 5km, April
- ☐☐ Oklahoma City Marathon (Oklahoma)
- ☐☐ Old Mutual Om Die Dam 50K (South Africa)
- ☐☐ Orange Colour City Running Festival - Orange, 42.2km, February
- ☐☐ Organise and direct a running race in Australia
- ☐☐ Outer Banks Marathon (North Carolina)
- ☑☐ Over Cliff Walk
- ☐☐ Oxfam Trail Walker Sydney - Hawkesbury, 100km, August
- ☐☐ Palma Marathon (Spain)
- ☐☐ Para River Classic - Salisbury, 10km, September
- ☐☐ Paris Marathon
- ☐☐ Paris-Versailles Run (France)
- ☐☐ Participate in a polar bear dip
- ☐☐ Participate in Australia Day Cockroach Race - Brisbane
- ☐☐ Participate in the Empire State Building Run Up (86 flights of stairs)
- ☐☐ Participate in the Great Cycle Challenge

- ☐☐ Participate in the Tough Mudder
- ☐☐ Patagonia International Marathon - Chile
- ☐☐ Pembrokeshire Coast Path National Trail, Wales
- ☐☐ People's Choice PJs Run
- ☐☐ Perimeter Trail
- ☐☐ Perth City to Surf Marathon
- ☐☐ Petra Marathon, Jordan
- ☐☐ Philadelphia Marathon (Pennsylvania)
- ☐☐ Polar Circle Marathon
- ☑☐ Pool of Siloam
- ☐☐ Prague International Marathon
- ☐☐ Prince Henry Cliff Walk
- ☐☐ Princes Pass to Blue Gum Forest
- ☑☐ Pub to Pub - The Strand, Dee Why, 13km, August
- ☐☐ Pulpit Rock
- ☐☐ Puma Glow Run
- ☐☐ Quebec City Marathon (Quebec)
- ☐☐ Queensland Half Marathon
- ☐☐ Quirindi Canter - Quirindi, 10km, April
- ☐☐ Rainbow Run - Geelong Showgrounds, Geelong, 5km, February
- ☐☐ Rainbow Run - Sydney Park, Sydney, 6km, February
- ☑☐ Rainforest Walk
- ☐☐ Raw Challenge: Doyalson, NSW - 6K - Obstacle Course
- ☐☐ Real Insurance – Spring Cycle
- ☐☐ Rebel Run Sydney - October, ANZ Stadium -Sydney Olympic Park
- ☑☐ Red Hands Cave
- ☐☐ Reggae Marathon (Jamaica)
- ☐☐ Resolute Track
- ☐☐ Reykjavik Marathon (Iceland)
- ☐☐ Richmond Marathon (Virginia)
- ☐☐ Ride bikes on the beach
- ☐☐ Ride the Tour De Cure Bike Ride for Cancer Charity
- ☐☐ Rio de Janeiro City Marathon (Brazil)
- ☐☐ Rio de Janeiro Marathon
- ☐☐ River Run 100 Ultramarathon
- ☐☐ River Tours Nepean & Warragamba Gorges
- ☐☐ Rock 'n' Roll Marathon (California)
- ☐☐ Rock 'n' Roll Seattle Marathon (Washington)
- ☐☐ Rock Solid Mud Run
- ☑☐ Rocket Point
- ☐☐ Rocks Walking Tour
- ☐☐ Rocky River Run - Sir Raymond Huish Drive, Rockhampton, 21.1km, May
- ☐☐ Rome Marathon (Italy)
- ☐☐ Romeo and Juliet Half-Marathon (Italy)
- ☑☐ Roseville Chase Rotary Fun Run, 10 km, July
- ☐☐ Rotterdam Marathon (Netherlands)
- ☐☐ Rottnest Marathon and Fun Run - Rottnest Island, 42.2km, October
- ☐☐ Round the Wolfgangsee 27K (Austria)
- ☑☐ Round Walk
- ☐☐ Route du VIN (Luxembourg)
- ☐☐ Royal National Park coastal walk - Bundeena to Otford, 31 km
- ☐☐ Ruined Castle Walk

- ☑☐ Run one race a month for one year (12 races)
- ☐☐ RUN 350
- ☑☐ Run 5km
- ☑☐ Run 10km
- ☑☐ Run 15km
- ☑☐ Run a course at night with glow gear
- ☑☐ Run a course in the rain
- ☑☐ Run a half-marathon
- ☑☐ Run a marathon
- ☐☐ Run a marathon in ACT
- ☐☐ Run a marathon in Africa
- ☐☐ Run a marathon in Antarctica
- ☐☐ Run a marathon in Asia
- ☐☐ Run a marathon in each state of Australia
- ☐☐ Run a marathon in Europe
- ☑☐ Run a marathon in New South Wales
- ☐☐ Run a marathon in North America
- ☐☐ Run a marathon in Northern Territory
- ☑☐ Run a marathon in Oceania
- ☐☐ Run a marathon in Queenstown
- ☐☐ Run a marathon in South Australia
- ☐☐ Run a marathon in Tasmania
- ☐☐ Run a marathon in Victoria
- ☐☐ Run a marathon in Western Australia
- ☐☐ Run a Mud Run
- ☑☐ Run a paint fight course
- ☐☐ Run a race in a crazy costume
- ☐☐ Run a race internationally
- ☐☐ Run a race on every inhabited continent
- ☐☐ Run a trail course
- ☑☐ Run an ultramarathon
- ☑☐ Run a zombie course
- ☐☐ Run Adelaide - Elder Park, Adelaide, 21.1km, April
- ☑☐ Run all the way up and down motion escalator
- ☑☐ Run an obstacle course
- ☐☐ Run Devonport - Roundhouse Park, Formby Rd, Devonport, 10km, March
- ☐☐ Run For the Hills Charity Event - Castle Hill, October
- ☐☐ Run For Your Freak'n Life
- ☐☐ Run For Your Lives - 5km Obstacle Zombie-Filled Course
- ☐☐ Run Melbourne
- ☐☐ Run or Dye
- ☐☐ Run Sunshine Coast
- ☐☐ Run the Big Five Marathon
- ☐☐ Run the Spoelana Naturist Race, Spain
- ☐☐ Run through a cornfield
- ☐☐ Run through a field of sunflowers
- ☐☐ Run to Rave
- ☐☐ Run to the Beat
- ☐☐ Run Townsville
- ☐☐ Run Warrandyte - The Warrandyte Sports Facility, Taroona Ave, Warrandyte, 12km, February
- ☐☐ Run Wild Missoula
- ☐☐ Run with the Wind
- ☐☐ Run4Autism
- ☐☐ Runner's World Zandvoort Circuit Run (Netherlands)
- ☐☐ Rwanda Marathon (Rwanda)
- ☐☐ Ryde Rivers Festival
- ☐☐ Ryde Rollercoaster, Bennelong Park, Ryde - 3.2 km
- ☐☐ Safaricom Marathon (Kenya)
- ☐☐ Sahara 100K (Tunisia)

- ☐☐ Salomon Chianti Ecomarathon (Italy)
- ☐☐ Salomon Trail Running Series
- ☐☐ Salt Lake City Marathon (Utah)
- ☐☐ Salvation loop trail
- ☐☐ San Francisco Marathon (California)
- ☐☐ San Silvestre Vallecana (Spain)
- ☐☐ Sandalford Vineyards Half-Marathon - Metricup Road, Wilyabrup, 21.1km, March
- ☐☐ Sandgate Sunset Run
- ☐☐ Scandinavian Adventure Run
- ☑☐ Scenic Walkway Blue Mountains
- ☐☐ Scotiabank Toronto Waterfront Marathon
- ☐☐ Seville Marathon (Spain)
- ☐☐ Seville to Los Palacios Half-Marathon (Spain)
- ☐☐ Shepparton Running Festival
- ☐☐ Sids Stampede
- ☐☐ Six Foot Track
- ☐☐ Six Foot Track Marathon – Blue Mountains, 42.2km, March
- ☐☐ Skovløberen Marathon (Denmark)
- ☐☐ Soft Sand Shuffle 4km
- ☐☐ Soft Sand Classic - Manly Beach
- ☐☐ South Australia Orroroo Half-Marathon - Orroroo, 21.1km, March
- ☐☐ South Kaibab Trail, Grand Canyon, Arizona, United States
- ☐☐ Southern Highland Challenge Half-Marathon, August
- ☐☐ Soweto Marathon (South Africa)
- ☐☐ Spartathlon (Greece)
- ☐☐ Sphinx Memorial to Bobbin Head Loop Track
- ☐☐ Splash 'n' Dash Festival: Wollongong, NSW - 5K
- ☐☐ Spray 'n' Run
- ☐☐ Springwood Sassatras Gully
- ☐☐ Sri Chinmoy Centennial Park Run - 7km, April
- ☐☐ St. Olavsloppet (Sweden)
- ☐☐ St. Peters Park run, November
- ☐☐ Stadium Stomp MCG
- ☐☐ Stadium Stomp SCG
- ☐☐ Standard Chartered Dubai Marathon (United Arab Emirates)
- ☐☐ Standard Chartered Hong Kong Marathon (Hong Kong)
- ☐☐ Standard Chartered Singapore Marathon (Singapore)
- ☐☐ Step Up for Down Syndrome (Sydney)
- ☐☐ Stockholm Marathon (Sweden)
- ☐☐ StonMarathon (Croatia)
- ☐☐ Stramilano Half (Italy)
- ☐☐ Strong Viking Run
- ☐☐ Suck It Up Buttercup 10 km Obstacle Course Tamworth, November
- ☐☐ Sunset Series - Tan - The Tan, 8km, February
- ☐☐ Sunset Series - Zoo -Melbourne Zoo, 8km, February
- ☐☐ Surf City USA Marathon (California)
- ☐☐ Sutherland Half-Marathon
- ☐☐ Swim across the English Channel
- ☐☐ Swiss Alpine Marathon (Switzerland)
- ☐☐ Swiss Alpine Running Festival
- ☐☐ Sydney Architecture Walks

- ☐☐ Sydney Marathon (Australia)
- ☑☐ Sydney Morning Herald Half Marathon - Sydney CBD, 21.1km, May
- ☐☐ Sydney Ride to Conquer Cancer
- ☑☐ Sydney Running Festival
- ☐☐ Sydney to the Gong Bike Ride for MS
- ☐☐ Sydney's Writers Walk
- ☐☐ Tallinn 21K (Estonia)
- ☐☐ Tamworth Running Festival - Tamworth, 21.1km, August
- ☐☐ Taroko Gorge Marathon (Taiwan)
- ☐☐ Tasmania Cadbury Marathon - Cadbury Chocolate Factory, Cadbury Estate in Claremont, 42.2km
- ☐☐ The Age Run Melbourne
- ☐☐ The Basin Track and Mackerel Track
- ☐☐ The Batemans Bay Fun Run - 5km
- ☑☐ The Bay Run – Iron Cove, Sydney Australia, 7km
- ☐☐ The Bloody Long Walk 35km Lighthouse to North Head to Cure Mito
- ☐☐ The Bondi to Coogee (Maroubra) Walk
- ☐☐ The Buffalo Stampede Ultra Run
- ☑☐ The Causeway
- ☐☐ The Charles Stuart University Bathurst Half-Marathon
- ☐☐ The Color Run Canberra- Canberra, 5km, February
- ☐☐ The Glo Run
- ☐☐ The Graffiti Run
- ☐☐ The Great Aussie Ram Run - Obstacles Course 5km
- ☐☐ The Great North Walk - Newcastle to Sydney 100km
- ☐☐ The Great Volcanic Mountain Challenge in Orange - 11km Off-Road
- ☐☐ The Honolulu Marathon
- ☐☐ The Husky Fun Runs at White Sands Park in Huskisson - 10km, February
- ☐☐ The Indy Mini Half-Marathon
- ☐☐ The Little Rock Marathon (Arkansas)
- ☐☐ The Lost Dutchman Marathon (Arizona)
- ☐☐ The North Face 100 - 50km Marathon
- ☑☐ The Real Insurance Sydney Harbour 10K
- ☐☐ The Stampede - Obstacle Course Sydney, November
- ☐☐ The Sydney Morning Herald Cole Classic
- ☑☐ The Sydney Morning Herald Sun Run
- ☐☐ The Sydney Skinny Ocean Swim - The Nude Event
- ☐☐ The TomTom Runner Western Sydney Marathon, October
- ☑☐ Three Sisters Walk
- ☐☐ Tjejmilen (Sweden)
- ☐☐ Tokyo Marathon (Japan)
- ☐☐ Top Ham Walking Track
- ☐☐ Tough Bloke Challenge
- ☐☐ Tour de Tirol (Austria)
- ☐☐ Townsville Running Festival
- ☐☐ TransVulcania (Spain)
- ☐☐ Trek through a jungle
- ☐☐ True Grit, Sydney
- ☐☐ Turin Marathon (Italy)

- ☐☐ Two Bays Trail Run - Dromana, Mornington Peninsula, 56km, January
- ☐☐ Two Oceans Marathon (South Africa)
- ☐☐ Ultimate Challenge Mud Run
- ☐☐ Ultra Trail Du Mont Blanc
- ☑☐ Undercliff Walk
- ☑☐ Unity Run and Walk
- ☐☐ Valencia Marathon (Spain)
- ☑☐ Variety Santa Fun Run
- ☐☐ Venice Marathon (Italy)
- ☐☐ Victory Track
- ☐☐ Vienna Marathon (Austria)
- ☐☐ Vila de Santa Pola Half-Marathon (Spain)
- ☐☐ Vilnius Marathon (Slovakia)
- ☐☐ Volunteer at a race
- ☐☐ Wagga Wagga Fun Run - Apex Park, Wagga Wagga, 11km, March
- ☐☐ Walk/run across hot coals
- ☑☐ Walk/run an overnight marathon
- ☐☐ Walk a high rope
- ☐☐ Walk across a country
- ☑☐ Walk across a railway track
- ☐☐ Walk across Capilano Suspension Bridge - British Columbia
- ☐☐ Walk across Golden Gate Bridge
- ☐☐ Walk across the Abbey Road Crosswalk "The Beatles Scene"
- ☐☐ Walk along an abandoned train line
- ☑☐ Walk around Chinatown
- ☑☐ Walk around Narrabeen Lakes
- ☑☐ Walk around the Woodcroft Lakeside
- ☐☐ Walk down Bourke Street, Melbourne, and see amazing Christmas shop window designs
- ☐☐ Walk in Jack the Ripper's footsteps
- ☐☐ Walk of Faith – glass walkway built on the side of a mountain – China
- ☐☐ Walk on a frozen lake
- ☐☐ Walk on stilts
- ☐☐ Walk on the Great Wall of China
- ☐☐ Walk on the Red Carpet
- ☑☐ Walk on the Scenic Skyway glass see-through platform, experience like walking on air
- ☑☐ Walk the Great Ocean Road
- ☐☐ Walk the Kokoda Track
- ☐☐ Walk the path of a volcano at Undara Lava Tubes and sleep in a converted train carriage
- ☐☐ Walk though and photograph an abandoned building
- ☐☐ Walk through Japan's Tunnel of Lights
- ☑☐ Walk through city of Sydney
- ☑☐ Walk through Hyde Park
- ☐☐ Walk under Madagascar's ancient baobab trees
- ☑☐ Walk up the 246 steps William Wallace monument, Scotland
- ☑☐ Walk/run distance of a beach
- ☐☐ Wallaroo Walking Track
- ☐☐ Walls Lookout Track
- ☐☐ Walt Disney World Marathon (Florida)
- ☐☐ Wanda Spring Beach Classic
- ☐☐ Waratah Walking Track
- ☐☐ Warsaw Marathon (Poland)

- ☐☐ Washpool/Gibraltar World Heritage Trails 50km
- ☐☐ We Can Walk It Out - Kings Domain, Alexandra Avenue, Melbourne, 8km, February
- ☑☐ Weeping Rock Circuit - Wentworth Falls
- ☑☐ Wentworth Falls - Lakes
- ☑☐ Wentworth Falls - Waterfalls
- ☑☐ West Head
- ☐☐ Western States Endurance Run
- ☐☐ Western Sydney Marathon
- ☐☐ Wiggins Track
- ☐☐ Wild Endurance 50km Team Challenge
- ☐☐ Wild Women on Top Sydney Coastrek 100km Team Challenge
- ☐☐ Willunga Trig Walking Track
- ☐☐ Winelands Marathon (South Africa)
- ☐☐ Wingello Trail Classic
- ☐☐ Winter Marathon (Sweden)
- ☐☐ Woronora "Dam Pipeline Trail Run"
- ☐☐ Yakima River Canyon Marathon (Washington)
- ☐☐ Yarra Bend Fun Run - Yarra Bend Park, Yarra Bend Road, Fairfield, 12km, February
- ☐☐ Yoma Yangon International Marathon - Myanmar
- ☐☐ Yurrebilla Trail 56 km Ultra
- ☐☐ Zazzle Bay-to-Breakers 12K San Francisco
- ☐☐ Zevenheuvelenloop (Netherlands)
- ☑☐ Zig Zag Railways Walkway
- ☐☐ Zombie Escape Survival Challenge (ZESC) - Be a Zombie for the Event
- ☐☐ Zombie Escape Survival Challenge (ZESC) - Sydney, May
- ☐☐ Zombie Walk - Sydney Hyde Park to Prince Alfred Park

Chapter 9: National Parks and National Beauty Worldwide

"From a small seed a mighty trunk may grow."

Aeschylus

Beautiful houses and expensive yachts, and a beach that is positioned with views: we spend so much time wanting the high-end line things in life but do we ever consider that the national parks and nature's landmarks are so beautiful? Do we ever take time to relax, unwind and soak in the atmosphere around us rather than a pollution-filled city with noises of traffic, honking horns and annoying sounds that blast out the sounds of nature? Birds singing, cicadas buzzing in the summertime: the sounds of nature are a great way of relaxing – and there is also fresh air to breath in. Rock faces and canyons and gorges: the Kimberley is one of the most known in Australia with beautiful red rock and water flowing from waterfalls. As you take it all in, consider a lot of the world is covered in houses. It's good to just look back at a piece of the past where it has not been taken over by man-made products and housing.

- ☐☐ The Heart River, a tributary of the Missouri River, approximately 180 mi (290 km), western North Dakota, USA
- ☐☐ Bungle Bungle National Park
- ☐☐ 2000-year-old tree in South Africa known as Tree of Life
- ☐☐ 300-year-old Oak trees, Oak Alley Plantation, Louisiana
- ☐☐ 659 steps to the top: The Guatape Rock in Colombia
- ☐☐ Antelope Canyon, Arizona
- ☐☐ Aurland Lookout, Norway
- ☐☐ Bald Hill Lookout
- ☐☐ Bali Province's Subak System, Indonesia
- ☐☐ Banff National Park
- ☐☐ Baobab Avenue, Madagascar
- ☐☐ Barossa Valley
- ☐☐ Black Turtle Cove
- ☑☐ Blow Hole, Kiama
- ☐☐ Bungle Bungle Range in Purnululu National Park
- ☑☐ Cadi Jam Ora
- ☐☐ Cahill's Lookout
- ☐☐ Canyon de Chelly National Monument, Arizona

- ☐☐ Cape of Good Hope, South Africa
- ☐☐ Cascate Del Mulino, Saturnia, Tuscany, Italy
- ☐☐ Cataract Gorge
- ☐☐ Chapada dos Veadeiros National Park
- ☐☐ Check out the view at the Amalfi Coast in Italy
- ☐☐ Clark Island on Port Jackson, Sydney Harbour
- ☐☐ Cling to a cliff, China
- ☐☐ Clingmans Dome, Great Smoky Mountains National Park, TN
- ☐☐ Cockatoo Island
- ☐☐ Colca Canyon
- ☐☐ Colored Fields of Yunnan, China
- ☐☐ Conguillío National Park
- ☐☐ Convict rampart on Mt Victoria pass
- ☐☐ Coorong National Park
- ☐☐ Copperfield Bay at Musha Cay, Bahamas
- ☐☐ Corcovado National Park
- ☐☐ Corona Arch near Moab Utah
- ☐☐ Corsica, France
- ☐☐ Cotopaxi National Park
- ☐☐ Den Fernella
- ☐☐ Devils Marbles
- ☐☐ Discovery Bay Coastal Park
- ☐☐ Douglas Apsley National Park
- ☐☐ El Cajas
- ☐☐ Erskine Lookout
- ☐☐ Étretat, France
- ☐☐ Federal Pass
- ☐☐ Fernando De Noronha, Brazil
- ☐☐ Finistère, France
- ☐☐ Fitz Roy
- ☐☐ Franklin-Gordon Wild Rivers National Park
- ☐☐ Fraser Island
- ☐☐ Freycinet National Park, Tasmania, Australia
- ☐☐ Galápagos National Park
- ☐☐ Geirangerfjord and Nærøyfjord, Norway
- ☐☐ General Sherman Tree Sequoia National Park - largest tree in the world
- ☐☐ Geothermal attraction Rotorua
- ☐☐ Glacier Bay National Park and surrounding Icy Straits in Southeast
- ☐☐ Glacier National Park (Montana)
- ☐☐ Glenbrook Gorge
- ☐☐ Golden Horn, Brac Island, Croatia
- ☐☐ Gorges de l'Areuse, Switzerland
- ☐☐ Grampians National Park
- ☐☐ Grand Canyon (Arizona)
- ☐☐ Granite Island
- ☐☐ Hawai'i Volcanoes National Park
- ☐☐ Heart Sea Arch, Portugal
- ☐☐ Hole n' the Rock, Moab, Utah
- ☐☐ Horseshoe Bend, Arizona, USA
- ☐☐ Huanglong, Tibetan China
- ☐☐ Iguazú National Park, Argentina
- ☐☐ Inishmore, Aran Islands, Ireland
- ☑☐ Isle of Skye, Scotland
- ☐☐ Jeju Island Lava Tubes, South Korea
- ☐☐ Jiuzhaigou National Park, Sichuan Province, China
- ☐☐ Jungle Safari in Khao Sok National Park
- ☐☐ Katherine Gorge
- ☐☐ Katherine Hot Springs

- ☐☐ Kimberley
- ☐☐ Kings Canyon NT, Australia
- ☐☐ Kjeragbolten, Norway
- ☐☐ Kruger National Park
- ☐☐ La cascada Del Limón (El Limón, Dominican Republic)
- ☐☐ Lava fields covered with moss in Vestur-Skaftafellssysla, Iceland
- ☐☐ Lavender Fields, South of France
- ☐☐ Lena Pillars Nature Park, Russia
- ☐☐ Lençóis Maranhenses National Park
- ☐☐ Leura Cascades
- ☐☐ Leura Forests
- ☐☐ Light and shade at Grand Sand Dunes National Park, Colorado
- ☐☐ Lion Park, South Africa Zoo
- ☐☐ Lion Rock, Hong Kong
- ☐☐ Lion's Head, Cape Town, South Africa
- ☐☐ Litchfield National Park
- ☐☐ Loch Ard Gorge
- ☐☐ Look into the mouth of a volcano
- ☐☐ Lookout "The Rock" Nepean Gorge
- ☐☐ Lookout on a New York rooftop
- ☐☐ Madagascar's Stone Forest
- ☐☐ Masada, Masada National Park, Israel
- ☑☐ McMahons Point Lookout
- ☐☐ Mesa Verde National Park (Colorado)
- ☑☐ Milson Point Lookout
- ☐☐ Mon, Denmark
- ☐☐ Moraine Lake, Banff National Park, Alberta, Canada
- ☐☐ Morning Glory Pool, Upper Geyser Basin, Yellowstone National Park, Wyoming
- ☐☐ Mossy Forest (White Peak), Cagayan Valley Province, Philippines
- ☐☐ Mount Portal, Lookout Point
- ☐☐ Mount Wellington Lookout Point
- ☐☐ Mountain Ash (Eucalyptus regnans) over Black Spur Drive, Victoria, Australia
- ☐☐ Mud Volcanoes of Gobustan, Azerbaijan
- ☐☐ Mungo National Park
- ☐☐ Na Pali Coast, Kauai, Hawaii, United States
- ☐☐ Nambung National Park
- ☐☐ National Pass
- ☐☐ Nature Track
- ☐☐ Navigating the world's highest climbing wall (nicknamed the "French Fry")
- ☑☐ Nepean Gorge
- ☐☐ Nitmiluk National Park
- ☐☐ Oneonta Gorge, Oregon
- ☑☐ Palm Grove
- ☑☐ Palm House
- ☐☐ Paracas National Reservation
- ☐☐ Paradise Cliffs, Norway
- ☐☐ Paria Canyon, Arizona, United States
- ☐☐ Patagonia is a region located at the Southern end of South America, territory shared by Argentina and Chile, boasting some of the most dramatic landscapes on Earth
- ☐☐ Pembrokshire Coast, National Park
- ☐☐ Pisgah Rock

- ☐☐ Pulpit Rock, Preikestolen, Norway
- ☐☐ Punkaharju Esker Nature Reserve, Finland
- ☐☐ Pu'uhonua o Honaunau Historical Park
- ☑☐ Queen Victoria Lookout
- ☑☐ Rare and threatened plants, gardens
- ☐☐ Rietvlei Nature Reserve
- ☐☐ Ring of Kerry, Ireland
- ☐☐ Rocky Mountains
- ☐☐ Sacred Valley
- ☐☐ Salt Flats
- ☐☐ Samariá Gorge
- ☐☐ Sea Horse: Camel Rock, Berguami, Australia
- ☐☐ Sea of Salt. National Park Salar de Uyuni, Bolivia
- ☐☐ See lava flowing from a volcano
- ☐☐ See Nelsons Column
- ☐☐ See Old Faithful (Wyoming)
- ☐☐ See sand dunes of Port Stephens
- ☐☐ See Tasmania's natural beauty
- ☐☐ See the Aphrodite's Rock in Cyprus
- ☐☐ See the Cherry Blossoms in Japan
- ☐☐ See the La Brea Tar Pits
- ☐☐ See the Redwood Forest
- ☐☐ See the Turpentine Tree, Kurrajong Heights, Blue Mountains
- ☐☐ Sitting Elephant, Valley of Fire State Park, Nevada
- ☐☐ Siwa Oasis, Egypt
- ☐☐ Skaftafell National Park, Iceland
- ☐☐ South Lawson Waterfalls
- ☐☐ Stara Fuzina, Triglav National Park, Slovenia
- ☐☐ Swiss National Park
- ☑☐ Sydney Fernery
- ☑☐ Sydney Tropical Centre
- ☐☐ Tanah's Lot is a rock formation off the Indonesian island of Bali
- ☐☐ Termite mound - Litchfield National Park, Australia
- ☐☐ The "Lost City" NT - Australia
- ☐☐ The Bay of Fundy, Canada
- ☐☐ The Door to Hell, Turkmenistan
- ☐☐ The Fjords of Norway
- ☐☐ The Fountains of Bellagio, Las Vegas
- ☐☐ The Hydrothermal Vents (Deep sea vents)
- ☑☐ The Prime Minister's Corridor of Oaks
- ☐☐ The Shilin Stone Forest, China
- ☐☐ The Totem Pole, Tasmania, Australia
- ☐☐ The Tyrol Overlook, Mount Isidor, Austria
- ☐☐ The Wizard's Hat, Bandon, Oregon
- ☑☐ The Wollemi Pine
- ☐☐ Torndirrup National Park
- ☐☐ Torres Del Paine National Park
- ☐☐ Totem Pole Dunes, Arizona, USA
- ☐☐ Tree Tunnel - Ballynoe, County Down, Northern Ireland
- ☐☐ Trolltunga is a piece of rock that stands horizontally out of the mountain above Skjeggedal in Odda, Norway
- ☐☐ Tsingy de Bemaraha Strict Nature Reserve, Madagascar
- ☐☐ Tsitskam National Park

- ☐☐ Tunnel of Trees Ukraine
- ☐☐ Tunnel View Lookout
- ☐☐ Unique Potato Chip Rock in San Diego
- ☐☐ Valley of Waters
- ☐☐ Verdon Gorge, Provence, France
- ☐☐ Visit a place with crystal clear waters
- ☐☐ Visit a volcano
- ☑☐ Visit Hunter Valley vineyards
- ☐☐ Visit Kakadu
- ☐☐ Visit National Arches Park
- ☑☐ Visit The Gap Park
- ☐☐ Visit the Mesa Verde, National Park in Colorado
- ☐☐ Visit the Serengeti
- ☐☐ Visit the Wave - Utah, USA
- ☐☐ Visit Uluru
- ☐☐ Visit Yosemite Valley (California)
- ☐☐ Volcan Isluga National Park
- ☐☐ Wave Rock, WA
- ☐☐ Weird Geology: Ringing Rocks
- ☐☐ West Head Lookout
- ☐☐ West MacDonnell National Park
- ☐☐ Whitsunday Islands
- ☐☐ William Bay National Park
- ☐☐ Wilpena Pound
- ☐☐ Windjana Gorge - NT, Australia
- ☐☐ Yarra Valley
- ☐☐ Yellowstone National Park, Wyoming
- ☐☐ YingXi Corridor of Stone Peaks, China
- ☐☐ Zimbabwe - Balancing Rocks

Chapter 10: Rainforests, Mountain Ranges, Craters and Deserts

"Love the moment and the energy of that moment will spread beyond all boundaries."

Corita Kent

Craters have been a fascination of man for decades. The moon is covered in craters created by meteorites and asteroids hitting on impact. We also have our own craters all around Earth where massive asteroids and meteorites have hit the Earth leaving their dint. One of the largest craters is located within Australia in Western Australia, another located in New Mexico and numerous other craters located around the world.

Australia's Tropical Rainforest covers approximately 900,000 square hectares and is internationally recognised as being one of the most ecologically fascinating natural areas in the world. Another rainforest that is truly recognisable by people around the world is the Amazon Rainforest covering 5,500,000 square kilometres, making Australia's dense rainforest minor in comparison. The view of the mountain ranges is breathtaking and a beautiful backdrop as commonly seen in calendars. The Himalayas, the Rocky Mountains and also the Great Dividing Range are the most iconic ranges around the world. They are sought after for photo moments and many adventures like the thrill of climbing them.

A desert is a barren area of land where little precipitation occurs and consequently, living conditions are hostile for plant and animal life. The largest (nonpolar) desert in the world is the Sahara, in North Africa, which spans an area measured at roughly 3.5 million square miles.

- ☐☐ Africa's Rift Valley
- ☐☐ Alice Springs Desert Park
- ☐☐ Alps
- ☐☐ Andes
- ☐☐ Appalachian Mountains
- ☑☐ Ben Nevis Mountain, Fort William, Scotland
- ☐☐ Big Hole
- ☐☐ Blue Ridge Mountains
- ☐☐ Borneo Rainforest Canopy Walkway, Malaysia/Indonesia/Burnei
- ☐☐ Carpathian Mountains
- ☐☐ Cascade Range
- ☐☐ Caucasus Mountains
- ☐☐ Central Station Rainforest
- ☐☐ Chimborazo
- ☐☐ Cradle Mountain Tasmania
- ☐☐ Cross a desert
- ☐☐ Daintree Rainforest
- ☐☐ Dalgaranga Crater
- ☐☐ Dandenong Ranges
- ☐☐ Diamond Head Crater, Oahu, Hawaii
- ☐☐ Dolomites Mountains, Italy
- ☐☐ Experience a sunrise in the desert
- ☐☐ Explore the Amazon Rainforest
- ☐☐ Fiji Zip Line - thrilling rainforest adventure
- ☐☐ Goat Paddock Crater
- ☐☐ Great Dividing Range
- ☐☐ Hill of Tara, Ireland
- ☐☐ Hillside, Hokkaido Japan
- ☐☐ Hindu Kush
- ☐☐ Ilhéu da Vila, Portugal
- ☐☐ Jeita Grotto, Nahr al-Kalb Valley, Lebanon
- ☐☐ Jiuzhaigou valley Sichuan
- ☐☐ Karakoram
- ☐☐ Lanin
- ☐☐ Lauterbrunnen Valley, Switzerland
- ☐☐ Magnificent Namib Desert
- ☑☐ Melba Gully Rainforest Walk
- ☐☐ Minnamurra Rainforest
- ☐☐ Mystery Hill, USA
- ☐☐ Nazca Desert, Peru
- ☐☐ Ngorongoro Crater, Tanzania
- ☐☐ Pacific Coast Ranges
- ☐☐ Pamir Mountains
- ☐☐ Piccaninny Crater
- ☐☐ Piz Bernina
- ☐☐ Pyrenees
- ☐☐ Rigi - Switzerland Mountain
- ☐☐ Rocky Mountains Ranges
- ☑☐ Roll down a hill
- ☑☐ Roll down a hill in a large tyre
- ☑☐ Roll down a really big hill
- ☐☐ Sahara Desert
- ☐☐ Schilthorn
- ☐☐ See Mt. Fuji - Shizuoka, Japan
- ☐☐ Shoemaker Crater
- ☐☐ Sierra Nevada
- ☐☐ Spider Crater
- ☐☐ Sugarloaf Mountain
- ☐☐ Swiss Alps, Switzerland
- ☐☐ Switzerland - Jungfrau Mountain
- ☐☐ Taygetus
- ☐☐ The Barringer Meteor Crater
- ☐☐ The mirny diamond mine in Russia is the world's biggest hole - it's 525 metres deep and 1.25km wide
- ☐☐ The multicoloured, volcanic crater Lakes of Mount Kelimutu, Indonesia
- ☐☐ Tian Shan
- ☐☐ Tianmen Mountain, China
- ☐☐ Travel through the Simpson Desert, NT, Australia

- ☐☐ Ural Mountains
- ☐☐ Veevers Crater
- ☐☐ Victoria Peak, Hong Kong
- ☐☐ Visit the Himalayas
- ☐☐ Wolfe Creek Crater
- ☐☐ Woodleigh Crater
- ☐☐ Yarrabubba Crater
- ☐☐ Zagros Mountains

Chapter 11: Board Games, Backyard Games, Puzzles and Toys

"My definition of an adventure game is an interactive story set with puzzles and obstacles to solve and worlds to explore."

Roberta Williams

Life is like a jigsaw puzzle, connecting the pieces together on a puzzle to work out where the pieces connect together. As a young child I grew up with puzzles and playing board games such as Monopoly, but nowadays a lot of board games are converted into video games. It's a shame since board games were a great way to get families together and play at least once a week and talk with one another. But technology changes and, yes, very few of us still play them because we play games on computers or our mobile phone. It's amazing how much we allow technology to change our lifestyles.

- ☐☐ Attend a board gamers café meet and greet
- ☐☐ Build a 3D puzzle
- ☐☐ Build a huge Lego model
- ☑☐ Finish a crossword puzzle
- ☑☐ Finish a find-a-word
- ☑☐ Finish a jigsaw puzzle
- ☑☐ Finish a Sudoku puzzle
- ☐☐ Go bobbing for apples
- ☑☐ Play a game of Poker
- ☐☐ Play 7 Wonders
- ☐☐ Play a Game of Thrones
- ☐☐ Play Acquire
- ☐☐ Play Agricola
- ☐☐ Play Alhambra
- ☐☐ Play Amazing Race
- ☐☐ Play Apples to Apples
- ☐☐ Play Arkham Horror
- ☐☐ Play Articulate
- ☐☐ Play Axis and Allies
- ☑☐ Play Backgammon
- ☑☐ Play Balderdash
- ☑☐ Play Barrel of Monkeys
- ☑☐ Play Battleship
- ☐☐ Play Battlestar Galactica
- ☐☐ Play Betrayal at House on the Hill
- ☑☐ Play Bingo
- ☐☐ Play Blokus
- ☐☐ Play Blood Bowl
- ☐☐ Play Boggle
- ☐☐ Play Bop It
- ☑☐ Play Buckaroo
- ☐☐ Play Candyland
- ☐☐ Play Carcassonne
- ☐☐ Play Cards against Humanity

- ☐☐ Play Catch Phrase
- ☐☐ Play Caylus
- ☐☐ Play Charades
- ☑☐ Play Chess
- ☑☐ Play Chinese Checkers
- ☑☐ Play Chutes-and-Ladders Game
- ☐☐ Play CLUE
- ☐☐ Play Cluedo
- ☑☐ Play Connect Four
- ☐☐ Play Cosmic Encounter
- ☑☐ Play Cranium
- ☐☐ Play Descent
- ☐☐ Play Diplomacy
- ☐☐ Play Dixit
- ☐☐ Play Dominant Species
- ☐☐ Play Dominion
- ☑☐ Play Dominoes
- ☐☐ Play Don't Break the Ice
- ☐☐ Play Dungeon Quest
- ☐☐ Play Dungeon
- ☑☐ Play Dungeons and Dragons
- ☐☐ Play Eclipse
- ☐☐ Play El Grande
- ☐☐ Play Fear Factor
- ☐☐ Play Go
- ☑☐ Play Guess Who?
- ☑☐ Play Hedbanz
- ☐☐ Play Hi Ho! Cherry-O
- ☐☐ Play Hot Potato with a real potato
- ☑☐ Play Hungry Hungry Hippo
- ☑☐ Play Jenga
- ☐☐ Play Jumanji
- ☐☐ Play Kerplunk
- ☐☐ Play Key to the Kingdom
- ☐☐ Play Knowledge
- ☐☐ Play Labyrinth
- ☐☐ Play Le Havre
- ☐☐ Play Logo
- ☑☐ Play Magic: The Gathering
- ☑☐ Play Mahjong
- ☐☐ Play Mancala
- ☑☐ Play Mastermind
- ☐☐ Play Messy Twister
- ☐☐ Play Mind Trap
- ☑☐ Play Monopoly
- ☑☐ Play Mouse Trap
- ☐☐ Play Munchkin
- ☐☐ Play Naked Twister
- ☐☐ Play Netrunner
- ☑☐ Play Operation
- ☐☐ Play Pac-Man
- ☐☐ Play Pandemic
- ☐☐ Play Pay Day
- ☑☐ Play Pictionary
- ☑☐ Play Pokemon
- ☑☐ Play Pop Up Pirate
- ☐☐ Play Power Grid
- ☐☐ Play Puerto Rico
- ☐☐ Play Qwirkle
- ☐☐ Play Reversi/Othello
- ☑☐ Play Risk
- ☐☐ Play Runewars
- ☐☐ Play Say Anything
- ☑☐ Play Scattergories
- ☐☐ Play Scene It
- ☐☐ Play Scotland Yard
- ☑☐ Play Scrabble
- ☐☐ Play Sequence
- ☐☐ Play Settlers of Catan
- ☐☐ Play Shadows over Camelot
- ☐☐ Play Shogun
- ☐☐ Play Skip Bo
- ☐☐ Play Small World
- ☐☐ Play Sorry
- ☐☐ Play StarCraft
- ☐☐ Play Stratego
- ☐☐ Play Summoner Wars
- ☐☐ Play Survivor
- ☐☐ Play Taboo
- ☑☐ Play Talisman
- ☑☐ Play Test Cricket

- ☐☐ Play The Game of Life
- ☐☐ Play The Invasion of Canada
- ☐☐ Play The Lord of the Rings
- ☐☐ Play Through the Ages: A Story of Civilization
- ☐☐ Play Ticket to Ride
- ☐☐ Play Tigris and Euphrates
- ☑☐ Play Trivial Pursuit
- ☑☐ Play Trouble
- ☐☐ Play Twilight Imperium
- ☐☐ Play Twilight Struggle
- ☑☐ Play UNO
- ☑☐ Play Uno Attack
- ☑☐ Play Upwords
- ☐☐ Play Warhammer
- ☐☐ Play Wasabi
- ☐☐ Play Wheel of Fortune
- ☐☐ Play Who Wants To Be A Millionaire
- ☐☐ Play Wits and Wagers
- ☑☐ Play Yahtzee
- ☑☐ Solve a Rubik's Cube

Chapter 12:
My Home Lifestyle Dreams

*"Where we love is home - home that our feet
may leave, but not our hearts."*

Oliver Wendell Holmes, Sr.

Ever dream of that perfect house that you have always wanted with everything you need in your life, or are you just happy to live the way you do now, in a house you call home? There are always split opinions by people, but most of us always turn to dreaming about that great lifestyle where the house we live in is built like a palace with nothing out of place and everything we need around us to live a happy life with our home comfortable and luxurious. We go home after a hard day's work and just want to relax. Sometimes we relax by watching our favourite television shows. Some have a beautiful kitchen to cook our delicious dinners in at night. Some of us finish work early enough to even look after our gardens. No matter how we live our lives, our homes are unique and we all desire in our lives to own one. Yet the true fact is a lot of us can't afford the extreme cost of housing and are turned away and need to rent most our lives. My aim is to own the perfect dream home, and with everything below I desire for my home.

- ☐☐ Built-in wardrobes
- ☐☐ Designed kitchen
- ☐☐ Double-bay parking garage
- ☐☐ Double-storey house
- ☐☐ Fire alarms
- ☐☐ Have a beautiful garden
- ☐☐ Have a pet dog
- ☐☐ Home office and study
- ☐☐ Home theatre room
- ☐☐ Internet
- ☐☐ Main ensuite
- ☐☐ Own a spa
- ☐☐ Pay television
- ☐☐ Renovate a house
- ☐☐ Safety locks and doors
- ☐☐ Sandstone front-yard fencing
- ☐☐ Solar power
- ☐☐ Spacious backyard
- ☐☐ Storage space
- ☐☐ Walk-in designer shower
- ☐☐ Walk-in wardrobe main
- ☐☐ Window shutters

Chapter 14: Theme Parks and Renowned Rides Wordwide

"Disney's something to be a little alarmed about. It's not just a little theme park anymore. It's now an ethic and outlook and strategy that goes way beyond central Florida."

Carl Hiaasen

Do yourself a favour and check out as many of these thrilling attractions as you can and hold on tight for the most spine-tingling, hair-raising roller coasters and excitement of theme parks all around the world. As kids, we love and enjoy the thrills and excitement that a theme park creates for us. But as adults, we appreciate the chance to embark on experiencing the rides we were too scared to go on as a child, not tall enough to ride, or even the factor of our parents not letting us go on the ride in fear that something will go wrong. We get the chance to take the plunge and go for it. As an adult, you might as well experience everything in the world you can because you never know the feeling of the excitement that a theme park can create until you explore one for yourself. Enjoy life and live like you're a kid once again. Fun times in life keep us happy and wanting more; we seek more adventures all the time, it's like a shot of adrenalin to keep you going.

- ☐☐ 0 to 240 km/hr, Ferrari World Abu Dhabi, United Arab Emirates
- ☐☐ 100-year-old Ferris Wheel Riesenrad - Vienna, Austria
- ☐☐ A Maze'N Things
- ☐☐ Adventure World
- ☐☐ Amaze n' Place
- ☐☐ Ashcombe Maze, Shoreham
- ☐☐ Aussie Waterballs, Broadbeach, Gold Coast
- ☐☐ Aussie World, QLD
- ☑☐ Australia's Wonderland
- ☐☐ Bakken Amusement Park
- ☐☐ Bellingham Maze | Tanawha, Sunshine Coast Area
- ☐☐ Conquer the "Big 8" thrill rides at Dreamworld
- ☐☐ CSI Experience
- ☐☐ Dinosaur Park
- ☐☐ Disney California Adventure
- ☐☐ Disney's Animal Kingdom
- ☐☐ Disney's Hollywood Studios

- ☐☐ Dracula's Haunted House, Surfers Paradise, Gold Coast
- ☐☐ Dreamworld
- ☐☐ Epcot
- ☐☐ Ferrari World, Dubai
- ☑☐ Fox Studios
- ☐☐ Go to an amusement park and go on every ride they have
- ☐☐ Go to Universal Studios, Hollywood, California
- ☐☐ Gold Reef City Theme Park
- ☐☐ Happy Magic Water Cube Water Park, Beijing
- ☐☐ Hopi Hari Theme Park
- ☐☐ Insano waterslide is located at the Beach Park in Fortaleza, Brazil
- ☐☐ Jambaroo Water Park
- ☐☐ King Arthur's Labyrith
- ☐☐ Kryal Castle Adventure Park
- ☐☐ La Feria Chapultepec Mágico
- ☐☐ Las Vegas Stratosphere Insanity Ride
- ☐☐ Legoland
- ☑☐ Luna Park, Sydney
- ☐☐ Luna Park, Melbourne
- ☐☐ Magic Kingdom
- ☐☐ Manly Waterworks
- ☐☐ Mazes of Infinity
- ☑☐ Melbourne Star Observation Wheel
- ☐☐ Movie World
- ☐☐ Old Mogo Town Gold Rush Theme Park
- ☐☐ Otway Fly Treetop Adventures
- ☐☐ Phantasialand
- ☐☐ Ride the scariest rollercoaster in the U.S - the Kingdom Ka at Six Flags in Jackson, NJ
- ☐☐ Ride the Vanish Roller Coaster in Japan
- ☐☐ Ride the world's longest zip line, South Africa
- ☐☐ Ride the world's tallest Ferris Wheel - Singapore Flyer
- ☐☐ Ripley's Believe It or Not, Queensland
- ☑☐ Scenic Cableway
- ☑☐ Scenic Railway
- ☑☐ Scenic Skyway
- ☑☐ Scenic World
- ☐☐ Sea World
- ☐☐ SeaWorld Orlando
- ☐☐ Techniquest
- ☑☐ Thomas the Tank Train Rides
- ☐☐ Timber Town, Wauchope, NSW
- ☐☐ Toboggan Hill Park, Nelson Bay
- ☐☐ Tree Top Adventure Park
- ☐☐ Underwater roller coaster in Japan
- ☐☐ Universal Orlando
- ☐☐ Visit the Coney Island Pier
- ☐☐ Visit the real Santa Claus in Lapland
- ☐☐ Walt Disney Imagineering
- ☐☐ Walt Disney Studios
- ☐☐ Walt Disney World
- ☐☐ Water slide through shark tank at Golden Nugget in Las Vegas
- ☐☐ Wet and Wild
- ☐☐ Whitewater World
- ☐☐ Wonders of the Orient – Chinese Theme park, Central Coast, New South Wales
- ☐☐ Xcaret Theme Park
- ☐☐ Xel-Ha Theme Park

Chapter 15: Zoos Worldwide

"People go to the zoo and they like the lion because it's scary. And the bear because it's intense, but the monkey makes people laugh."

Lorne Michaels

Every zoo around the world has their own unique experiences, from different zoo keepers to animals unique to that area of the world. Some are large mass in size and others are small. Some zoos mainly focus on specific animals, for example the big large cats, or like my local zoo, Featherdale, focuses around Australian wildlife. Visiting different zoos allows us to view many types of animals, find out about different animals and to help the zoos to fight extinction of your favourite animals. A lot of people judge zoos as cruel as they lock the animals up in captivity. However, if you view the other side of the scale and see the difference they do for animals and protecting them, keeping them healthy and safe from harm. You will understand, yes, they may lock them in cages, behind big walls or even glass cabinets, but out in the wild they are unfortunately shot by poachers for their skins, their tusks and many other things used to make cruel man-made products on the black markets.

I support the zoos and the abilities they have to keep species around the world from extinction and continuing to breed the animals for future generations to come so our children and relatives can see them in the future and are able to view such amazing, beautiful animals throughout our world.

- ☐☐ Aalborg Zoo
- ☐☐ Adelaide Zoo
- ☐☐ Air Zoo
- ☐☐ Akron Zoo
- ☐☐ Alabama Gulf Coast Zoo
- ☐☐ Alexandria Zoo
- ☐☐ Alice Springs Desert Park, Alice Springs
- ☐☐ Alice Springs Reptile Centre, Alice Springs
- ☐☐ Armadale Reptile Centre, Armadale
- ☐☐ Auckland Zoo
- ☐☐ Audubon Zoo
- ☐☐ Austin Zoo & Animal Sanctuary
- ☐☐ Australia Walkabout Wildlife Park, Calga, Central Coast

- ☐☐ Australian Reptile Centre
- ☑☐ Australian Reptile Park
- ☐☐ Australian Shark and Ray Centre
- ☐☐ Australia Zoo
- ☐☐ Bali Zoo
- ☐☐ Ballarat Wildlife Park
- ☐☐ Banham Zoo
- ☐☐ Barefoot Bushman Wildlife Park, Airlie Beach
- ☐☐ Big Swamp Wildlife Park, Bunbury
- ☐☐ Billabong Koala and Wildlife Park
- ☐☐ Billabong Sanctuary, Nome, Townsville
- ☐☐ Binder Park Zoo
- ☐☐ Birdland Animal Park, Batemans Bay
- ☐☐ Blackbutt Reserve, Kotara
- ☐☐ Blackpool Zoo
- ☐☐ Blank Park Zoo
- ☐☐ Bonorong Wildlife Conservation Centre, Brighton
- ☐☐ Brevard Zoo
- ☐☐ Brisbane Forest Park, Brisbane
- ☐☐ Bristol Zoo Gardens
- ☐☐ Bronx Zoo
- ☐☐ Brookfield Zoo
- ☐☐ Buenos Aires Zoo
- ☐☐ Burgers' Zoo
- ☐☐ Buttonwood Park Zoo
- ☐☐ Cairns Tropical Zoo
- ☐☐ Cairns Zoo and Wildlife Dome -Cairns, Cairns Area
- ☐☐ Cameron Park Zoo
- ☐☐ Caversham Wildlife Park, Whiteman, Perth
- ☐☐ Central Florida Zoo & Botanical Gardens
- ☐☐ Central Park Zoo, NY
- ☐☐ Chapultepec Zoo
- ☐☐ Chattanooga Zoo
- ☐☐ Chester Zoo
- ☐☐ Cheyenne Mountain Zoo
- ☑☐ Churchill Island and Farm
- ☐☐ Cincinnati Zoo & Botanical Garden
- ☐☐ Cleland Conservation Park
- ☐☐ Cleveland Metroparks Zoo
- ☐☐ Cohunu Koala Park, Perth
- ☐☐ Colchester Zoo
- ☐☐ Como Park Zoo & Conservatory
- ☐☐ Creation Kingdom Zoo
- ☐☐ Crocodylus Park, Darwin
- ☐☐ Currumbin Wildlife Sanctuary, Gold Coast
- ☐☐ Daisy Hill Koala Centre - Daisy Hill
- ☐☐ Dallas Zoo
- ☐☐ Darling Downs Zoo, Clifton
- ☐☐ David Fleay Wildlife Park
- ☐☐ Denver Zoo
- ☐☐ Detroit Zoo
- ☐☐ Dickerson Park Zoo
- ☐☐ Diergaarde Blijdorp/Rotterdam Zoo
- ☐☐ Dubai Mall Aquarium & Underwater Zoo
- ☐☐ Dublin Zoo
- ☐☐ Dudley Zoo
- ☐☐ Duisburg Zoo
- ☐☐ Dusit Zoo
- ☐☐ East Coast Natureworld, Bicheno
- ☐☐ Edinburgh Zoo
- ☐☐ El Paso Zoo
- ☐☐ Elmwood Park Zoo
- ☐☐ Ettamogah Wildlife Sanctuary, Ettamogah, Albury
- ☐☐ Fairfield City Farm, Abbotsbury, City of Fairfield

- ☑☐ Featherdale Zoo
- ☐☐ Flying High Bird Sanctuary
- ☐☐ Flying High Bird Sanctuary, Apple Tree Creek
- ☐☐ Folly Farm Adventure Park and Zoo
- ☐☐ Fort Worth Zoo
- ☐☐ Franklin Park Zoo
- ☐☐ Fresno Chaffee Zoo
- ☐☐ Gaia Zoo
- ☐☐ Georgia Aquarium, largest aquarium in the world
- ☐☐ Givskud Zoo
- ☐☐ Gladys Porter Zoo
- ☐☐ Gorge Wildlife Park, Cudlee Creek
- ☐☐ Granby Zoo
- ☐☐ Greenville Zoo
- ☐☐ Grizzly Zoo
- ☐☐ Gulf Breeze Zoo
- ☐☐ Halls Gap Zoo
- ☐☐ Hanover Zoo
- ☐☐ Happy Hollow Park & Zoo
- ☐☐ Hartley's Crocodile Adventure - Cairns, Australia
- ☐☐ Hattiesburg Zoo
- ☑☐ Healesville Sanctuary
- ☐☐ Henry Vilas Zoo
- ☐☐ Hobart Zoo
- ☐☐ Houston Zoo
- ☐☐ Hovatter's Wildlife Zoo
- ☐☐ Hunter Valley Zoo, Nulkaba
- ☐☐ Indianapolis Zoo and White River Gardens
- ☐☐ Jacksonville Zoo and Gardens
- ☐☐ Johannes Zoo
- ☐☐ Johannesburg Zoo
- ☐☐ John Ball Zoo
- ☐☐ Kansas City Zoo
- ☐☐ Knoxville Zoo
- ☑☐ Koala Park Sanctuary, West Pennant Hills, Sydney
- ☑☐ Koala Conservation Park, Phillip Island
- ☐☐ Kölner Zoo
- ☐☐ Korat Zoo
- ☐☐ Kula Eco Park, Sigatoka
- ☐☐ Kumbartcho Sanctuary, Eatons Hill, Brisbane
- ☐☐ Kyabram Fauna Park, Kyabram
- ☐☐ Lehigh Valley Zoo
- ☐☐ Lincoln Children's Zoo
- ☐☐ Lincoln Park Zoo
- ☐☐ Lisbon Zoo
- ☐☐ Little Ray's Reptile Zoo
- ☐☐ Little Rock Zoo
- ☐☐ Lone Pine Koala Sanctuary
- ☐☐ Loro Parque - Zoo
- ☐☐ Los Angeles Zoo and Botanical Gardens
- ☐☐ Louisville Zoo
- ☑☐ Mansfield Zoo, Mansfield
- ☐☐ Marty's Ozzie Reptiles at Morelia Zoo
- ☐☐ Maru Koala and Animal Park, Grantville, Victoria
- ☑☐ Melbourne Sealife Aquarium
- ☑☐ Melbourne Zoo
- ☐☐ Memphis Zoo
- ☐☐ Mesker Park Zoo & Botanic Garden
- ☐☐ Milwaukee County Zoo
- ☐☐ Minnesota Zoo
- ☑☐ Mogo Zoo
- ☐☐ Mon Repos Conservation Park - Bundaberg, Bundaberg Area
- ☐☐ Monarto Zoo
- ☐☐ Moonlit Sanctuary Wildlife Conservation Park
- ☐☐ Naples Zoo at Caribbean Gardens

- ☐☐ Nashville Zoo
- ☐☐ National Wetlands Centre
- ☑☐ National Zoo & Aquarium Canberra
- ☐☐ NEW Zoo
- ☐☐ Niabi Zoo
- ☐☐ Noah's Ark Zoo Farm
- ☐☐ North Carolina Zoo
- ☐☐ Oakland Zoo
- ☑☐ Oceanworld Manly
- ☐☐ Odense Zoo
- ☐☐ Okinawa Churaumi Aquarium - Japan
- ☐☐ Oklahoma City Zoo and Botanical Garden
- ☐☐ Olson Pheasant Farm
- ☐☐ Omaha's Henry Doorly Zoo and Aquarium
- ☐☐ Opel Zoo Kronberg
- ☐☐ Orana Wildlife Park in Christchurch, New Zealand
- ☐☐ Osaka Aquarium Kaiyukan - Japan
- ☐☐ Paignton Zoo Environmental Park
- ☐☐ Palm Beach Zoo
- ☐☐ Paradise Wildlife Park, UK
- ☐☐ Parken Zoo
- ☐☐ Parndana Wildlife Park, Parndana, Kangaroo Island
- ☐☐ Peel Zoo, Mandurah
- ☐☐ Penguin Encounter at Sea World
- ☐☐ Peoria Zoo
- ☐☐ Perth Zoo
- ☐☐ Philadelphia Zoo
- ☐☐ Phoenix Zoo
- ☐☐ Pittsburgh Zoo & PPG Aquarium
- ☐☐ Plumpton Park Zoo
- ☐☐ Point Defiance Zoo & Aquarium
- ☐☐ Potawatomi Zoo
- ☐☐ Potoroo Palace Native Animal Sanctuary, Merimbula
- ☐☐ Potter Park Zoo
- ☐☐ Racine Zoo
- ☐☐ Reid Park Zoo
- ☐☐ Riverbanks Zoo and Garden
- ☐☐ Rockhampton Zoo, Rockhampton
- ☐☐ Rolling Hills Zoo
- ☐☐ Rosamond Gifford Zoo
- ☐☐ Sacramento Zoo
- ☐☐ Saint Louis Zoo
- ☐☐ San Diego Zoo
- ☐☐ San Diego Zoo Safari Park
- ☐☐ San Francisco Zoo
- ☐☐ Santa Ana Zoo
- ☐☐ Santa Barbara Zoo
- ☐☐ Scovill Zoo
- ☐☐ Sea World - Gold Coast
- ☐☐ Sedgwick County Zoo
- ☐☐ Seneca Park Zoo
- ☑☐ Shoalhaven Zoo, Nowra
- ☐☐ Singapore Zoo, Night Safari and River Safari
- ☐☐ Sloth Sanctuary in Costa Rica
- ☐☐ Smithsonian's National Zoo
- ☐☐ Southwick's Zoo
- ☐☐ Sriracha Tiger Zoo
- ☐☐ Staten Island Zoo
- ☐☐ Stone Zoo
- ☑☐ Sydney Sea life Aquarium
- ☑☐ Sydney Wildlife World
- ☑☐ Symbio Wildlife Park
- ☐☐ Taipei Zoo
- ☐☐ Tampa's Lowry Park Zoo
- ☐☐ Tangalooma Wild Dolphin Resort, Moreton Island
- ☑☐ Taronga Zoo

- ☐☐ Tasmania Zoo, Launceston
- ☐☐ Territory Wildlife Park, Berry Springs
- ☐☐ The Alaska Zoo
- ☐☐ The Birmingham Zoo
- ☐☐ The Buffalo Zoo
- ☐☐ The Calgary Zoo
- ☐☐ The Camargue in Provence, Unique French Wetlands
- ☐☐ The Columbus Zoo and Aquarium
- ☐☐ The GW Zoo
- ☐☐ The Honolulu Zoo
- ☐☐ The Malcolm Douglas Crocodile Park
- ☐☐ The Maryland Zoo in Baltimore
- ☐☐ The Reptile Zoo
- ☐☐ The Toledo Zoo
- ☐☐ The Toronto Zoo
- ☐☐ The Wildlife Habitat Sanctuary, Port Douglas
- ☐☐ Topeka Zoo
- ☐☐ Trowunna Wildlife Park, Mole Creek
- ☐☐ Tulsa Zoo
- ☐☐ Turtle Back Zoo
- ☐☐ Two Oceans Aquarium
- ☐☐ Twycross Zoo
- ☐☐ Underwater World, Brisbane
- ☐☐ Underwater World, Mooloolaba
- ☐☐ Unforgettable Wildlife Safari
- ☐☐ Urimbirra Wildlife Park, Victor Harbor
- ☐☐ UShaka Marine World
- ☐☐ Utah's Hogle Zoo
- ☐☐ Visit AK Wildlife Conservation Center - Alaska
- ☑☐ Visit Bee House Coffs Harbour
- ☑☐ Visit Butterfly House in Coffs Harbour
- ☑☐ Visit Pet Porpoise Pool Coffs Harbour
- ☐☐ Visit Raptor Domain - Kangaroo Island, South Australia, Australia
- ☐☐ Visit Vancouver Aquarium
- ☐☐ Wagga Wagga Zoo, Wagga Wagga
- ☐☐ Walkabout Creek Wildlife Centre, The Gap
- ☐☐ Wanpi World Safari Zoo
- ☐☐ Waratah Park Earth Sanctuary, Duffys Forest, Sydney
- ☐☐ Warrawong Wildlife Sanctuary, Stirling
- ☐☐ Warszawskie ZOO
- ☐☐ Waterways Wildlife Park, Gunnedah
- ☐☐ Wellington Zoo
- ☑☐ Werribee Open Range Zoo
- ☐☐ West Australian Reptile Park, Henley Brook
- ☐☐ Western Plains Zoo, Dubbo
- ☐☐ Wild Action Zoo Melbourne
- ☐☐ Wild Life Hamilton Island, Hamilton Island
- ☐☐ Wildlife World Zoo & Aquarium
- ☐☐ Wing's Wildlife Park, Gunns Plains
- ☐☐ Woodland Park Zoo
- ☐☐ Wyndham Zoological Gardens and Crocodile Park, Wyndham
- ☐☐ Zoo America
- ☐☐ Zoo Antwerpen
- ☐☐ Zoo Aquarium de Madrid
- ☐☐ Zoo Atlanta
- ☐☐ Zoo Basel
- ☐☐ Zoo Berlin
- ☐☐ Zoo Boise
- ☐☐ Zoo da Maia
- ☐☐ Zoo de Barcelona

- ☐☐ Zoo de Beauval
- ☐☐ Zoo Heidelberg
- ☐☐ Zoo Johor
- ☐☐ Zoo Leipzig
- ☐☐ Zoo Liberec
- ☐☐ Zoo Magdeburg
- ☐☐ Zoo Melaka
- ☐☐ Zoo Miami
- ☐☐ Zoo Negara Malaysia
- ☐☐ Zoo Osnabrück
- ☐☐ Zoo Parc de Beauval
- ☐☐ ZOO Plzeň
- ☐☐ Zoo Praha
- ☐☐ Zoo Rostock & Darwineum
- ☐☐ Zoo Safaripark Stukenbrock
- ☐☐ Zoo Santo Inácio
- ☐☐ ZOO Wrocław
- ☐☐ Zoo Zürich
- ☐☐ Zoodoo Wildlife Park, Richmond
- ☐☐ Zoosiana - Zoo of Acadiana
- ☐☐ ZSL London Zoo
- ☐☐ ZSL Whipsnade Zoo

Chapter 16: Health, Beauty Therapy and Body Imaging

"Massage therapy has been shown to relieve depression, especially in people who have chronic fatigue syndrome; other studies also suggest benefit for other populations."

Andrew Weil

Health and beauty has been traditionally a women's culture for a long time. However, nowadays a lot more men are giving facials and massages a try and are reaping the benefits. They are surprised at how much they have been missing out on in their lifetime. It's about time men started getting pampered as well, so why not everyone give it a go? Traditionally men never used to have bathroom accessories and, at most, had a form of gel to put into their hair called Brylcreem.

These days they have cologne, aftershave and many other bathroom accessories. In the last few years I have come to realise what men have been missing out on all this time. So all you men out there, if you haven't already given it a go, go ahead – you will be surprised on what you have been missing.

- ☐☐ Bathe in chocolate
- ☑☐ Bathe in dead sea salts
- ☑☐ Bathe in ice water
- ☐☐ Bathe in jelly
- ☐☐ Bathe in milk
- ☐☐ Bathe in oil
- ☐☐ Bathe in the mineral baths in Italy
- ☑☐ Dye my hair
- ☑☐ Experience a facial cleansing
- ☐☐ Experience a scalp massage
- ☐☐ Experience a Turkish bath massage
- ☐☐ Experience body cocoon
- ☐☐ Experience cupping
- ☐☐ Experience ear waxing candles
- ☑☐ Experience hot stone massage
- ☐☐ Experience reflexology
- ☐☐ Experience sitting in a sauna
- ☐☐ Get a henna tattoo
- ☐☐ Get a tattoo
- ☐☐ Get A UV reflective tattoo

- ☑☐ Get an adjustment from a chiropractor
- ☐☐ Get body painted
- ☑☐ Get piercing
- ☐☐ Have a candlelit bath
- ☐☐ Have a closecut shave
- ☐☐ Have a fish pedicure done
- ☐☐ Have a spray tan
- ☐☐ Have something waxed
- ☐☐ Hell's Gate Geothermal Park and Mud Bath Spa
- ☐☐ Onsen, Natural Hot Springs, Kinosaki, Japan
- ☐☐ Polynesian spa
- ☐☐ Relax in a natural hot spring
- ☐☐ Sabeto Hot Springs and Mud Baths
- ☐☐ Salt therapy treatment
- ☐☐ Survive a cold sauna, Canada
- ☐☐ Try acupuncture

Chapter 17: Comedians of the World

"Laugh and the world laughs with you, snore and you sleep alone."

Anthony Burgess

A comedian is a person who seeks to entertain an audience, primarily by making them laugh. This might be through jokes or amusing situations, or acting a fool or employing prop comedy. A comedian who addresses an audience directly is called a stand-up comedian. We all love to be entertained by a comedian every once in a while; it puts a big smile on our faces and brings laughter to us all, and helps us release any stress that we hold on to. Every comedian has their own unique personal style to help their audience enjoy every moment of the entertainment; some comedians have such a natural talent they could just walk into a room and start a show with no preparation necessary. They can have the audience involved and get them to run the show by their great input, such as choosing what the comedian is to talk about or add into a song the comedian makes up including someone chosen from the crowd on the spot. No matter who the comedian and how skilled they are at their work, they all end up making us laugh and entertain us for a great night out. Even local people can give it a go at a stand-up mic night in nearby city locations. Just enjoy the moment: laugh, clap and cheer the whole night through.

- ☑☐ Akmal Saleh
- ☐☐ Gabriel Iglesias
- ☐☐ Henning When
- ☐☐ Jim Owen
- ☐☐ Joe Lycett
- ☑☐ Peter Helliar
- ☐☐ Louis Ck
- ☐☐ Sean Lock
- ☐☐ Richard Pryor
- ☐☐ Michael Mcintyre
- ☐☐ Bill Bailey
- ☐☐ Billy Connolly
- ☐☐ Eddie Izzard
- ☐☐ Chris Rock
- ☐☐ Jimmy Carr
- ☑☐ Dylan Moran
- ☐☐ Peter Kay
- ☐☐ Lee Evans
- ☐☐ Russell Howard
- ☐☐ Bill Hicks
- ☐☐ Micky Flanagan
- ☐☐ Russell Brand

- ☐☐ George Carlin
- ☐☐ Stewart Lee
- ☐☐ Dane Cook
- ☐☐ Russell Kane
- ☐☐ Jack Dee
- ☐☐ Ricky Gervais
- ☐☐ Eddie Murphy
- ☐☐ Al Murray
- ☐☐ Zach Galifianakis
- ☐☐ Ross Noble
- ☐☐ Sarah Millican
- ☑☐ The Umbilical Brothers
- ☐☐ Omid Djalili
- ☐☐ Lee Mack
- ☐☐ Russell Peters
- ☐☐ Harry Hill
- ☐☐ Frankie Boyle
- ☐☐ Alan Carr
- ☐☐ Dara O'Briain
- ☐☐ Rhod Gilbert
- ☐☐ Chris Ramsey
- ☐☐ John Bishop
- ☐☐ Jack Whitehall
- ☐☐ Kevin Bridges
- ☐☐ Ed Byrne
- ☐☐ Woody Allen
- ☐☐ Jon Richardson
- ☐☐ Victoria Wood
- ☐☐ Jeff Dunham
- ☐☐ Chris Addison
- ☐☐ Daniel Kitson
- ☐☐ Doc Brown
- ☐☐ Dave Gorman
- ☐☐ Jo Brand
- ☐☐ Tony Law
- ☐☐ Tim Minchin
- ☐☐ Johnny Vegas
- ☐☐ Dave Chapelle
- ☐☐ Tim Vine
- ☐☐ Anh Do
- ☐☐ Josie Long
- ☐☐ Denis Leary
- ☐☐ Jason Manford
- ☐☐ Frank Skinner
- ☐☐ Kevin Hart
- ☐☐ Stephen K. Amos
- ☐☐ Joan Rivers
- ☐☐ Alexei Sayle
- ☐☐ Trevor Noah
- ☐☐ Sam Kinison
- ☐☐ Josh Widdecombe
- ☐☐ Aziz Ansari
- ☐☐ Seann Walsh
- ☐☐ Jerry Seinfield
- ☐☐ Rufus Hound
- ☐☐ Dr Brown
- ☐☐ Stewart Francis
- ☐☐ Julian Clary
- ☐☐ Sean Hughes
- ☐☐ Bill Cosby
- ☐☐ Chubby Brown
- ☐☐ Milton Jones
- ☐☐ Stephen Merchant
- ☐☐ Shappi Khorsandi
- ☐☐ Jasper Carrott
- ☐☐ Patrick Kielty
- ☐☐ Richard Herring
- ☐☐ David Baddiel
- ☐☐ Lenny Henry
- ☐☐ Greg Davies
- ☐☐ Andrew Maxwell
- ☐☐ Sarah Silverman
- ☐☐ Reg D Hunter
- ☐☐ Tom Stade
- ☑☐ Wayne Brady
- ☐☐ Jenny Éclair
- ☐☐ Simon Amstell
- ☐☐ Marcus Brigstocke
- ☐☐ Tracy Morgan
- ☐☐ Andrew Lawrence
- ☐☐ Tom Green
- ☐☐ Robin Ince

- ☐☐ Rob Beckett
- ☐☐ Daniel Sloss
- ☐☐ See the top 100 comedians of 2013
- ☑☐ See live comedy show

Chapter 18: Memorials of the World and Days of Remembrance "Lest We Forget"

"I know not age, nor weariness nor defeat."

Rose Kennedy

We honour the fallen on Remembrance Day (also known as Poppy Day or Armistice Day), which is a memorial day observed in Commonwealth countries since the end of World War I to remember the members of their armed forces who have died in the line of duty. There are many other days we stop for a moment and honour the troops that go to war and fight in honour for our countries. One of the most known is Anzac Day for Australian and New Zealand people, the day Australian and New Zealand Army Corps landed at Gallipoli in 1915 and is annually commemorated on 25 April. This year *2015* will be the 100-year anniversary of the event.

Anzac Day is one of Australia's most important memorable national commemorative occasions. It marks the anniversary of the first major military action fought by Australian and New Zealand forces during the First World War. There are many more memorials and memorial days to honour our fallen, though these are the two biggest known in the world. We remember the fallen by placing poppy flowers and wreaths of flowers for memorial services for our troops to appreciate what they have done for us.

- ☑ Anzac War Memorial, Hyde Park
- ☐ Attend a Gallipoli Service on Anzac Day
- ☐ Attend the National Ceremony for Anzac Day, Canberra
- ☑ Australian War Memorial, ACT
- ☑ Dawn Service Anzac Day, Sydney
- ☐ Georgia Guidestones, Elberton, GA
- ☐ Holocaust Memorial, Miami Beach
- ☐ Jefferson Memorial, Washington, USA

- ☐☐ Lion Monument, Lucerne, Switzerland
- ☐☐ Monument Valley, UT/AZ
- ☐☐ Phar Lap Statue, Flemington, Victoria
- ☐☐ Place a poppy flower at the Shrine of Remembrance to remember the Australian war heroes
- ☐☐ Sigiriya the "Mount of Remembrance," Sri Lanka
- ☐☐ Visit Mount Rushmore National Memorial, South Dakota
- ☐☐ Visit the 9/11 Memorial, New York
- ☐☐ Visit the Eternal Flame
- ☐☐ Visit the Jewish Memorial in Berlin
- ☐☐ Visit the Lincoln Memorial, USA
- ☑☐ Visit the Shrine of Remembrance, St. Kilda, Victoria
- ☑☐ Visit William Wallace monument, Scotland
- ☐☐ Voortrekker Monument
- ☐☐ Washington Monument, Washington, D.C
- ☑☐ Watch Anzac Day March, Sydney
- ☐☐ White Sands National Monument, New Mexico

Chapter 19: Festival Events Wordwide

> *"Each year, every city in the world that can should have a multiday festival. More people meeting each other, digging new types of music, new foods, new ideas. You want to stop having so many wars? This could be a step in the right direction."*
>
> Henry Rollins

Witness some of the most unique and fabulous celebrations from all around the world, festivals that have gathered millions of people from around the world partying, drinking and having the time of their lives. Experience life the way it should be lived. Chinese New Year is the biggest holiday, with dragons, fireworks, symbolic clothing, flowers, lanterns, and celebration, and is China's most important and significant day of the year.

Also known as the Spring Festival, Chinese New Year celebrations traditionally run from Chinese New Year's Eve, the last day of the last month of the Chinese calendar, to the Lantern Festival on the 15th day of the first month, making the festival the longest in the Chinese calendar!

Burning Man is an annual event when up to 48,000 people gather in Nevada's Black Rock Desert to create art and express their individuality. It takes its name from the ritual burning of a large wooden effigy, which is set alight on Saturday evening.

The event is described as an experiment in community, art, radical self-expression and radical self-reliance. People who have gone to Burning Man gatherings claim you need to attend to truly understand. So many famous gatherings to talk about, so many looking to explore, but only a few I hear about from friends and family visiting them for themselves. I'm personally looking forward to the experiences for myself one day in the future.

- ☐☐ Adelaide Festival of Arts
- ☐☐ Adelaide Film Festival
- ☐☐ Annual Sydney Comedy Festival Gala
- ☐☐ Attend a grease pole festival
- ☐☐ Attend a Hawaiian luau
- ☐☐ Attend a masquerade party
- ☐☐ Attend a Native American sweat lodge
- ☐☐ Attend a pow wow
- ☐☐ Attend a sci-fi convention
- ☐☐ Attend the Highland Games
- ☐☐ Attend Up-Helly-Aa in Scotland
- ☐☐ Bathurst auto fest
- ☐☐ Battle of Oranges, Ireva, Italy
- ☐☐ Battle of the Oranges Festival, Ivrea Italy
- ☐☐ Be Part of International Pillow Fight Day
- ☐☐ Bluesfest
- ☐☐ Boryeong Mud Festival, South Korea
- ☐☐ Burning Man in the Black Rock Desert of Nevada
- ☐☐ Byron Bay International Film Festival
- ☐☐ Byron Latin Fiesta
- ☐☐ Campbelltown City Festival of Fishers Ghost
- ☐☐ Carnival in Venice, Italy
- ☐☐ Celebrate St. Patrick's Day in Dublin, Ireland
- ☐☐ Chinese New Year's Festival
- ☐☐ Cobargo Folk Festival
- ☐☐ Cooper's Hill Cheese Rolling and Wake
- ☐☐ El Colacho Festival, Castrillo de Murcia Spain
- ☐☐ Elephant Day, Thailand
- ☐☐ Empire Asparagus Festival, Empire, Mich.
- ☐☐ Experience the Yi Peng Festival in Northern Thailand
- ☐☐ Festival of the Sea, Nelson Bay
- ☐☐ Festival of the Winds, Bondi
- ☐☐ Fireside Festival
- ☐☐ Four Winds Festival
- ☐☐ Go and watch the annual Festival of Water Buffalo Racing, Indonesia
- ☐☐ Go To Full Moon Party, Thailand
- ☐☐ Go to Macy's Thanksgiving Parade
- ☐☐ Havaiana's Thong Challenge - Australia Day, Bondi Beach
- ☐☐ Ironfest Festival Lithgow
- ☐☐ La Tomatina Festival, Bunol Spain
- ☐☐ Lantern Festival in Honolulu, Hawaii
- ☐☐ Lightning Ridge Easter Festival
- ☐☐ Loy Krathong Festival, Parramatta
- ☐☐ Loy Krathong, the Sky Lantern Festival in Thailand
- ☐☐ Melbourne Arts Festival
- ☐☐ Melbourne Film Festival
- ☐☐ Melbourne Food and Wine Festival
- ☐☐ Melbourne Fringe Festival
- ☐☐ Mind, Body, Spirit Festival, Sydney
- ☐☐ Monkey Buffet Festival, Lopburi, Thailand
- ☑☐ My Lords and Ladies Medieval Fayre
- ☐☐ Nelson Bay Foreshore Festival
- ☐☐ Next Wave Festival
- ☐☐ Night of the Radishes, Oaxaca, Mexico
- ☐☐ Oktoberfest, Munich, Germany

- ☐☐ Parramatta Wellness Community Festival
- ☐☐ Partake in a Japanese Tea Ceremony. This timeless tradition is at the heart of Japanese culture
- ☐☐ Participate in Cosplay at an event
- ☐☐ Participate in the Amazing Race
- ☐☐ Participate in the Russian Subways Now Accepting Squats for Ticket Payments
- ☐☐ Participate in the Tomato Battle
- ☐☐ Participate in the Traditional Maasai Dancing Gathering
- ☐☐ Party at the Rio Carnival
- ☐☐ Perth Arts Festival
- ☐☐ Revelation Perth Film Festival
- ☐☐ Roswell UFO Festival
- ☐☐ Running of the Bulls - San Fermin Festival in Pamplona, Spain
- ☐☐ Singularity Festival
- ☐☐ Slip, slide and smash your way through the Chinchilla Melon Festival from 14-17 February
- ☐☐ Snow Castle, Harbin Snow Festival, China
- ☑☐ Spend New Year's Eve in Sydney, Australia Festival
- ☐☐ Stomping Of the Grapes Festival
- ☐☐ Sydney Comedy Festival
- ☐☐ Sydney Film Festival
- ☐☐ Sydney Writers Festival
- ☐☐ Tamaki Maori Village Ceremony
- ☐☐ The Ati-Atihan Festival, the Philippines
- ☐☐ The Day of the Dead, Mexico
- ☐☐ The Galway International Oyster Festival, Galway, Ireland
- ☐☐ The Holi Festival, Festival of Colours, India
- ☐☐ The largest hot air balloon gathering in the world at dawn in Chambley, France
- ☐☐ The marvelous floating stage of the Bregenz Festival in Austria
- ☐☐ Top Gear Festival, Sydney
- ☐☐ Tullamore Irish Festival
- ☐☐ Visit India during Diwal Festival
- ☑☐ Vivid Festival Sydney
- ☐☐ Waitangi Festival
- ☐☐ Watch Mardi Gra Festival live
- ☐☐ Water Fights, Songkran Ongkran, Thailand
- ☐☐ Wife Carrying World Championship, Sonkajärvi, Finland
- ☐☐ Woolgoolga Curryfest
- ☐☐ World Championship Pumpkin Chuckin Festival
- ☐☐ World's Biggest Water Fight - New Year's Eve, Thailand

Chapter 20: Music Festival Events

"My favourite festival experience is a show at midnight with the moon blazing and a crowd full of open hearts ready to dance."

Lykke Li

Everybody in the world loves music; we listen to it to relax after a hard day's work and throughout the work days. Music festivals make it 10 times better than just listening to the music. They are a large gathering of people for the love of music. Of course, we all like different kinds of music, but there are festivals of all types of music cultures that help us enjoy our own unique taste. In Tamworth there is the Big Country Festival or Soundwave for the louder rock and roll, death metal fans. The span of music culture and music genres is amazing; personally, my favourite types of genres are dance, trance and rock music, depending on the mood. It changes from time to time. I'm willing to experience all other musical festivals around the world outside my comfort zone; as they say, you only live once and you never know what you're missing unless you see what it is like for yourself. Experience all genres you can: it's a great experience to be able to meet all the new and interesting people throughout the world and how they react to their chosen music – people jumping on shoulders, people stage diving, enjoying the moment and enjoying their lives. Young or old, it's never too late to get up and enjoy the rhythm of good music.

- ☐☐ "The Roo" - Bonnaroo, Tennessee, United States
- ☐☐ A Day on the Green
- ☐☐ Australia's Regional Musical Odyssey Groovin The Moo
- ☐☐ Baybeats Music Festival, Singapore
- ☐☐ Benicassim, Spain
- ☐☐ Berlin Festival, Berlin, Germany
- ☐☐ Bestival, Isle of Wight, England
- ☐☐ Big Red Bash Music Festival in the Desert, Northern Territory
- ☐☐ Bilbao BBK Live, Bilbao, Basque Country
- ☐☐ Boom, Idanha-a-Nova, Portugal
- ☐☐ Bumbershoot, Seattle, United States
- ☐☐ Cambridge Folk Festival, Cambridge, England
- ☐☐ Canberra Music Festival

- ☐☐ Coachella
- ☐☐ Creamfields, Cheshire, England
- ☐☐ Dour Festival, Dour, Belgium
- ☐☐ Download Festival, Derby, England
- ☐☐ Endorse it in Dorset, Dorset, England
- ☐☐ Eurockeennes, Malsaucy, France
- ☐☐ Exit, Novi Sad, Serbia
- ☐☐ Festival Au Bord De l'Eau, Sierre, Switzerland
- ☐☐ Finger Lakes Grassroots Festival of Music and Dance, New York, United States
- ☐☐ Fuji Rock, Naeba, Japan
- ☐☐ Glastonbury Festival
- ☐☐ Global Gathering, Warwickshire, England
- ☐☐ Go to Defqon
- ☑☐ Go to Future Music Festival
- ☑☐ Go to Soundwave
- ☐☐ Go to Stereo Sonic
- ☐☐ Go to the Big Day Out
- ☐☐ Go to the Eurovision Song Contest
- ☐☐ Hellfest, Rue du Champ Louet, France
- ☐☐ Hip Hop Kemp, Hradec Králové, Czech Republic
- ☐☐ INmusic, Zagreb, Croatia
- ☐☐ Jisan Valley Rock Festival, Seoul, South Korea
- ☐☐ Lollapalooza, Chicago, United States
- ☐☐ Melbourne Jazz Festival
- ☐☐ Meredith Music Festival
- ☐☐ Midi, French Riviera, France
- ☐☐ National Folk Festival
- ☐☐ Nickelodeon SLIMEFEST
- ☐☐ Obscene Extreme, Trutnov, Czech Republic
- ☐☐ Open'er, Gdynia, Poland
- ☐☐ Outside Lands, San Francisco, United States
- ☐☐ Pitchfork, Chicago, United States
- ☐☐ Pohoda, Trenčín, Slovakia
- ☐☐ Reading/Leeds Festival, Reading and Leeds, England
- ☐☐ Rock Al Parque, Bogota, Colombia
- ☐☐ Rock Werchter, Werchter, Belgium
- ☐☐ Roskilde, Copenhagen, Denmark
- ☐☐ Satchmo Summer Fest, New Orleans, United States
- ☐☐ Secret Garden Party, Abbots Ripton, England
- ☐☐ Shambala, Northamptonshire, England
- ☐☐ Sonar, Barcelona, Spain
- ☐☐ Splendor in the Grass, New South Wales, Australia
- ☐☐ Standon Calling, Hertfordshire, England
- ☐☐ Stop Making Sense, Tisno, Croatia
- ☐☐ Summer Sonic Festival, Osaka and Chiba, Japan
- ☐☐ Summerfest, Wisconsin, United States
- ☐☐ SXSW Festival
- ☐☐ Sziget, Budapest, Hungary
- ☐☐ Tamworth's Country Music Festival
- ☐☐ Tomorrowland, Boom, Belgium
- ☐☐ Ultra Music Festival
- ☐☐ Wacken Open Air, Schleswig-Holstein, Germany

- ☐☐ Way Out West, Göteborg, Sweden
- ☐☐ World Electronic Music Festival, Ontario, Canada

Chapter 21: Live Bands and Singer Performances

"Music should always be an adventure."

Coleman Hawkins

The screaming of fans, the cheers from the bottom of everybody's lungs, watching, trying to get front row to see their most favourite bands and singers they have always wanted to see, to watch in envy as everyone rushes to get the best views, to try and be noticed by the stage in the hope of being asked to come up on stage and dance or sing a few words. It sometimes happens, but not always, unfortunately. A lot of singers and bands judge on how wealthy you are to get the best views of what you have come to see. If you're a real devoted fan paying the VIP access it can cost you a fortune, but it's worth it for the chance at getting to meet your favourite bands and singers in person and a chance for a signed CD or autograph. We enjoy the moment to share in the glory of our favourites and we listen to them with our hearts and sing along with them to the words of the song.

- ☑☐ Have A CD signed by a band/singer
- ☐☐ See 3 Doors Down live
- ☐☐ See AC/DC live
- ☐☐ See Alicia Keys live
- ☑☐ See Amon Amarth live
- ☐☐ See Audioslave live
- ☐☐ See Avenged Sevenfold live
- ☐☐ See Bastille live
- ☐☐ See Beyoncé Knowles live
- ☐☐ See Birds of Tokyo live
- ☐☐ See Capital Cities live
- ☐☐ See Coldplay live
- ☐☐ See Counting Crows live
- ☐☐ See Creed live
- ☐☐ See Eminem live
- ☐☐ See Empire of the Sun live
- ☐☐ See Evanescence live
- ☐☐ See Faith No More live
- ☐☐ See Fall Out Boy live
- ☑☐ See Five Finger Death Punch live
- ☐☐ See Foster the People live
- ☐☐ See Godsmack live
- ☐☐ See Gorillaz live
- ☑☐ See Greenday live
- ☑☐ See Hinder live
- ☐☐ See Imagine Dragons live
- ☐☐ See Incubus live
- ☐☐ See Justice Crew live

- ☐☐ See Justin Timberlake live
- ☐☐ See Katy Perry live
- ☑☐ See Korn live
- ☐☐ See Lady Gaga live
- ☐☐ See Lamb of God live
- ☐☐ See Lighthouse live
- ☐☐ See Limp Bizkit live
- ☐☐ See Linkin Park live
- ☐☐ See Marilyn Manson live
- ☐☐ See Mariah Carey live
- ☐☐ See Metallica live
- ☐☐ See MGMT live
- ☐☐ See Mumford and Sons live
- ☑☐ See New Empire live
- ☑☐ See New Found Glory live
- ☐☐ See Nickelback live
- ☐☐ See Oasis live
- ☐☐ See Of Mice & Men live
- ☐☐ See Offspring live
- ☐☐ See Pantera live
- ☐☐ See Papa Roach live
- ☐☐ See Pearl Jam live
- ☑☐ See Pennywise live
- ☐☐ See Pink live
- ☑☐ See Placebo live
- ☐☐ See Queens of the Stone Age live
- ☐☐ See Rammstein live
- ☐☐ See Red Hot Chilli Peppers live
- ☐☐ See REM live
- ☑☐ See Riot in Belgium live
- ☐☐ See Rob Zombie live
- ☐☐ See Sepultura live
- ☑☐ See Sheppard live
- ☑☐ See Sick Puppies live
- ☐☐ See Slash live
- ☐☐ See Slayer live
- ☐☐ See Slipknot live
- ☑☐ See Sneaky Sound System live
- ☐☐ See Sound Garden live
- ☐☐ See System of a Down live
- ☐☐ See The Calling live
- ☐☐ See The Foo Fighters live
- ☐☐ See The Killers live
- ☑☐ See The Living End live
- ☐☐ See The Lonely Island live
- ☑☐ See The Potbelleez live
- ☑☐ Watch Pharrell Williams live
- ☑☐ Watch Rudimental live
- ☐☐ Watch Thirty Seconds to Mars live

Chapter 22:
Top DJs of the World

"Sometimes it's not the song that makes you emotional. It's the people and things that come to your mind when you hear it."

Tiesto

We all come across at least one DJ throughout our lives, whether it be at a wedding or to see a DJ play live. My goal is to view all the top 100 DJs from 2013, as this was when I started ticking them off my list. I have always liked dance music but to see them live is another honour in itself. The list changes all the time of who is the better DJ who is leading the charts with a new song. No matter what you do the list will always be different, so I selected one top list from 2013 and that's my list of all the ones I would like to see play live. I also have viewed a few extra DJs along the way that are not on the top 100 list.

- ☑☐ DJ Alison Wonderland
- ☑☐ DJ Joel Fletcher
- ☑☐ DJ Kaz James
- ☑☐ DJ New World Sound
- ☑☐ DJ Stafford Brothers and Timmy Trumpet Live
- ☑☐ DJ Riot in Belgium
- ☑☐ DJ Throttle
- ☑☐ DJ TJR
- ☑☐ DJ Will Sparks
- ☐☐ Hardwell
- ☐☐ Armin van Buuren
- ☑☐ Avicii
- ☑☐ Tiesto
- ☐☐ David Guetta
- ☐☐ Dimitri Vegas & Like Mike
- ☐☐ Nicky Romero
- ☑☐ Steve Aoki
- ☐☐ Afrojack
- ☑☐ Dash Berlin
- ☑☐ Skrillex
- ☐☐ Deadmau5
- ☑☐ Alesso
- ☑☐ W&W
- ☑☐ Calvin Harris
- ☑☐ NERVO
- ☐☐ Above and Beyond
- ☐☐ Sebastian Ingrosso
- ☐☐ Axwell
- ☐☐ Aly & Fila
- ☐☐ Markus Schulz
- ☐☐ Daft Punk
- ☐☐ Headhunterz
- ☐☐ Zedd
- ☐☐ Knife Party
- ☐☐ Swedish House Mafia
- ☑☐ Showtek
- ☐☐ Andrew Rayel

- ☐☐ Fedde Le Grand
- ☑☐ Dyro
- ☑☐ Laidback Luke
- ☐☐ Paul Van Dyk
- ☐☐ ATB
- ☐☐ Angerfist
- ☑☐ Dada Life
- ☑☐ Kaskade
- ☐☐ Frontliner
- ☐☐ Steve Angello
- ☐☐ Sander Van Doorn
- ☑☐ Martin Garrix
- ☐☐ Porter Robinson
- ☐☐ Ferry Corsten
- ☑☐ Chuckie
- ☐☐ Krewella
- ☐☐ Coone
- ☐☐ Carl Cox
- ☐☐ Bobina
- ☐☐ Omnia
- ☐☐ Orjan Nielsen
- ☑☐ Zatox
- ☐☐ Gareth Emery
- ☐☐ Bingo Players
- ☐☐ Infected Mushroom
- ☑☐ Eric Prydz
- ☐☐ Tommy Trash
- ☐☐ Wildstylez
- ☑☐ Arty
- ☑☐ R3hab
- ☐☐ Madeon
- ☐☐ Vicetone
- ☐☐ Brennan Heart
- ☐☐ DJ Feel
- ☐☐ Gunz for Hire
- ☐☐ Diplo
- ☐☐ Tenishia
- ☐☐ Noisecontrollers
- ☐☐ Mike Candys
- ☐☐ DJ Antoine
- ☐☐ Quentin Mosimann
- ☐☐ Project 46
- ☐☐ Blasterjaxx
- ☐☐ D Block and S Te Fan
- ☐☐ Dillon Francis
- ☐☐ Dannic
- ☐☐ Adaro
- ☐☐ Richie Hawtin
- ☐☐ Martin Solveig
- ☐☐ Felguk
- ☐☐ Myon and Shane 54
- ☐☐ Cosmic Gate
- ☐☐ Heatbeat
- ☐☐ John O'Callaghan
- ☐☐ Wasted Penguinz
- ☐☐ Tiddey
- ☐☐ Skazi
- ☐☐ Da Tweekaz
- ☐☐ Tenashar
- ☐☐ Bob Sinclar
- ☐☐ Benny Benassi
- ☐☐ Bl3nd
- ☐☐ Paul Oakenfold
- ☐☐ Mat Zo
- ☐☐ Diego Miranda
- ☐☐ DJs from Mars
- ☐☐ Matt Darey
- ☐☐ Umek
- ☐☐ Solar Stone
- ☐☐ Ummet Ozcan
- ☐☐ Ran D
- ☐☐ See the Top 100 DJs of 2013

Chapter 23: Photo Opportunities

"Photography is a way of feeling, of touching, of loving. What you have caught on film is captured forever . . . it remembers little things, long after you have forgotten everything."

Aaron Siskind

Photo opportunities are all around us. You can take a photo of anything in the world that fascinates you and you want to have as a keepsake stored away to view in years to come so you can say to your future family, I have been there. You can have a photo taken with that famous celebrity you have always dreamed about meeting, or even special projects like taking a photo in the same spot or of the same person for a month, year or even longer to see how the image changes over time and see how every day is a different story to tell. For example, taking a photo of the sky is always different from the day before rainy days, sunny days, cloud formations in different ways; there are always changes in the way it looks no matter how big or small an image, but it's a very hard technique to get one photo exactly the same as one you have taken in the past because the world is ever changing.

- ☐☐ Visit a state
- ☐☐ Take pictures in said state
- ☐☐ Cut them out in the shape of said state, and adhere to map
- ☐☐ Be part of a Spencer Tunik photo
- ☐☐ Get a photo hung somewhere in public
- ☐☐ Get a photo I've taken published
- ☐☐ Have a photo with Captain Hook
- ☐☐ Have a photo with Donald Duck
- ☐☐ Have a photo with Goofy
- ☐☐ Have a photo with Mickey Mouse
- ☐☐ Have a photo with Minnie Mouse
- ☐☐ Have a photo with Pluto
- ☐☐ Have a photo with the Chipmunks
- ☐☐ Have an underwater picture taken of me
- ☐☐ Have my photo taken with a sports team
- ☑☐ Have my photo taken with Craig Lowndes - Red Bull V8 Holden Car

- ☐☐ Have my photo taken with Mario
- ☐☐ Have my picture taken holding a massive cheque
- ☑☐ Photobomb a random person's photo
- ☑☐ Photobomb someone's picture
- ☑☐ Photograph an endangered species. Aside from an image you can keep for a lifetime, it will remind you, and others, how fragile life can be
- ☐☐ Photograph the Aurora Borealis
- ☑☐ Photograph the sunrise
- ☐☐ Photograph tulips in Holland
- ☐☐ Process pictures in a dark room
- ☐☐ Publish a photo in National Geographic
- ☑☐ Represent the seasons: autumn
- ☐☐ Represent the seasons: spring
- ☐☐ Represent the seasons: summer
- ☐☐ Represent the seasons: winter
- ☐☐ Sydney Photography Tours
- ☐☐ Take a photo booth picture
- ☐☐ Take a photo every day for a year
- ☐☐ Take a photo of the sunrise every day for a year
- ☐☐ Take a photo of the sunset every day for a year
- ☐☐ Take a picture from each hour of the day
- ☐☐ Take a picture of myself every day for a year
- ☐☐ Take a picture with a celebrity
- ☐☐ Take a selfie every day for a year
- ☑☐ Take pictures of graffiti in a city
- ☑☐ Take up photography
- ☐☐ Win photography competitions

Chapter 24: Career Achievements

"Choose a job you love, and you will never have to work a day in your life."

Confucius

Our career working lifestyle is a major part of our adult lives. We need to work to pay bills, to buy things we need, to pay for food and groceries – we need to work to live. Some of us are happy just to go into work, do our hours and go home. Others strive to do overtime for extra funds in their pockets for the weekend. The more career-orientated people strive for higher positions in the company, a boss-like figure that gives them power in the workplace, and people look to them for advice and leadership skills.

We all like to be honoured and thanked for our hard efforts at work, and to be presented with an employee-of-the-month award is one way that we are recognised for our hard work in companies.

- ☑☐ Be a business manager
- ☑☐ Be a night department manager
- ☑☐ Be a trainee manager
- ☑☐ Build a team
- ☑☐ Employee of the month
- ☐☐ Employee of the year
- ☑☐ Work in door-to-door sales
- ☑☐ Work in hospitality
- ☑☐ Work in retail
- ☑☐ Work in warehouse and logistics

Chapter 25:
Live Sporting Events

"The way a team plays as a whole determines its success. You may have the greatest bunch of individual stars in the world, but if they don't play together, the club won't be worth a dime."

Babe Ruth

We all have our favourite sports teams – whether it be footy, rugby or AFL, soccer, or basketball we love to spend weekends watching a good sports battle between teams on television. However, watching our sports live-up close and in person changes the perspective of the way we view the sports games. Rather than depending on the camera man to capture the best views for us to view on television, we can see the whole field ourselves and enjoy the atmosphere of everyone around us chanting from the bottom of their lungs for their selected sports teams, wearing jerseys and enjoying time with loved ones and family and friends. We experience waving flags up high in the air, proud to see everyone immersing themselves in the atmosphere, taking advantage of the moment and watching the game in rain, hail or shine.

- ☐☐ AFL live game
- ☐☐ Attend a boxing match
- ☐☐ Attend a Harlem Globetrotters game
- ☐☐ Attend a medal ceremony at Olympic games
- ☐☐ Attend a medal ceremony at the winter Olympic games
- ☐☐ Attend a NASCAR race
- ☐☐ Attend an NRL grand final
- ☐☐ Attend a rodeo
- ☐☐ Attend an AFL grand final MCG Stadium, Victoria
- ☐☐ Attend Ascot Races
- ☐☐ Attend closing ceremony of the Olympic games
- ☐☐ Attend closing ceremony of the winter Olympic games
- ☐☐ Attend Daytona 500
- ☑☐ Attend Olympic games
- ☐☐ Attend opening ceremony of Olympic games
- ☐☐ Attend opening ceremony of the winter Olympic games
- ☐☐ Attend the Commonwealth Games
- ☐☐ Attend the FIFA World Cup
- ☐☐ Attend the Monaco Grand Prix
- ☐☐ Attend the Paralympics
- ☐☐ Attend winter Olympics
- ☐☐ Brisbane Racing Behind the Scenes Tour

- ☑☐ Go Drag Racers Eastern Creek
- ☑☐ Go Horse Racers
- ☐☐ Go to a Legend Football Game (Ladies Football Game)
- ☐☐ Go to a Super Bowl Game
- ☐☐ Go to Dubai World Cup - World's Richest Horse Race
- ☐☐ Go to greyhound racing
- ☐☐ Go to Melbourne Cup
- ☐☐ Go to the Tour De France
- ☐☐ Harness racing
- ☑☐ Live basketball game
- ☐☐ Live football game
- ☐☐ Live soccer match
- ☐☐ Penrith Nitro Race Night
- ☐☐ See a destruction derby
- ☐☐ See a live wrestling match
- ☐☐ See sumo wrestling live
- ☐☐ State of Origin game
- ☐☐ Sydney Speedway
- ☐☐ V8 Supercars pit lane experience
- ☐☐ V8 Supercars Sydney Telstra 500 Race, Olympic Park, Sydney
- ☐☐ V8s Bathurst Telstra 1000
- ☐☐ Watch a live cage fight
- ☐☐ Watch a live ice hockey game
- ☐☐ Watch Sydney-Hobart yacht race
- ☐☐ Watch Tennis Live Australian Open
- ☑☐ Watch the Australian Open Live - Golf
- ☐☐ Watch the Kentucky Derby
- ☐☐ Watch the Monster Trucks
- ☐☐ Watch a rugby game
- ☐☐ Watch an AFL game, Adelaide Crows
- ☐☐ Watch an AFL game, Brisbane Lions
- ☐☐ Watch an AFL game, Carlton
- ☐☐ Watch an AFL game, Collingwood
- ☐☐ Watch an AFL game, Essendon
- ☐☐ Watch an AFL game, Fremantle
- ☐☐ Watch an AFL game, Geelong Cats
- ☐☐ Watch an AFL game, Gold Coast Suns
- ☐☐ Watch an AFL game, GWS Giants
- ☐☐ Watch an AFL game, Hawthorn Hawks
- ☐☐ Watch an AFL game, Melbourne
- ☐☐ Watch an AFL game, North Melbourne
- ☐☐ Watch an AFL game, Port Adelaide
- ☐☐ Watch an AFL game, Richmond
- ☐☐ Watch an AFL game, St. Kilda
- ☐☐ Watch an AFL game, Sydney Swans
- ☐☐ Watch an AFL game, West Coast Eagles
- ☐☐ Watch an AFL game, Western Bulldogs
- ☐☐ Watch an NBL game, Adelaide 36ers
- ☐☐ Watch an NBL game, Australia Boomers "Men's"
- ☐☐ Watch an NBL game, Australia Opals "Women's"
- ☑☐ Watch an NBL game, Cairns Taipans
- ☐☐ Watch an NBL game, Melbourne UTD
- ☐☐ Watch an NBL game, NZ Breakers
- ☐☐ Watch an NBL game, Perth Wildcats

- ☑☐ Watch an NBL game, Sydney Kings
- ☐☐ Watch an NBL game, Townsville Crocodiles
- ☐☐ Watch an NBL game, Wollongong Hawks
- ☐☐ Watch an NRL game, Team Broncos
- ☐☐ Watch an NRL game, Team Bulldogs
- ☐☐ Watch an NRL game, Team Cowboys
- ☐☐ Watch an NRL game, Team Dragons
- ☐☐ Watch an NRL game, Team Eels
- ☐☐ Watch an NRL game, Team Knights
- ☐☐ Watch an NRL game, Team Panthers
- ☐☐ Watch an NRL game, Team Rabbitohs
- ☐☐ Watch an NRL game, Team Raiders
- ☐☐ Watch an NRL game, Team Roosters
- ☐☐ Watch an NRL game, Team Sea Eagles
- ☐☐ Watch an NRL game, Team Sharks
- ☐☐ Watch an NRL game, Team Storms
- ☐☐ Watch an NRL game, Team Titans
- ☐☐ Watch an NRL game, Team Warriors
- ☐☐ Watch an NRL game, Team West Tigers
- ☐☐ Watch a rugby game, All Blacks
- ☐☐ Watch a rugby game, Blues
- ☐☐ Watch a rugby game, Brumbies
- ☐☐ Watch a rugby game, Bulls
- ☐☐ Watch a rugby game, Cheetahs
- ☐☐ Watch a rugby game, Chiefs
- ☐☐ Watch a rugby game, Crusaders
- ☐☐ Watch a rugby game, Force
- ☐☐ Watch a rugby game, Highlanders
- ☐☐ Watch a rugby game, Hurricanes
- ☐☐ Watch a rugby game, Lions
- ☐☐ Watch a rugby game, Pumas
- ☐☐ Watch a rugby game, Rebels
- ☐☐ Watch a rugby game, Reds
- ☐☐ Watch a rugby game, Sharks
- ☐☐ Watch a rugby game, Springboks
- ☐☐ Watch a rugby game, Stormers
- ☐☐ Watch a rugby game, Wallabies
- ☐☐ Watch a rugby game, Waratahs
- ☐☐ Watch a soccer game, Adelaide United FC
- ☐☐ Watch a soccer game, Brisbane Roar FC
- ☐☐ Watch a soccer game, Central Coast Mariners FC
- ☐☐ Watch a soccer game, Melbourne City FC
- ☐☐ Watch a soccer game, Melbourne Victory FC
- ☐☐ Watch a soccer game, Newcastle Jets FC
- ☐☐ Watch a soccer game, Perth Glory FC
- ☐☐ Watch a soccer game, Sydney FC
- ☐☐ Watch a soccer game, Western Sydney Wanderers FC
- ☐☐ World Wrestling Entertainment "WWE" Live

Chapter 26: Expos and Family Events

"The privilege I've had as a curator is not just the discovery of new works . . . but what I've discovered about myself and what I can offer in the space of an exhibition - to talk about beauty, to talk about power, to talk about ourselves, and to talk and speak to each other."

Thelma Golden

Expos are a great way of viewing things we don't normally see. Designers show off and expose their products to everyone who visits to get their name out there and viewing in people's minds, to see if the products are going to sell or if it won't be a good seller. It's a way of exhibiting to get people's opinions about how they feel about the product and if they want to use it for their own planned events, like a cake or dress designer for a wedding. Family events are special times throughout our lives like attending a baby shower, christening or even a wedding. Milestones occur throughout our lives when we go visit each other or big events hit our city that may be a once-in-a-lifetime opportunity – we must see it or it's very unlikely to be seen again – so we take the whole family to enjoy the moment.

- ☑☐ Attend a christening
- ☑☐ Attend a wedding
- ☑☐ Attend a baby shower
- ☑☐ Attend a wedding expo
- ☑☐ Australian Fleet Review Ships into Sydney
- ☑☐ Camden Country - Quilters Guild
- ☐☐ Car Motor Show
- ☑☐ EB Games Expo, Sydney
- ☑☐ Game Masters Expo
- ☐☐ Go to Comic Con
- ☐☐ Go To Sexpo Expo
- ☐☐ Hunters Hill Quilters Show
- ☑☐ Sydney Royal Easter Show
- ☑☐ Visit the Australian Garden Show
- ☑☐ Visit the Better Homes and Gardens Expo, Sydney

Chapter 27: Historic Houses, Cottages, Buildings and Museums

"Computers let people avoid people, going out to explore. It's so different to just open a website instead of looking at a Picasso in a museum in Paris."

Raf Simons

Historic places, buildings, houses or cottages tell a story from past years of how they used to live and why they lived the way they did; having servants make the beds and food for them and special rooms for men's and ladies' lounges for different occasions, their beds made of straw, duck feathers and many mattress layers. Small in size compared to today's beds but very high. People used to lie up against the pillow upright, not lie down like today's standards. Many things have changed since the old times, but viewing such a time makes you realise how life was maintained and how life was without all the gadgets and computers of today's society. People actually talked to one another and communicated over a piano being played or during a game of cards – a lot more than what we do today where everywhere you look in lunch rooms at work or on the streets people are so addicted to using their mobile phones.

Museums are unique experiences showing interesting things from around the world such as planes, fossils, dinosaurs, even art works. We learn a lot from museums and it increases the knowledge we learn about the history of our past generations.

- ☐☐ 86 Hartley St
- ☐☐ A treasure trove of human history: Berlin's Museum Island
- ☐☐ Abandoned Mill, Sorrento, Italy
- ☐☐ Abandoned Village in Russia
- ☐☐ Acropolis Museum
- ☐☐ Admiralty House
- ☐☐ Albert Kersten Mining & Minerals Museum
- ☐☐ Alcatraz Island, San Francisco, California
- ☑☐ Alexander the Great Expedition
- ☐☐ Alfa Planetarium
- ☐☐ Ardrossan Museum
- ☐☐ Army Museum, WA

- ☐☐ Art Science Museum, Singapore
- ☐☐ Art Space
- ☐☐ Auburn Old Police Station and Courthouse Museum
- ☐☐ Audit House
- ☐☐ Australian Age of Dinosaurs, Winton, Central West
- ☐☐ Australian Aviation Heritage Centre
- ☐☐ Australian Centre for Photography
- ☑☐ Australian Museum, Sydney
- ☐☐ Australian Pearling Exhibition
- ☐☐ Australian Pioneer Village
- ☐☐ Australian Sailing Museum
- ☐☐ Aviation Heritage Centre, Darwin
- ☐☐ Aviation Museum, S.A
- ☐☐ Ayers House Museum
- ☐☐ Ballenberg Open Air Museum
- ☐☐ Balmain Watch House; one of Balmain's historic sandstone buildings
- ☐☐ Bandiana Army Barracks Museum
- ☐☐ Barwon Grange
- ☐☐ Barwon Park
- ☐☐ Bassett Boys' Schoolroom
- ☐☐ Bathurst District Hospital Museum
- ☐☐ Beachport Old Wool & Grain Store Museum
- ☐☐ Beaubourg Museum, Paris, France
- ☐☐ Beaumont House
- ☐☐ Bederval, Braidwood
- ☐☐ Benaki Museum
- ☐☐ Berry Museum
- ☐☐ Blue Mountains Heritage Center, Blackheath
- ☐☐ Blue Mountains Honey Shed
- ☐☐ Bob Marley Museum, Jamaica
- ☐☐ Bob Marley's House, Jamaica
- ☐☐ Bon Accord Cottage
- ☐☐ Bon Accord Mine Complex
- ☐☐ Brennan & Geraghty's Store Museum
- ☐☐ Brett Whiteley Studio
- ☐☐ Bridgedale
- ☐☐ Brislington House, Parramatta
- ☐☐ British Museum
- ☐☐ Bundanon Homestead
- ☐☐ Burnett House
- ☐☐ Burra Mine Site Grassland
- ☐☐ Burra Miner's Dugouts
- ☐☐ Burra Police Lockup and Stables
- ☑☐ Bygone Beauty's Antiques and Tearooms
- ☐☐ Byzantine & Christian Museum
- ☐☐ Cabazon Dinosaurs, Cabazon, California
- ☐☐ Caboolture Historical Village
- ☑☐ Cadman's Cottage
- ☑☐ Campbell's Storehouse
- ☐☐ Cape Jaffa Lighthouse
- ☐☐ Caricature Museum, Mexico City
- ☐☐ Ceduna School House Museum
- ☐☐ Central Greenough historic settlement
- ☐☐ Centre for Alternative Technology
- ☐☐ Charles Darwin Research Station
- ☐☐ Chinese Museum
- ☐☐ Clare Old Police Station and Courthouse Museum
- ☐☐ Clarendon, Tasmania
- ☐☐ Cleve Old Council Chambers
- ☐☐ Clontarf Cottage

- ☐☐ Coal Mines Historic Site
- ☐☐ Cobdogla Irrigation Museum
- ☐☐ Collin Grove Homestead
- ☐☐ Como House and Gardens
- ☐☐ Cooma Cottage, Yass
- ☐☐ Coptic Museum
- ☐☐ Creswick Woollen Mills Museum
- ☐☐ Crystal Kingdom Fossil Museum
- ☐☐ Cube House, Netherlands
- ☐☐ Currumbin Wildlife Sanctuary
- ☐☐ Cusco Historic Center
- ☑☐ Customs House
- ☐☐ Dalwood House, Dalwood
- ☐☐ Davidson Cottage
- ☐☐ De Gooyer Windmill
- ☐☐ Defense of Darwin Experience
- ☐☐ Defense of Darwin Experience & Military Museum
- ☐☐ Den Fynske Landsby
- ☐☐ Dive Cancún Underwater Museum, Cancún, Mexico
- ☐☐ Dow's Pharmacy
- ☐☐ Dubrovnik Old Town
- ☐☐ Dunbar House
- ☐☐ Dundullimal Homestead, Dubbo
- ☐☐ Duntroon Dairy
- ☐☐ East Perth Cemeteries
- ☐☐ Egyptian Museum
- ☐☐ El Ateneo, Guinness World Record Library in Buenos Aires, Argentina
- ☑☐ Elizabeth Bay House
- ☑☐ Elizabeth Farm
- ☐☐ Ellensbrook
- ☐☐ Erawan Museum
- ☐☐ Eryldene Historic House and Garden
- ☐☐ Estádio Nacional de Brasília, Football Stadium
- ☐☐ Estonia - City of Tallinn, Old Town which is a medieval era township
- ☑☐ Everglass House and Gardens, Leura
- ☐☐ Experiment Farm Cottage
- ☐☐ Explore the old saw mill ruins in Faulconbridge
- ☐☐ Explore the Secrets of Odense
- ☐☐ Fiji Museum, Suva
- ☑☐ Fitzroy Melbourne, Cooks' Cottage
- ☐☐ Fleet Air Arm Museum
- ☐☐ Former Outpatients Building aka Tuxworth Fullwood
- ☐☐ Fort Bourtange, Groningen, Netherlands
- ☑☐ Fort Denison Island
- ☑☐ Fort Phillip Signal Station Observatory Hill, Sydney
- ☐☐ Fossils and Minerals Museum
- ☐☐ Franklin House
- ☐☐ Franz Mayer Museum
- ☐☐ Gamble Cottage
- ☐☐ Gammon Cottage
- ☐☐ Gawler Old Telegraph Station Museum
- ☐☐ Gettysburg Battlefield, Gettysburg, Pennsylvania
- ☐☐ Glass Museum
- ☐☐ Gledwood Homestead
- ☐☐ Glencoe Woolshed
- ☑☐ Go aboard James Cook Endeavor
- ☐☐ Golden Pipeline Heritage Trail
- ☐☐ Goolwa Museum
- ☐☐ Goolwa Old Railway Superintendent's Cottage
- ☑☐ Government House

- ☐☐ Grand Prix Museum, Macua
- ☐☐ Grandchester Railway Station
- ☐☐ Gravity Discovery Centre
- ☐☐ Grossmann House and Bragh House, Maitland
- ☐☐ Guggenheim Museum in Bilbao, Spain
- ☐☐ Gulf Station
- ☐☐ Gum San Chinese Heritage Centre
- ☑☐ Hambleton Cottage, Parramatta
- ☐☐ Harpers Mansion, Berrima
- ☑☐ Hars Aircraft Museum
- ☐☐ Hartley Street School Museum
- ☐☐ Hawksbury Museum and Gallery
- ☐☐ Henry Ford Museum Dearborn, MI
- ☑☐ Henry Kendall Cottage and Historical Museum
- ☐☐ Heritage Railway Discovery Tour
- ☐☐ Herning Museum
- ☐☐ Historic Abercrombre House, Bathurst
- ☐☐ Historic Mt Victoria Toll House
- ☐☐ Historic Tarella
- ☐☐ Historical Museum of Bern
- ☐☐ Home Hill
- ☐☐ Hood Milk Bottle, Boston, Massachusetts
- ☐☐ Hope Cottage
- ☐☐ Hou Wang Temple
- ☑☐ Houses of Parliament
- ☐☐ Hughes Pump House
- ☐☐ Humberstone and Santa Laura Saltpeter Works
- ☑☐ Hyde Park Barracks Museum
- ☑☐ Immigration Museum
- ☐☐ Institute for Sound and Vision, Hilversum, Netherlands
- ☐☐ Iraklion Archaeological Museum
- ☑☐ James Cook birth place, Great Ayton, Yorkshire, England
- ☐☐ James Cook Museum
- ☐☐ Jamestown Local History Centre
- ☐☐ Jamestown Railway Station and Goods Shed Museum
- ☐☐ Jones Store
- ☐☐ José Luis Cuevas Museum
- ☑☐ Justice and Police Museum
- ☐☐ Kalgoorlie Boulder Pure Gold - Audio Tour
- ☐☐ Keith 1910 Congregational Church
- ☐☐ Keith Early Settler's Cottage
- ☐☐ Kennedy Space Center Cape Canaveral, FL
- ☐☐ Kingston National Trust Museum
- ☐☐ Kirribilli House
- ☐☐ Klementinum Library, Prague, Czech Republic
- ☐☐ Koppio Smithy Museum
- ☐☐ Krzywy Domek (Crooked House) Sopot, Poland
- ☐☐ Kunsthalle Basel
- ☐☐ La Perouse Museum
- ☐☐ La Trobe's Cottage
- ☐☐ Labassa
- ☐☐ Lady Denman Maritime and Heritage Complex
- ☐☐ Lake Boga Flying Boat Museum
- ☐☐ Lake View House
- ☐☐ Lancer Barracks Building, Parramatta
- ☐☐ Les Hansen House

- ☐☐ Limestone Tunnel Cave, Orange
- ☐☐ Lindesay House
- ☐☐ Lofotr Borg Viking Museum
- ☐☐ Lyall's Store
- ☐☐ Macleay Museum
- ☐☐ Madame Tussauds Wax Museum London
- ☑☐ Madame Tussauds Wax Museum Sydney
- ☐☐ Magistrates House
- ☐☐ Maitland Museum
- ☐☐ Malowen Lowarth Cottage
- ☐☐ Mamre House
- ☐☐ Mangowine Homestead
- ☐☐ Market Square Museum
- ☐☐ Mary Mackillop Place Museum
- ☐☐ Matta House
- ☐☐ May Gibbs's "Nutcote Cottage"
- ☐☐ McCrae Homestead
- ☐☐ Melbourne Museum
- ☐☐ Memento Park, Budapest
- ☐☐ Meroogal
- ☐☐ Millicent Museum
- ☐☐ Mines House
- ☐☐ Minlaton Museum
- ☐☐ Miss Potter's House, Newcastle
- ☐☐ Miss Traill's House, Bathurst
- ☐☐ Moonta Miners Cottage and Heritage Garden
- ☐☐ Moonta Mines Model School Museum
- ☐☐ Moonta Mines Sweet Shop
- ☐☐ Moonta Railway Station
- ☐☐ Moonta School of Mines
- ☐☐ Mooramong Historic Site, Victoria
- ☐☐ Motor Museum of WA
- ☐☐ Moundsville Penitentiary, West Virginia, America
- ☐☐ Mount Gambier Courthouse Museum
- ☐☐ Mount Laura Station
- ☐☐ Mt Victoria Museum
- ☐☐ Mulberry Hill
- ☐☐ Mus'ee D Orsay
- ☐☐ Museo Antropologico P. Sebastian Englert
- ☐☐ Museo de Arte Contemporáneo de Monterrey
- ☐☐ Museo de Arte Moderno
- ☐☐ Museo de la Secretaría de Hacienda y Crédito Público
- ☐☐ Museo Del Romanticsmo
- ☐☐ Museo Nacional de Antropología
- ☐☐ Museo Nacional de Arte
- ☐☐ Museo Nacional de las Culturas
- ☐☐ Museo Rufino Tamayo, Mexico City
- ☐☐ Museo Soumaya
- ☐☐ Museu Paraense Emílio Goeldi
- ☐☐ Museu Picasso
- ☐☐ Museum of Australian Currency Notes
- ☐☐ Museum of Australian Democracy at Eureka (M.A.D.E)
- ☑☐ Museum of Fire
- ☐☐ Museum of Human Disease
- ☐☐ Museum of Islamic Art, Cairo
- ☐☐ Museum of Macau
- ☐☐ Museum of Old and New Art
- ☑☐ Museum of Sydney
- ☐☐ Museum Victoria
- ☐☐ Nambucca Heads Historical Museum
- ☐☐ Nappers Accommodation House
- ☐☐ National Air and Space Museum (Smithsonian), Washington, D.C

- ☐☐ National Archaeological Museum, Athens
- ☐☐ National Artillery Museum
- ☑☐ National Maritime Museum
- ☑☐ National Museum of Australia
- ☐☐ Natural History Museum of Basel
- ☐☐ Natural History Museum of Geneva
- ☐☐ Nicholson Museum
- ☐☐ No. 1 Pump Station
- ☐☐ Norfolk Plains Heritage Centre
- ☑☐ North Fort Museum, North Head
- ☐☐ Northkapp Museum
- ☐☐ Norweigen Folk Museum
- ☐☐ Nowra Museum
- ☐☐ Oberon Sapphire Fossicking
- ☐☐ O'Keeffe House
- ☐☐ Old Blythewood
- ☐☐ Old Farm, Strawberry Hill
- ☑☐ Old Government House, Parramatta
- ☐☐ Old Highercombe Hotel Museum
- ☑☐ Old Melbourne Gaol (Ned Kelly placed there)
- ☑☐ Old Parliament House
- ☐☐ Old Police Station, Borroloola
- ☐☐ Old Police Station precinct
- ☐☐ Old Umbrella Shop
- ☐☐ Olivewood
- ☐☐ Olympic Museum
- ☐☐ Ophir Reserve - Site of Australia's First Payable Gold
- ☐☐ Oscar Niemeyer Museum
- ☐☐ Overland Corner Hotel
- ☑☐ Oxford University England
- ☑☐ Parliament House Canberra
- ☑☐ Parliament Square
- ☐☐ Peacocks Chimney Stack
- ☐☐ Penghana
- ☐☐ Peninsula Farm (Tranby)
- ☐☐ Penitentiary Chapel Historic Site
- ☐☐ Penneshaw Maritime and Folk Museum
- ☐☐ Penola Telegraph Station and Post Office
- ☐☐ Penrith Museum of Printing
- ☐☐ Pioneer Museum Park
- ☐☐ Polar Museum
- ☐☐ Port Elliot Railway Station
- ☐☐ Port Pirie Railway Station
- ☐☐ Portable Iron Houses, Vic, Australia
- ☐☐ Portarlington Mill
- ☑☐ Powerhouse Museum/Harry Potter Exhibition
- ☑☐ Pylon Lookout Harbour Bridge
- ☐☐ Qantas Founders Museum, Longreach, Queensland
- ☑☐ Queen Victoria Building
- ☐☐ Queen Victoria Museum and Art Gallery
- ☐☐ R.P. Gustavo Le Paige Archaeological Museum
- ☐☐ Rail Heritage Center
- ☐☐ Railway Station Katherine
- ☐☐ Railway Station Pine Creek
- ☐☐ Redruth Gaol
- ☐☐ Rietberg Museum
- ☐☐ Rijks Museum
- ☐☐ Rippon Lea House and Gardens
- ☐☐ Riverside, Goulburn
- ☐☐ Robe CSIRO Research Station
- ☐☐ Robe Customs House
- ☑☐ Rose Seidler House
- ☑☐ Rouse Hill House and Farm
- ☐☐ Royal Bull's Head Inn
- ☐☐ Royal Klunkehjem Museum
- ☐☐ Royal Ontario Museum

- ☐☐ Runnymede
- ☐☐ Rupert Wood Mansion, Vic, Australia
- ☐☐ Sampsons Cottage
- ☐☐ San Ildefonso College
- ☐☐ Sandstone Courthouse at Hartley
- ☐☐ São Paulo Museum of Art
- ☐☐ Saumarez Homestead, Armidale
- ☐☐ Science Works Museum
- ☐☐ Seavey Family Homestead, Seward, Alaska *summertime*
- ☑☐ See Kirribilli House from water
- ☐☐ See the large heart of famous Horse Phar Lap
- ☐☐ See where the declaration of independence was signed
- ☑☐ Selwood Science and Puzzles
- ☐☐ Sharam Cottages
- ☐☐ Small Arms Factory Museum
- ☑☐ Sovereign Hill Gold Adventures and Historic Buildings
- ☑☐ Sovereign Hill - Gold Museum
- ☐☐ St. Fagans National History Museum
- ☐☐ Stangate House and Garden
- ☐☐ Stationmasters House
- ☐☐ Steamtown Heritage Rail Centre
- ☐☐ Stock Exchange Building and Arcade
- ☐☐ Stone House, Guimaraes, Portugal
- ☐☐ Stratford-upon-Avon, birth place William Shakespeare
- ☐☐ Strathalbyn Police Station and Courthouse Museum
- ☐☐ Streaky Bay Museum
- ☑☐ Susannah Place Museum
- ☐☐ Svalbald Museum
- ☐☐ Swarovski Switzerland entrance + inside
- ☐☐ Swiss Museum of Transport
- ☐☐ Swiss Re Building, London
- ☐☐ Sydney Jewish Museum
- ☐☐ Sydney Tramway Museum
- ☐☐ Tandanya National Aboriginal Cultural Institute
- ☐☐ Tanilba House, Tanilba Bay
- ☐☐ Tate Modern, London
- ☐☐ Te Papa Museum
- ☑☐ The Arms of Australian Inn
- ☐☐ The Briars
- ☐☐ The conic "Trulli" dwellings in Apulia, Italy
- ☐☐ The Dragon Gate of Harlech House, Dublin
- ☐☐ The Farm Shed Museum
- ☐☐ The Federal Standard Printing Works
- ☐☐ The Heights Heritage House and Garden
- ☐☐ The Infinity Room at House on the Rock, Spring Green, WI
- ☐☐ The Mystery Spot, Santa Cruz, California, USA
- ☑☐ The National Opal Collection
- ☐☐ The Perth Mint, WA
- ☑☐ The Rocks Discovery Museum
- ☐☐ The Rose Cottage c 1876
- ☐☐ The Sheeps Back Museum
- ☐☐ The Vines Cottage Tool Museum
- ☐☐ The Workshops Rail Museum
- ☐☐ Thyssen Museum
- ☐☐ Tobuk Outback Sheep Station
- ☐☐ Tokyo National Museum, Samurai Era of Japan
- ☐☐ Tomago House, Tomago
- ☐☐ Tongwynlais
- ☐☐ Townsville Heritage Centre

- ☑ Toy and Railway Museum
- ☐ Train Works
- ☐ Trapholt Museum
- ☐ Tree House, Revelstoke, British Columbia
- ☐ Tuggeranong Homestead
- ☐ Tumby Bay Branch Museum
- ☐ Turf Houses, Faroe Islands
- ☑ Ultimate sport tour - MCG, Rod Laver Arena and Sports Museum, Melbourne
- ☐ Union Buildings
- ☐ Upside down house, Szymbark, Poland
- ☑ Vaucluse House
- ☐ Valley Heights Locomotive Depot Heritage Museum
- ☐ Van Gogh Museum
- ☐ Vatican Museums
- ☐ Victor Harbor Station Master's Residence
- ☐ Victoria Barracks
- ☐ Victory Theater Antique Center
- ☐ Vienna Cottage, Hunters Hill
- ☐ Viking Ship Museum
- ☑ Visit Cartoon Bunker Coffs Harbour
- ☑ Visit site Ned Kelly (Glenn Rowen)
- ☐ Visit "The Shire" in New Zealand
- ☐ Visit the Anne Frank house
- ☐ Visit the Auschwitz Concentration Camp
- ☐ Visit the Cairo Museum, Egypt
- ☐ Visit the famous Santa Monica pier
- ☐ Visit the famous Wall Street
- ☐ Visit the Four Corners - Arizona, New Mexico, Utah, and Colorado, USA
- ☑ Visit the Louvre Museum
- ☐ Visit the Mint
- ☐ Visit the Smithsonian
- ☐ Visit where Captain James Cook first set foot on Australian soil at Kurnell Peninsula Headland, Botany Bay
- ☐ Volcano Adventure, Hawaii
- ☐ Wallaroo Heritage and Nautical Museum
- ☐ Warden Finnerty's Residence
- ☐ Watch House
- ☐ Waterman's Cottage
- ☐ Wengerhalpbahn Railway
- ☐ Werribee Park Historic Farm
- ☐ Westpac Museum
- ☐ Willunga Courthouse Museum
- ☐ Willunga Slate Museum
- ☐ Wilson's Cottage
- ☐ Winns Bakehouse
- ☐ Witch Monument, Vardø, Norway
- ☐ Wolston House
- ☐ Wonnerup
- ☐ Woodbridge
- ☐ Woodford Academy, Woodford Great Western Hwy
- ☐ Wyoming Dinosaur Center Thermopolis, WY
- ☐ Yellow House, Potts Point
- ☐ York Courthouse Complex
- ☐ Zara Clark Museum
- ☐ Zentrum Paul Klee Museum

Chapter 28: Caving Experiences

"You can go into caves, and they can maintain constant conditions of temperature and humidity over long periods of time, even though the outside temperature may be way above what it is inside the cave."

Hendrik Poinar

Discover an underground labyrinth of limestone caves and formations. Stalagmites are a type of rock formation that rises from the floor of a cave due to the accumulation of material deposited on the floor from ceiling drippings. Stalactites are a tapering structure hanging like an icicle from the roof of a cave, formed of calcium salts deposited by dripping water. When both combine, they make marvellous columns. As compound cave formations, they include among their ranks as the tallest freestanding speleothems in the world.

There are many wonderful cave adventures around the world and all unique in their own special way: diamond caves, mud caves, crystal caves, underwater caves. Each one has their own personality to impress any visitors that wish to explore them and they are all formed over decades.

- ☐☐ Ajanta Caves, India
- ☐☐ Aladdin Adventure Tour
- ☐☐ Archway by Night
- ☐☐ Archway Cave (self-guided tour)
- ☐☐ Bushrangers Cave
- ☐☐ Cango Caves
- ☐☐ Carols in the Caves, Jenolan Caves
- ☐☐ Cathedral Cave Tour
- ☐☐ Cave City of Vardzia in Georgia
- ☐☐ Cave of Melody, Scotland
- ☐☐ Caves of Aggtelek Karst and Slovak Karst, Hungary and Slovakia
- ☐☐ Central River Adventure Cave Tour
- ☐☐ Chifley Cave
- ☐☐ Cradle of Humankind
- ☐☐ Cueva de los Cristales/Cave of Crystals, Mexico
- ☐☐ Diamond Cave
- ☐☐ Ellora Caves, India
- ☐☐ Explore a Cava Cave in Spain
- ☑☐ Explore a cave internationally

- ☐☐ Explore the Giant Crystal Caves, Chihuahua, Mexico
- ☐☐ Explore the Paleolithic Cave Art in Altamira, Spain
- ☐☐ Figtree Cave (self-guided tour)
- ☐☐ Fingal's Cave, Staffa, Scotland
- ☐☐ Go cave diving
- ☐☐ Grove Cave
- ☑☐ Imperial Cave
- ☐☐ Incredible ice cave inside the Mutnovsky volcano in Russia
- ☐☐ Jalan Batu Caves, Selangor, Malaysia
- ☑☐ Jubilee Cave
- ☐☐ Junction Cave
- ☐☐ Kayak through caves
- ☐☐ King Solomon's Temple
- ☐☐ Kooringa Cave
- ☐☐ Legends, Mysteries & Ghost Tour
- ☐☐ Llechwedd Slate Caverns
- ☑☐ Lucas Cave
- ☐☐ Mammoth Adventure Tour
- ☐☐ Marble Caverns of Carrera Lake, Chile
- ☐☐ Marble Caves in Patagonia
- ☐☐ Marble Caves, Chile Chico, Chile
- ☐☐ Mini Adventure Tour
- ☐☐ Mogao Grottoes (Caves of the Thousand Buddhas), Dunhuang, China
- ☐☐ Mulwaree Cave
- ☐☐ Opera and Orchestra in the caves
- ☑☐ Orient Cave
- ☐☐ Palawan Underground River Caves
- ☑☐ Plughole Adventure Tour
- ☐☐ Pool of Cerberus Cave
- ☐☐ Rapelling into Krubera Cave
- ☐☐ Reed Flute Cave in China
- ☐☐ Rent Your Own Cave, Blue Mountains
- ☐☐ Ribbon Cave
- ☐☐ River Cave
- ☐☐ See the Cave paintings at Bhopal, India
- ☐☐ Slovenian Caves - the Grand Canyon of the underground
- ☐☐ Swim the Cave of the Crystal Sepulcher
- ☐☐ Temple of Baal Cave
- ☐☐ Thermal baths inside a cave, Miskolc Tapolca, Hungary
- ☐☐ Visit all Abercrombie Caves
- ☐☐ Visit all Jenolan Caves
- ☐☐ Visit all Wombeyan Caves
- ☐☐ Visit Australia's Crystal Caves
- ☐☐ Waitomo Glowworm Caves
- ☐☐ Wellington Caves & Phosphate Mine
- ☐☐ Wollondilly Cave

Chapter 29: Art Galleries and Famous Artworks

"A work of art is above all an adventure of the mind."

Eugene Ionesco

Photographs, people, objects, paintings, creations that make you stop just a moment and view the beautiful artworks people have taken a lot of time in designing, and breathtaking paintings that have survived decades. The world is a beautiful place yet the canvas tells us much more: the way someone was feeling when they painted, photographed, even made a sculpture of something they foresaw in front of their eyes. It's not just the art that is marvelous: the time and effort that has gone into designing the art galleries around the world is astonishing. For example, The Louvre is a pyramid shape and aboveground, but when you go downstairs it's a maze of beautiful art, sculptures, photographs and much more. A lot of us just live closed-in lives and don't really appreciate the true beauty of things around us. A lot of us even have art galleries a town or so away from where we live and still never walk in to view the galleries. Take a chance; I'm sure you'll like what you see.

- ☐☐ "Badenixe" (bathing beauty), sculpture in Hamburg, Germany
- ☐☐ "Rhythms of Life" Sculpture, Kenya
- ☐☐ "The Scream," Edvard Munch, National Gallery, Oslo
- ☐☐ A Sunday Afternoon on the Island of La Grande Jatte, artwork by Georges Seurat
- ☐☐ Aboriginal Art and Culture, Arnhem Land
- ☐☐ American Gothic, artwork by Grant Wood
- ☑☐ Angel Place Birdcages, Sydney, Australia
- ☐☐ Art Gallery of Ballarat
- ☐☐ Art Gallery of Western Australia
- ☑☐ Arts of Circular Quay, Sydney
- ☐☐ Arts Village
- ☑☐ Bilarong Reserve & Playground - Sculptures
- ☑☐ Billich Art Gallery
- ☑☐ Caricature artist to draw personalised sketch
- ☐☐ Carving of Jesus Christ the Cedars of Lebanon

- ☐☐ Create a piece of art and sell it
- ☐☐ Dogs Playing Poker, artwork by C.M. Coolidge
- ☑☐ Falls Gallery, Wentworth Falls
- ☑☐ Gannon House
- ☐☐ Girl with a Pearl Earring artwork by Johannes Vermeer
- ☑☐ Grotto Point Aboriginal Markings
- ☐☐ Hawksbury Regional Gallery
- ☑☐ Ken Duncan Gallery
- ☐☐ Ken Duncan Gallery, Erina Heights
- ☐☐ Kunsthaus, Zurich
- ☐☐ Kunstmuseum, Basel
- ☐☐ Lost Bear Gallery, Katoomba
- ☑☐ Manly Art and Museum
- ☐☐ Metropol Parasol, Seville, Spain
- ☑☐ Museum of Contemporary Art
- ☐☐ National Galleries
- ☑☐ Norman Lindsay Gallery, Faulconbridge
- ☐☐ Ordrupgaard Gallery
- ☑☐ Own a replica copy of Mona Lisa
- ☑☐ Own a replica copy of Venus de Milo sculpture
- ☑☐ Penrith Regional Art Gallery
- ☐☐ S.H Erviz Gallery, Rocks
- ☐☐ Sand sculptures
- ☐☐ School of Athens, artwork by Raphael
- ☐☐ See a Van Gogh painting
- ☐☐ See Da Vinci's the Last Supper
- ☐☐ See Michelangelo's David
- ☐☐ See Statue of David in Florence, Italy
- ☐☐ See the Bayeux Tapestry
- ☑☐ See the Mona Lisa in Louvre, Paris
- ☐☐ See the Turin Shroud
- ☑☐ See the Venus De Milo in Louvre, Paris
- ☐☐ The Birth of Venus, artwork by Sandro Botticelli
- ☐☐ The Night Watch (De Nachtwacht), artwork by Rembrandt van Rijn
- ☐☐ The Persistence of Memory, artwork by Salvador Dali
- ☐☐ The Sistine Chapel Ceiling, artwork by Michelangelo
- ☐☐ The Starry Night, artwork by Vincent van Gogh
- ☐☐ Uffizi Gallery, Florance, Italy
- ☐☐ Umbrella Street, Portugal
- ☐☐ Whistler's Mother, artwork by James McNeill

Chapter 30: Mountain Peak Challenges

"Great things are done when men and mountains meet."

William Blake

Since I was in my early teens it has been a wish of mine to climb Mount Kosciuszko. It is a mountain located in the Snowy Mountains in Kosciuszko National Park, New South Wales. With a height of 2,228 metres above sea level, it is the highest mountain on the Australian continent. It will allow me to stand above my country of Australia and look over its majestic beauty: a glorious achievement to stand so high in the world and look down at where I have come from and how far I have travelled – and it is high on my bucket list. It's a great way to see how much you can achieve in life if you just push your body to its limits. Don't picture the pain of the journey, picture the end and the beauty and glory of any achievements we do in our lives. It will go down in my life as one of my greatest achievements and I am so looking forward to conquering this challenge before me.

- ☐☐ Three Peaks Challenge of Africa
- ☐☐ Australian Capital Territory - Bimberi Peak - 1913 metres
- ☐☐ Climb Aconcagua
- ☐☐ Climb Carstensz Pyramid Mountain
- ☐☐ Climb Elbrus, Russia
- ☐☐ Climb Mont Blanc
- ☐☐ Climb Mount Everest
- ☐☐ Climb Mount Kilimanjaro
- ☐☐ Climb Mount McKinley
- ☐☐ Climb Mt K2
- ☐☐ Climb Mt Kangchenjunga
- ☐☐ Climb Mt Kinabalu via Ferata, Malaysia
- ☐☐ Climb Mt Chimborazo
- ☐☐ Climb Mt Aconcagua
- ☐☐ Climb Mt Broad Peak
- ☐☐ Climb Mt Cho Oyu
- ☐☐ Climb Mt Gasherbrum I
- ☐☐ Climb Mt Ihotse
- ☐☐ Climb Mt Ismoil Somoni Peak
- ☐☐ Climb Mt Logan
- ☐☐ Climb Mt Makalu
- ☐☐ Climb Mt Manaslu
- ☐☐ Climb Mt Mauna Kea
- ☐☐ Climb Mt Nanga Parbat
- ☐☐ Climb Mt Shishapangma
- ☐☐ Climb the Matterhorn, Switzerland
- ☐☐ Climb Pigeon House Mountain
- ☐☐ Climb to all eight states' summits of Australia

- ☐☐ Climb Vinson Massif
- ☐☐ Complete the Seven Summits of the World
- ☐☐ Mount Bromo, Indonesia
- ☐☐ Mount Lofty
- ☐☐ Mount Roraima
- ☐☐ Mount Sinai
- ☐☐ Mount Tomanivi
- ☐☐ Mount Roraima, Brazil
- ☐☐ Mount St. Helens
- ☐☐ Mt Everest Base Camp
- ☐☐ New South Wales - Mount Kosciuszko - 2228 metres
- ☐☐ Northern Territory - Mount Zeil - 1531 metres
- ☐☐ Queensland - Bartle Frere - 1622 metres
- ☐☐ South Australia - Mount Woodroffe - 1435 metres
- ☐☐ Tasmania - Mount Ossa - 1617 metres
- ☐☐ Victoria - Mount Bogong - 1986 metres
- ☐☐ Western Australia - Mount Meharry - 1253 metres

Chapter 31:
Animal Encounters

"Until one has loved an animal a part of one's soul remains unawakened."

Anatole France

Unique animal encounters: come face to face with native and exotic animals from around the globe. Many of us are scared, if not terrified, from a fraction of fear to hearts beating to the thrill and adrenalin of coming up face to face with our favourite animals. Some of us do it to overcome fears, such as a fear of spiders or snakes. Some of us love animals so much we are willing to touch, hold or even feed animals to show our affection from the heart towards our animals around the world. Once we enter with the zoo keepers, we discover a lot of knowledge about the animals and are able to ask questions of things we don't understand. No matter what animal, we have the wonderful experience which we always come out with after it's all over of feeling accomplished and wanting to experience more. I loved my first animal experience and I couldn't believe how close I was to it, so much that I now strive to have a photo animal encounter with every possible animal that we can imagine, or find and experience the way they are, the way they play, eat, and have adapted to captivity. Animals are a big part of our world and mean the world to me; how about you?

- ☐☐ Have my picture taken with an arctic fox
- ☐☐ Have my picture taken with an ant eater
- ☐☐ Have my picture taken with an armadillo
- ☐☐ Have my picture taken with an American black bear
- ☐☐ Have my picture taken with an Asian black bear
- ☑☐ Have my picture taken with an alligator
- ☐☐ Have my picture taken with an ant
- ☐☐ Have my picture taken with an aardvark
- ☐☐ Have my picture taken with an alpaca
- ☐☐ Have my picture taken with an African civet
- ☐☐ Have my picture taken with an African palm civet
- ☐☐ Have my picture taken with an adeline penguin

- ☐☐ Have my picture taken with an African penguin
- ☐☐ Have my picture taken with an aldabra giant tortoise
- ☐☐ Have my picture taken with an antelope
- ☐☐ Have my picture taken with an Arctic hare
- ☐☐ Have my picture taken with an Arctic wolf
- ☐☐ Have my picture taken with an Asian palm civet
- ☐☐ Have my picture taken with an Asiatic black bear
- ☐☐ Have my picture taken with an axolotl
- ☐☐ Have my picture taken with an aye aye
- ☐☐ Have my picture taken with a brown bear
- ☐☐ Have my picture taken with a barracuda
- ☐☐ Have my picture taken with a blue tongue lizard
- ☐☐ Have my picture taken with a baboon
- ☐☐ Have my picture taken with a bandicoot
- ☐☐ Have my picture taken with a bactrian camel
- ☐☐ Have my picture taken with a badger
- ☐☐ Have my picture taken with a banded palm civet
- ☐☐ Have my picture taken with a beaver
- ☐☐ Have my picture taken with a buffalo
- ☐☐ Have my picture taken with a bat
- ☐☐ Have my picture taken with a binturong
- ☐☐ Have my picture taken with a barn owl
- ☐☐ Have my picture taken with a basking shark
- ☐☐ Have my picture taken with a bearded dragon
- ☐☐ Have my picture taken with a bengal tiger
- ☐☐ Have my picture taken with a black bear
- ☐☐ Have my picture taken with a black rhinoceros
- ☐☐ Have my picture taken with a blue whale
- ☐☐ Have my picture taken with a bobcat
- ☐☐ Have my picture taken with a bongo
- ☐☐ Have my picture taken with a bison
- ☐☐ Have my picture taken with a bare-eared squirrel monkey
- ☐☐ Have my picture taken with a black lion tamarind
- ☐☐ Have my picture taken with a beluga whale
- ☑☐ Have my picture taken with a butterfly
- ☐☐ Have my picture taken with a bonobo
- ☑☐ Have my picture taken with a bottle nosed dolphin
- ☐☐ Have my picture taken with a budgerigar
- ☐☐ Have my picture taken with a bull shark
- ☐☐ Have my picture taken with a caracal

- ☐☐ Have my picture taken with a cassowary
- ☐☐ Have my picture taken with a centipede
- ☐☐ Have my picture taken with a chamois
- ☐☐ Have my picture taken with a chinstrap penguin
- ☐☐ Have my picture taken with a chipmunk
- ☐☐ Have my picture taken with a cockroach
- ☑☐ Have my picture taken with a cockatoo
- ☐☐ Have my picture taken with a collared peccary
- ☐☐ Have my picture taken with a common buzzard
- ☐☐ Have my picture taken with a common toad
- ☐☐ Have my picture taken with a coral
- ☐☐ Have my picture taken with a crane
- ☐☐ Have my picture taken with a crested penguin
- ☐☐ Have my picture taken with a cuscus
- ☐☐ Have my picture taken with a cuttlefish
- ☐☐ Have my picture taken with a chinchilla
- ☐☐ Have my picture taken with a chimpanzee
- ☐☐ Have my picture taken with a chicken
- ☐☐ Have my picture taken with cattle
- ☐☐ Have my picture taken with a caterpillar
- ☐☐ Have my picture taken with a cat
- ☐☐ Have my picture taken with a capybara
- ☑☐ Have my picture taken with a coati
- ☐☐ Have my picture taken with a crab
- ☐☐ Have my picture taken with a crab eating macaque
- ☐☐ Have my picture taken with a crocodile
- ☑☐ Have my picture taken with a common marmoset
- ☑☐ Have my picture taken with a cotton top tamarins monkey
- ☐☐ Have my picture taken with a catfish
- ☐☐ Have my picture taken with a chameleon
- ☐☐ Have my picture taken with a camel
- ☐☐ Have my picture taken with a coyote
- ☐☐ Have my picture taken with a clouded leopard
- ☑☐ Have my picture taken with a coastal python
- ☐☐ Have my picture taken with a cougar
- ☑☐ Have my picture taken with a cheetah
- ☑☐ Have my picture taken with a deer
- ☐☐ Have my picture taken with a dhole
- ☐☐ Have my picture taken with a dusky dolphin
- ☐☐ Have my picture taken with a dwarf crocodile

- ☐☐ Have my picture taken with a dugong
- ☐☐ Have my picture taken with a dragonfly
- ☑☐ Have my picture taken with a dog
- ☑☐ Have my picture taken with a duck
- ☑☐ Have my picture taken with a donkey
- ☑☐ Have my picture taken with a dingo
- ☐☐ Have my picture taken with a douc languor monkey
- ☐☐ Have my picture taken with an Eskimo dog
- ☐☐ Have my picture taken with an electric eel
- ☐☐ Have my picture taken with an elephant seal
- ☐☐ Have my picture taken with an Elephant Shrew
- ☐☐ Have my picture taken with an emperor penguin
- ☐☐ Have my picture taken with an emperor tamarind
- ☐☐ Have my picture taken with an elk
- ☐☐ Have my picture taken with an echidna
- ☑☐ Have my picture taken with an eland
- ☐☐ Have my picture taken with an eagle
- ☐☐ Have my picture taken with an elephant
- ☐☐ Have my picture taken with an eastern quoll
- ☑☐ Have my picture taken with a European fallow deer
- ☑☐ Have my picture taken with an emu
- ☐☐ Have my picture taken with a falcon
- ☐☐ Have my picture taken with a fennec fox
- ☐☐ Have my picture taken with a fin whale
- ☐☐ Have my picture taken with a fish
- ☐☐ Have my photo taken with a firefly
- ☐☐ Have my picture taken with a fishing cat
- ☐☐ Have my picture taken with a fossa
- ☐☐ Have my picture taken with a fur seal
- ☐☐ Have my picture taken with a fox
- ☑☐ Have my picture taken with a fresh water eel
- ☐☐ Have my picture taken with a frill necked lizard
- ☐☐ Have my picture taken with a frog
- ☐☐ Have my picture taken with a flamingo
- ☐☐ Have my picture taken with a ferret
- ☐☐ Have my picture taken with a glow worm
- ☐☐ Have my picture taken with a gentoo penguin
- ☐☐ Have my picture taken with a galapagos penguin
- ☐☐ Have my picture taken with a galapagos tortoise
- ☐☐ Have my picture taken with a gecko

- ☐☐ Have my picture taken with a Geoffrey's tamarin
- ☐☐ Have my picture taken with a giant clam
- ☐☐ Have my picture taken with a gibbon
- ☐☐ Have my picture taken with a giant panda
- ☐☐ Have my picture taken with a gila monster
- ☐☐ Have my picture taken with a golden lion tamarin
- ☐☐ Have my picture taken with a golden retriever
- ☐☐ Have my picture taken with a great dane
- ☐☐ Have my picture taken with a goose
- ☐☐ Have my picture taken with a gopher
- ☐☐ Have my picture taken with a great white shark
- ☐☐ Have my picture taken with a grey mouse lemur
- ☐☐ Have my picture taken with a grey reef shark
- ☐☐ Have my picture taken with a grey seal
- ☐☐ Have my picture taken with a greyhound
- ☐☐ Have my picture taken with a guinea fowl
- ☐☐ Have my picture taken with a goanna
- ☐☐ Have my picture taken with a grasshopper
- ☐☐ Have my picture taken with a goose
- ☐☐ Have my picture taken with a gerbil
- ☐☐ Have my picture taken with a gaur
- ☐☐ Have my picture taken with a gazelle
- ☐☐ Have my picture taken with a guinea pig
- ☐☐ Have my picture taken with a genet
- ☐☐ Have my picture taken with a goat
- ☐☐ Have my picture taken with a grivet
- ☐☐ Have my picture taken with a gabon talapoin
- ☐☐ Have my picture taken with a gelada
- ☐☐ Have my picture taken with a golden snub-nosed monkey
- ☐☐ Have my picture taken with a grizzly bear
- ☑☐ Have my picture taken with a giraffe
- ☐☐ Have my picture taken with a golden tree snake
- ☐☐ Have my picture taken with a gorilla
- ☐☐ Have my picture taken with a giant turtle
- ☐☐ Have my picture taken with a glider
- ☐☐ Have my picture taken with a hummingbird
- ☐☐ Have my picture taken with a humboldt penguin
- ☐☐ Have my picture taken with a howler monkey
- ☐☐ Have my picture taken with a hamster
- ☐☐ Have my picture taken with a hare

- ☐☐ Have my picture taken with a heron
- ☐☐ Have my picture taken with a highland cattle
- ☐☐ Have my picture taken with a humpback whale
- ☐☐ Have my picture taken with a hammerhead shark
- ☐☐ Have my picture taken with a hedgehog
- ☐☐ Have my picture taken with a hippopotamus
- ☐☐ Have my picture taken with a hyena
- ☐☐ Have my picture taken with a horse
- ☐☐ Have my picture taken with a hermit crab
- ☐☐ Have my picture taken with a hive of bees
- ☐☐ Have my picture taken with a honey badger
- ☐☐ Have my picture taken with an ibis
- ☐☐ Have my picture taken with an impala
- ☐☐ Have my picture taken with an indri
- ☐☐ Have my picture taken with an Indian sloth bear
- ☑☐ Have my picture taken with an iguana
- ☐☐ Have my picture taken with a jellyfish
- ☐☐ Have my picture taken with a Japanese macaque
- ☐☐ Have my picture taken with a jackal
- ☐☐ Have my picture taken with a jaguar
- ☐☐ Have my picture taken with a kudu
- ☐☐ Have my picture taken with a kiwi
- ☐☐ Have my picture taken with a king crab
- ☐☐ Have my picture taken with a killer whale
- ☐☐ Have my picture taken with a keel billed toucan
- ☐☐ Have my picture taken with a kakapo
- ☐☐ Have my picture taken with a king penguin
- ☐☐ Have my picture taken with a komodo dragon
- ☐☐ Have my picture taken with a kestrel (falcon)
- ☐☐ Have my picture taken with a kinkajou
- ☐☐ Have my picture taken with a king columbus
- ☐☐ Have my picture taken with a kirundi
- ☐☐ Have my picture with a kookaburra
- ☑☐ Have my picture taken with a kangaroo
- ☑☐ Have my picture taken with a koala
- ☐☐ Have my picture taken with a liger
- ☐☐ Have my picture taken with a leopard tortoise
- ☐☐ Have my picture taken with a leopard seal
- ☐☐ Have my picture taken with a ladybird
- ☐☐ Have my picture taken with a leaf-tailed gecko

- ☑☐ Have my picture taken with a little penguin
- ☐☐ Have my picture taken with a long-eared owl
- ☐☐ Have my picture taken with a lobster
- ☑☐ Have my picture taken with a long nosed potoroo
- ☐☐ Have my picture taken with a llama
- ☐☐ Have my picture taken with a leopard
- ☐☐ Have my picture taken with a lynx
- ☐☐ Have my picture taken with a lion
- ☐☐ Have my picture taken with a macaroni penguin
- ☐☐ Have my picture taken with a mule
- ☐☐ Have my picture taken with a magellanic penguin
- ☐☐ Have my picture taken with a malayan civet
- ☐☐ Have my picture taken with a mandrill
- ☐☐ Have my picture taken with a mink
- ☐☐ Have my picture taken with a manta ray
- ☐☐ Have my picture taken with a markhor
- ☐☐ Have my picture taken with a masked palm civet
- ☐☐ Have my picture taken with a millipede
- ☐☐ Have my picture taken with a minke whale
- ☐☐ Have my picture taken with a monitor lizard
- ☐☐ Have my picture taken with a moth
- ☐☐ Have my picture taken with a moustache guenon
- ☐☐ Have my picture taken with a mouse
- ☐☐ Have my picture taken with a mole
- ☐☐ Have my picture taken with a mongoose
- ☐☐ Have my picture taken with a manatee
- ☐☐ Have my picture taken with a moose
- ☑☐ Have my picture taken with a meerkat
- ☐☐ Have my picture taken with a mona monkey
- ☐☐ Have my picture taken with a monk saki
- ☐☐ Have my picture taken with macaws
- ☐☐ Have my picture taken with a moray eel
- ☑☐ Have my picture taken with a musk lorikeet
- ☐☐ Have my picture taken with a newt
- ☐☐ Have my picture taken with a nurse shark
- ☐☐ Have my picture taken with a numbat
- ☐☐ Have my picture taken with a narwhal
- ☑☐ Have my picture taken with an ostrich
- ☐☐ Have my picture taken with an opossum
- ☐☐ Have my picture taken with an ocelot

- ☐☐ Have my picture taken with an okapi
- ☐☐ Have my picture taken with an otter
- ☐☐ Have my picture taken with an octopus
- ☐☐ Have my picture taken with an orangutan
- ☐☐ Have my picture taken with an oyster
- ☑☐ Have my picture taken with a powerful owl
- ☐☐ Have my picture taken with a pademelon
- ☐☐ Have my picture taken with a parrot
- ☐☐ Have my picture taken with a pony
- ☐☐ Have my picture taken with a patas monkey
- ☐☐ Have my picture taken with a pelican
- ☐☐ Have my picture taken with a pheasant
- ☐☐ Have my picture taken with a pied tamarin
- ☐☐ Have my picture taken with a pink fairy armadillo
- ☐☐ Have my picture taken with a porcupine
- ☐☐ Have my picture taken with a pig
- ☑☐ Have my picture taken with a peacock
- ☐☐ Have my picture taken with a praying mantis
- ☑☐ Have my picture taken with a platypus
- ☐☐ Have my picture taken with a patas monkey
- ☐☐ Have my photo taken with a puffin bird
- ☐☐ Have my picture taken with a panther
- ☐☐ Have my picture taken with a pygmy hippopotamus
- ☐☐ Have my picture taken with a pangolin
- ☐☐ Have my picture taken with a proboscis monkey
- ☑☐ Have my picture taken with a pygmy marmoset
- ☑☐ Have my picture taken with a possum
- ☐☐ Have my picture taken with a polar bear
- ☐☐ Have my picture taken with a quail
- ☐☐ Have my picture taken with a quokka
- ☐☐ Have my picture taken with a reef shark
- ☐☐ Have my picture taken with a rooster
- ☐☐ Have my picture taken with a raccoon
- ☑☐ Have my picture taken with a rainbow lorikeet
- ☐☐ Have my picture taken with a reindeer
- ☐☐ Have my picture taken with a rabbit
- ☐☐ Have my picture taken with a raccoon dog
- ☐☐ Have my picture taken with a radiated tortoise
- ☐☐ Have my picture taken with a red-handed tamarin
- ☐☐ Have my picture taken with a red leaf monkey

- ☑☐ Have my picture taken with a ring tailed lemur
- ☑☐ Have my picture taken with a red panda
- ☐☐ Have my picture taken with a river dolphin
- ☐☐ Have my picture taken with a royal penguin
- ☐☐ Have my picture taken with a river turtle
- ☐☐ Have my picture taken with a rock hyrax
- ☐☐ Have my picture taken with a rock hopper penguin
- ☑☐ Have my picture taken with a rough knob tailed gecko
- ☐☐ Have my picture taken with a roseate spoonbill
- ☐☐ Have my picture taken with a saola
- ☐☐ Have my picture taken with a Siamese fighting fish
- ☑☐ Have my picture taken with a shingleback lizard
- ☑☐ Have my picture taken with a shingleback lizard - western "yellow colour"
- ☐☐ Have my picture taken with a snail
- ☐☐ Have my picture taken with a snapping turtle
- ☐☐ Have my picture taken with a snowy owl
- ☐☐ Have my picture taken with a sperm whale
- ☐☐ Have my picture taken with a spider monkey
- ☑☐ Have my picture taken with a spot tailed quoll
- ☐☐ Have my picture taken with a squid
- ☑☐ Have my picture taken with a stick insect
- ☐☐ Have my picture taken with a sumatran rhinoceros
- ☐☐ Have my picture taken with a sea lion
- ☐☐ Have my picture taken with a sumatran tiger
- ☑☐ Have my picture taken with a sugar glider
- ☑☐ Have my picture taken with a squirrel glider
- ☑☐ Have my picture taken with a spotted tree monitor
- ☐☐ Have my picture taken with a spectacled bear
- ☐☐ Have my picture taken with a snow leopard
- ☑☐ Have my picture taken with a sun bear
- ☐☐ Have my picture taken with a salamander
- ☐☐ Have my picture taken with a stingray
- ☐☐ Have my picture taken with a scorpion
- ☐☐ Have my picture taken with a sloth
- ☐☐ Have my picture taken with a squirrel
- ☐☐ Have my picture taken with a serval african wild cat
- ☐☐ Have my picture taken with a sheep
- ☐☐ Have my picture taken with a skunk
- ☑☐ Have my picture taken with a squirrel monkey
- ☐☐ Have my picture taken with a seahorse

- ☐☐ Have my picture taken with a sea dragon
- ☑☐ Have my picture taken with a snake
- ☑☐ Have my picture taken with a seal
- ☐☐ Have my picture taken with a starfish
- ☐☐ Have my picture taken with a sea urchin
- ☑☐ Have my picture taken with a southern bettong
- ☐☐ Have my picture taken with a swan
- ☐☐ Have my picture taken with a tarantula
- ☐☐ Have my picture taken with a tree kangaroo
- ☐☐ Have my picture taken with a turkey
- ☐☐ Have my picture taken with a Tasmanian devil
- ☐☐ Have my picture taken with a toucan
- ☐☐ Have my picture taken with a tapir
- ☐☐ Have my picture taken with a tarsier
- ☑☐ Have my picture taken with a tortoise
- ☐☐ Have my picture taken with a tawny frogmouth owl
- ☐☐ Have my picture taken with a termite
- ☐☐ Have my picture taken with a tiger salamander
- ☐☐ Have my picture taken with a tiger shark
- ☐☐ Have my picture taken with a tree frog
- ☐☐ Have my picture taken with a tuatara
- ☐☐ Have my picture taken with a uakari
- ☐☐ Have my picture taken with a vampire bat
- ☐☐ Have my picture taken with a vervet monkey
- ☑☐ Have my picture taken with a Victorian carpet python
- ☐☐ Have my picture taken with a vulture
- ☑☐ Have my picture taken with a wallaby
- ☐☐ Have my picture taken with a warthog
- ☑☐ Have my picture taken with a wombat
- ☐☐ have my picture taken with a walrus
- ☐☐ Have my picture taken with wild dogs
- ☑☐ Have my picture taken with a white lion
- ☐☐ Have my picture taken with a water buffalo
- ☐☐ Have my picture taken with a wildebeest
- ☑☐ Have my picture taken with a water dragon
- ☐☐ Have my picture taken with a weasel
- ☐☐ Have my picture taken with a whale shark
- ☐☐ Have my picture taken with a wolf
- ☐☐ Have my picture taken with a white faced capuchin
- ☐☐ Have my picture taken with a white rhinoceros

- ☐☐ Have my picture taken with a white tiger
- ☐☐ Have my picture taken with a wild boar
- ☐☐ Have my picture taken with a wildebest
- ☐☐ Have my picture taken with a wolverine
- ☐☐ Have my picture taken with a woolly monkey
- ☐☐ Have my picture taken with a yak
- ☑☐ Have my picture taken with a yellow bellied glider
- ☐☐ Have my picture taken with a yellow-eyed penguin
- ☐☐ Have my picture taken with a zorse
- ☐☐ Have my picture taken with a zonkey
- ☐☐ Have my picture taken with a zebu
- ☐☐ Have my picture taken with a zebra shark
- ☐☐ Have my picture taken with a zebra
- ☐☐ Adopt a mistreated animal and aid in its recovery
- ☐☐ Adopt an animal from the zoo
- ☐☐ African safari
- ☐☐ Attend Running with the Bulls, Spain
- ☐☐ Bathe an elephant
- ☐☐ Be a zookeeper for a day
- ☑☐ Be able to make bird calls with my hands
- ☐☐ Be attacked in a body suit by an attack dog
- ☐☐ Breed a caterpillar into a butterfly
- ☐☐ Camel ride in Sahara Desert
- ☐☐ Catch a fish with your bare hands
- ☐☐ Collect honey from a beehive
- ☐☐ Come face to face with a snow monkey in Nagano, Japan
- ☐☐ Dive at an aquarium
- ☐☐ Dive with whale sharks
- ☐☐ Elephant Art behind the Scenes, Perth Zoo
- ☑☐ Feed animals at the zoo
- ☐☐ Feed swimming pigs in Exuma, the Bahamas
- ☑☐ Feed the ducks
- ☐☐ Feed wild bottlenose dolphins at Monkey Mia
- ☐☐ Free diving in Jellyfish Lake, Palau - marine sanctuary home to the Golden Jellyfish
- ☑☐ Gather eggs from chickens
- ☑☐ Give a coin donation to Taronga zoo birds, watch them fly it into the donation box
- ☐☐ Go bird watching in Costa Rica
- ☐☐ Go horseback riding
- ☐☐ Go on a bird watching tour
- ☐☐ Go on a cattle drive
- ☐☐ Go water buffalo racing, Indonesia
- ☐☐ Hand feed fish at Aqua Scene, Doctors Gully, Darwin
- ☐☐ Hold a baby tiger
- ☐☐ Husky Dog Safari Kakslauttanen
- ☐☐ Magnetic Termite Mounds
- ☐☐ Make a bird house
- ☐☐ Marine Biologist for a Day, Sea Life, Sydney Aquarium
- ☑☐ Milk a cow
- ☐☐ Milk a goat
- ☐☐ Nurse an injured animal back to health and release it
- ☐☐ Orang-utans, Borneo

- ☐☐ Pat a Panda - Chengdu, China
- ☐☐ Ride a bull at a rodeo
- ☐☐ Ride a camel along the beaches of Western Australia
- ☐☐ Ride a camel down Broome's Cable Beach at sunset
- ☑☐ Ride a donkey
- ☐☐ Ride a horse along a trail
- ☐☐ Ride a horse bareback
- ☐☐ Ride an elephant
- ☐☐ Ride an elephant in India
- ☐☐ Ride an ostrich
- ☑☐ See a large bat colony
- ☐☐ See fireflies
- ☐☐ See penguins in their natural habitat, Phillip Island
- ☐☐ See salmon jump up stream
- ☐☐ See the big five cats in Kruger Park, South Africa
- ☐☐ Send a message by carrier pigeon
- ☐☐ Serengeti migration
- ☐☐ Sleep over at the zoo
- ☐☐ Starfish Colony, west coast of New Zealand
- ☐☐ Swim with a school of fish
- ☐☐ Swim with dolphins
- ☐☐ Swim with great white sharks, South Africa
- ☐☐ Swim with manatees
- ☐☐ Swim with sea turtles
- ☐☐ Swim with sharks
- ☐☐ Swim with stingrays
- ☑☐ Teach a dog tricks
- ☐☐ Teach a parrot to say something
- ☐☐ Try falconry
- ☐☐ Try sheep herding
- ☑☐ Up-close picture of a snake
- ☐☐ Visit a ranch
- ☐☐ Visit Christmas Island and see the amazing wildlife
- ☑☐ Visit the Entrance to see them feed the pelicans
- ☐☐ Visit the Living Legends - Victoria (retirement home of the great horses of Australia)
- ☐☐ Volunteer with animals
- ☐☐ Watch a tadpole evolve into a frog
- ☑☐ Watch Black Caviar run a race
- ☐☐ Watch the charmers use their flute to hypnotise a cobra in a trance/dance
- ☐☐ Watch the great wildebeest migration
- ☐☐ Watch turtles hatch and run for the ocean
- ☑☐ Whale watching cruise
- ☐☐ Witness the birth of a baby animal
- ☐☐ Wrestle an alligator/crocodile

Chapter 32: Social Media

"Social media is changing the way we communicate and the way we are perceived, both positively and negatively. Every time you post a photo, or update your status, you are contributing to your own digital footprint and personal brand."

Amy Jo Martin

Our lives today revolve around social media – from news happening around the world to being able to talk to family, relatives and friends around the globe. We seek information from each other and find out what is happening around the world and what is new and popular in today's society. We hear about famous people who have passed away, we find out about different landmarks to see around the world and inspirational stories shared between each other. A lot of us use social media to get our name, company or even our voice from YouTube out there, so it's seen throughout the world, more than just the surrounding city you live in.

We use social media for social interaction, information seeking, passing time, entertainment, relaxation, expression of opinions, things to talk about, convenience, sharing information and knowing about others.

- ☐☐ Be retweeted by someone famous on Twitter
- ☑☐ Create a bucket list blog
- ☑☐ Create a Facebook group page
- ☑☐ Create a Facebook page
- ☑☐ Create a Pinterest page
- ☑☐ Create a Twitter page
- ☑☐ Create a website
- ☐☐ Get 1,000 views on a YouTube video
- ☐☐ Make a viral video
- ☑☐ Make a YouTube video
- ☐☐ Reach 25,000 followers on my blog

Chapter 33:
Play Musical Instruments

"It's easy to play any musical instrument: all you have to do is touch the right key at the right time and the instrument will play itself."

Johann Sebastian Bach

A musical instrument is an instrument created or adapted to make musical sounds. In principle, any object that produces sound can be a musical instrument; it is through purpose that the object becomes a musical instrument. Instruments have been played for many years and have always been a part of various cultures around the world and used for sacred dances in certain countries. They are also used throughout the world as part of every music group, the most commonly used instruments guitars (bass and acoustic) and the drums. It's always great to just relax with a classical orchestra or jazz and hear the sounds of trumpets, harps and others you don't always hear in modern pop and rock music bands.

Music is a big part of today's society. We listen to it when we want to relax, we listen to it while driving around in our cars, we listen throughout the work day, and every song has its own unique sound and instruments they play. The way I play an instrument will sound different to the way someone else plays it – it's what makes instruments so interesting. The way they're tuned or the ability the person playing has for the instrument makes them sound so unique to the person using the instruments.

- ☑☐ Play a (acoustic) guitar
- ☑☐ Play a (bass) guitar
- ☐☐ Play a balalaika
- ☐☐ Play a banjo
- ☐☐ Play a bass clarinet
- ☐☐ Play a bassoon
- ☐☐ Play a cello
- ☐☐ Play a clarinet
- ☐☐ Play a conga (drum)
- ☐☐ Play a djembe drum
- ☐☐ Play a dulcian
- ☐☐ Play a flute
- ☐☐ Play a French horn
- ☐☐ Play a gong
- ☑☐ Play a harmonica
- ☐☐ Play a harp
- ☐☐ Play a kettledrum
- ☐☐ Play a mandolin
- ☑☐ Play a musical instrument
- ☑☐ Play a piano

- ☐☐ Play a piccolo
- ☑☐ Play a recorder
- ☐☐ Play a saxophone
- ☐☐ Play a snare drum
- ☑☐ Play a tambourine
- ☑☐ Play a triangle
- ☐☐ Play a trombone
- ☐☐ Play a trumpet
- ☐☐ Play a tuba
- ☑☐ Play a ukulele
- ☐☐ Play a vibraphone
- ☐☐ Play a viola
- ☐☐ Play a violin
- ☐☐ Play a xylophone
- ☐☐ Play a zither
- ☐☐ Play an accordion
- ☑☐ Play an electric guitar
- ☑☐ Play an electric keyboard
- ☐☐ Play an English horn
- ☐☐ Play an oboe
- ☐☐ Play an organ
- ☐☐ Play the bagpipes
- ☐☐ Play the bongos
- ☑☐ Play the castanets
- ☑☐ Play the cymbals
- ☐☐ Play the didgeridoo
- ☑☐ Play the drums
- ☑☐ Play the maracas
- ☑☐ Sing on a microphone

Chapter 34:
Food Challenges, Baking and Making Food, Restaurants and Desired Tastes

"Follow your dreams, work hard, practice and persevere. Make sure you eat a variety of foods, get plenty of exercise and maintain a healthy lifestyle."

Sasha Cohen

Food, the human life line, whether it be something as simple as a boiled egg or as complicated as a five-star chef course dinner, we all love food. Some of us are born with the ability to make whatever our minds think of, and some of us learn from parents or grandparents. We all have the skill to make things and we all like to eat it, but what about the people that haven't got it? When you sit at your table to a big roast dinner that someone has prepared, do you think of the people that have none when you are saying grace?

Some of us have too much food; we buy and buy with no thought of anyone else. When you're throwing away food that is out of date because you have so much. You forget about the pack of burgers which have sat in the back of the freezer, but throw them away without a second thought. We all love food, there is no doubt about that: from a simple pizza to a special night out. We all know that no birthday or wedding is complete without a cake and lots of food, but do we all really need more than our fair share? Next time you're at the supermarket and you're wondering whether to get the doughnuts or the choc bar and decide to get both, think of that child or the family that have nothing – maybe grab a bag of pasta or a tin of soup and donate it and give someone else a warm meal tonight.

- ☐☐ Airplane restaurant in Costa Rica
- ☐☐ Bake a cake
- ☐☐ Bake a loaf of bread
- ☐☐ Bake cookies
- ☑☐ Bake muffins
- ☐☐ Bird's Nest Restaurant, Thailand
- ☐☐ Catch a Jafflechuting in Victoria alley way

- ☐☐ Celebrate Thanksgiving
- ☐☐ Centrepoint Tower Revolving Restaurant
- ☑☐ Chang Lai Yuan Chinese Gardens
- ☑☐ Chinese food
- ☑☐ Chocolate by Max Brenner
- ☐☐ Chocolate making class
- ☑☐ Complete a food challenge
- ☐☐ Cook a barbie on the beach
- ☑☐ Cook a homemade pizza
- ☑☐ Cook a traditional dish from a different culture
- ☑☐ Cook an entire meal including dessert
- ☐☐ Cook every recipe in a cook book
- ☐☐ Dine in the dark
- ☐☐ Dine in the Sky, Worldwide *www.dinnerinthesky.com*
- ☐☐ Dine under the Opera House sails at Guillaume at Bennelong
- ☐☐ Drink from a coconut
- ☑☐ Eat a 1kg steak
- ☑☐ Eat a cake with a picture of my own face on it
- ☐☐ Eat a fried tarantula
- ☐☐ Eat a fried Twinkie
- ☐☐ Eat a hotdog from a hotdog stand
- ☐☐ Eat alligator
- ☑☐ Eat alone at a restaurant
- ☑☐ Eat an insect
- ☐☐ Eat at 1889 Enoteca, Brisbane, Queensland
- ☐☐ Eat at five-star restaurant
- ☐☐ Eat at an underwater restaurant
- ☐☐ Eat at Aria, Brisbane, Queensland
- ☐☐ Eat at Attica Restaurant, Melbourne, Victoria
- ☐☐ Eat at Bacchus, Brisbane, Queensland
- ☐☐ Eat at Botin Restaurant, Madrid, Spain. The world's oldest operating restaurant, opened in 1725
- ☐☐ Eat at Carton King Restaurant, Taiwan
- ☐☐ Eat at Esquire, Brisbane, Queensland
- ☐☐ Eat at Est., Sydney, New South Wales
- ☐☐ Eat at Gerard's Bistro, Brisbane, Queensland
- ☐☐ Eat at Marque, Sydney, New South Wales
- ☐☐ Eat at Momofuku Seibo, Sydney, New South Wales
- ☐☐ Eat at Quay Restaurant, Sydney, New South Wales
- ☐☐ Eat at Rockpool, Sydney, New South Wales
- ☐☐ Eat at Royal Mail Hotel, Dunkeld, Victoria
- ☐☐ Eat at Sepia, Sydney, New South Wales
- ☐☐ Eat at Stokehouse, Brisbane, Queensland
- ☐☐ Eat at Tartufo, Brisbane, Queensland
- ☐☐ Eat at Tetsuya's, Sydney, New South Wales
- ☐☐ Eat at the Euro, Brisbane, Queensland
- ☐☐ Eat at Urbane, Brisbane, Queensland
- ☐☐ Eat at Vue De Monde, Melbourne, Victoria
- ☐☐ Eat caviar

- ☑☐ Eat chicken
- ☑☐ Eat chilli
- ☑☐ Eat cow
- ☐☐ Eat crab
- ☑☐ Eat dinner at Hooters
- ☐☐ Eat donuts at Voodoo donuts in Portland, Oregon
- ☑☐ Eat duck
- ☐☐ Eat escargot (snails)
- ☑☐ Eat fish
- ☑☐ Eat fried ice-cream
- ☐☐ Eat frog legs
- ☐☐ Eat from Harry's Cafe de Wheels, Sydney
- ☐☐ Eat grasshoppers
- ☑☐ Eat haggis
- ☐☐ Eat kangaroo meat
- ☐☐ Eat lobster
- ☑☐ Eat pig
- ☑☐ Eat prawns
- ☐☐ Eat rabbit
- ☐☐ Eat scorpion
- ☑☐ Eat sheep
- ☐☐ Eat snake
- ☐☐ Eat Southern BBQ in the South *America*
- ☑☐ Eat squid (calamari)
- ☐☐ Eat sushi
- ☑☐ Eat tofu
- ☑☐ Eat turkey
- ☑☐ Eat with chopsticks
- ☑☐ Fry ice cream
- ☑☐ German food
- ☐☐ Golden Sakura in Japan
- ☐☐ Have breakfast at Tiffany's
- ☑☐ Have chocolate fondue
- ☐☐ Have something on a menu named after myself
- ☑☐ Hog's Breath Cafe
- ☐☐ Hunt for truffles
- ☑☐ Indian food
- ☑☐ Italian food
- ☐☐ Kill, prepare, cook and eat an animal
- ☑☐ Korean food
- ☑☐ Lebanese food
- ☑☐ Lindt Cafe in the city
- ☐☐ Make a rainbow cake
- ☐☐ Make and eat a giant chocolate chip cookie
- ☐☐ Make Anzac biscuits
- ☐☐ Make caramel apples
- ☑☐ Make designs for coffees
- ☐☐ Make gingerbread men
- ☐☐ Make homemade cheese cake
- ☐☐ Make homemade ice-cream
- ☐☐ Make homemade jam
- ☐☐ Make homemade lemonade
- ☑☐ Make homemade pasta
- ☐☐ Make snow cones
- ☐☐ Minus 5 Bar
- ☐☐ Order Subways giant sub
- ☑☐ Panarottis Pizza & Pasta
- ☑☐ Pancakes on the Rocks
- ☑☐ Phillipino food
- ☐☐ Pizza making class
- ☐☐ Randy's Donuts, Inglewood, California
- ☐☐ Restaurant near Sanyou Cave above Chang Jiang River, Hubei, China
- ☐☐ Saffire Freycinet's Marine Farm experience, Coles Bay, TAS, Australia *Experience Eating in the Water*
- ☐☐ Shave a coconut
- ☐☐ Sit in the ocean on tables and chairs in Hawaii
- ☐☐ Take a cake-decorating class
- ☐☐ Take a cooking course
- ☐☐ Tali Wiru dining experience, Uluru, NT, Australia

- ☑☐ Thai food
- ☑☐ The Paragon Cafe at Katoomba, Blue Mountains
- ☐☐ Theme restaurant in Tokyo
- ☑☐ Toast marshmallows on a stick
- ☐☐ Tree dining in Thailand
- ☐☐ Try every flavour ice-cream at Cold Rock Ice Creamery
- ☐☐ Apple pie
- ☐☐ Aussie vanilla
- ☐☐ Banana
- ☐☐ Boysenberry
- ☐☐ Bubble-gum
- ☐☐ Butterscotch
- ☐☐ Caramel
- ☐☐ Caramel mud cake
- ☐☐ Cheesecake
- ☐☐ Choc hazelnut
- ☐☐ Choc mint
- ☐☐ Coconut
- ☐☐ Coffee
- ☑☐ Cookies & cream
- ☐☐ Donut
- ☑☐ Double chocolate
- ☐☐ English toffee
- ☐☐ Honeycomb
- ☐☐ Irish cream
- ☐☐ Licorice
- ☐☐ Macadamia
- ☐☐ Mango
- ☐☐ Meringue
- ☐☐ Natural cream
- ☐☐ Passionfruit
- ☐☐ Pistachio
- ☐☐ Rum & raisin
- ☐☐ Sticky date
- ☐☐ Strawberry
- ☐☐ Tia maria
- ☐☐ Tiramisu
- ☑☐ White chocolate
- ☑☐ White cookies & cream
- ☐☐ Try vodka gummy bears
- ☑☐ Vietnamese food
- ☑☐ Visit Hard Rock Café, Darling Harbour, Sydney, Australia

Chapter 35:
Camping and the Outdoors

"Another thing I like to do is sit back and take in nature. To look at the birds, listen to their singing, go hiking, camping and jogging and running, walking along the beach, playing games and sometimes being alone with the great outdoors. It's very special to me."

Larry Wilcox

The thrill of thinking about the great outdoors fascinates me. Sitting around the campfire at night, roasting marshmallows and having a singalong with family or mates, camping down by the riverside and bushwalking down sturdy hills into the bushlands. Experiencing the beauty of sounds and echoes throughout the nighttime where your imagination runs wild in thought and gets you away from the focus of stress and bumper-to-bumper city lifestyles. To relax, unwind and enjoy the beauty of nature at its finest.

My intentions are to complete the outdoor camping experience in many forms of the camping lifestyle, while knowing full well there is a chance you have to rough it without modern conveniences and the chances of bad weather along the way.

- ☐☐ Biggest tent: Khan Shatyr Tent, Astana, Kazakhstan
- ☐☐ Camp in a teepee
- ☐☐ Camp in a tent
- ☐☐ Camp in a yurt
- ☐☐ Camp in the forest
- ☐☐ Camp in the snow
- ☐☐ Camp on the beach
- ☐☐ Camp to a Wildlife Lullaby, Africa
- ☐☐ Experience camping outdoors
- ☐☐ Experience glamping
- ☐☐ Have a campfire
- ☐☐ Live in a different country
- ☐☐ Live on a deserted island for one week
- ☐☐ Live with a tribe for a week
- ☐☐ Sleep in a hammock
- ☐☐ Sleep under stars
- ☐☐ Spend a night under the stars on the Mongolian Steppes
- ☐☐ Tree camping in Elk, California, USA
- ☐☐ Tree camping in Germany

Chapter 36:
Find, Search, Seek and Discover

"Our greatest weakness lies in giving up. The most certain way to succeed is always to try just one more time."

Thomas A. Edison

Have you ever lost something and tried to search and seek the thing you're missing? Ever been on the beach using a metal detector and finding trinkets along the beach shoreline, or hidden jewels within the landscape? Dug up fossils or gold and gems and other minerals from underground?

I myself wish to discover the glory of finding something interesting, even prehistoric dinosaur bones during an archaeological dig. Now that will be most interesting: millions of years old bones waiting to be explored and discovered. Or even find something that has never been found before and you could be first in the world to ever find it. The thrill of being the only person in the world to see something before anyone else would be an extraordinary experience in itself.

- ☐☐ Bury a time capsule
- ☐☐ Bury something and make a treasure map
- ☐☐ Find a fossil
- ☑☐ Find a four-leaf clover
- ☐☐ Find a message in a bottle
- ☐☐ Find a meteorite
- ☐☐ Find a missing animal
- ☐☐ Find an opal
- ☐☐ Find out what happened in the newspaper on my birthday in 19.06.1985
- ☑☐ Find someone else with the same bucket list item as me and complete it together
- ☐☐ Find the end of the rainbow
- ☐☐ Get a metal detector and look for hidden treasure
- ☐☐ Go diamond mining at Crater of Diamonds State Park, Murfreesboro
- ☐☐ Go on an archaeology dig expedition
- ☑☐ Google search my name and have at least one page of stuff
- ☐☐ Place a letter inside a balloon and send it off into the air

Chapter 37:
Astrology and the Stars

"Keep your eyes on the stars, and your feet on the ground."

Theodore Roosevelt

There are millions of stars located throughout our galaxy, the Milky Way, and many more we are yet to discover further into the unseen galaxy beyond. We have so much to learn about outer space. We know very little of the stars and planets. We strive to learn by robots digging for sand samples, looking for water; a good example of this is the planet Mars. We also have a robot powering throughout the galaxy exploring the unknown and gathering information through a satellite and reporting back to earth. Man has landed on the moon, but where else will they land next? What are we going to seek and find out down the track? Is there a possibility that worm holes are short cuts to power through the galaxy faster? Some things we will never know until we try, or until someone is willing to take the plunge and learn – to go down in history for taking that huge step for mankind.

We enjoy the chance to look up into the beautiful skies at night and view the beautiful stars and identify certain constellations and asterisms. We even take the chance to view from observatories and telescopes to get close-up views of the beautiful planets and sparkling stars throughout the Milky Way galaxy.

- ☐☐ Capture lightening in a photograph
- ☐☐ Catadioptrics telescope
- ☐☐ Go to Roswell, New Mexico and look for UFOs
- ☐☐ Kings Tableland Observatory
- ☑☐ Learn astrology
- ☑☐ Name a star (Red Balloon)
- ☐☐ Radio telescope
- ☐☐ Reflector telescope
- ☑☐ Refractor telescope
- ☑☐ See a cluster of stars through a telescope
- ☑☐ See a full moon
- ☑☐ See a shooting star
- ☑☐ See a super moon
- ☐☐ See comet fly through sky
- ☐☐ See Jupiter through telescope
- ☑☐ See lunar eclipse
- ☐☐ See Mars through telescope
- ☐☐ See Mercury through telescope

- ☐☐ See meteor shower
- ☑☐ See Milky Way galaxy
- ☐☐ See Neptune through telescope
- ☐☐ See Pluto through telescope
- ☑☐ See Saturn through telescope
- ☑☐ See solar eclipse
- ☐☐ See stars in bush area
- ☐☐ See stars out in the desert
- ☐☐ See the moon through telescope
- ☐☐ See Uranus through telescope
- ☑☐ See Venus through telescope
- ☐☐ Space Guard Centre
- ☐☐ Stargaze at the Atacama Desert in Chile
- ☑☐ Sydney Observatory
- ☐☐ Tebbutts Observatory Windsor
- ☐☐ University of Western Sydney Observatory
- ☐☐ Find all the constellations in the skies
- ☐☐ Andromeda - "Chained Maiden"
- ☐☐ Antlia - "The Air Pump"
- ☐☐ Apus - "The Bird of Paradise"
- ☐☐ Aquarius - "The Water Bearer"
- ☐☐ Aquila - "The Eagle"
- ☐☐ Ara - "The Altar"
- ☐☐ Aries - "The Ram"
- ☐☐ Auriga - "The Charioteer"
- ☐☐ Boötes - "The Herdsman"
- ☐☐ Caelum - "The Chisel"
- ☐☐ Camelopardalis - "The Giraffe"
- ☐☐ Cancer - "The Crab"
- ☐☐ Canes Venatici - "The Hunting Dogs"
- ☐☐ Canis Major - "The Big Dog"
- ☐☐ Canis Minor - "The Small Dog"
- ☐☐ Capricornus - "The Sea Goat"
- ☐☐ Carina - "The Keel of the Argo Navis"
- ☐☐ Cassiopeia - "The Queen"
- ☐☐ Centaurus - "The Centaur"
- ☐☐ Cepheus - "The King"
- ☐☐ Cetus - "The Whale"
- ☐☐ Chamaeleon - "The Chamaeleon"
- ☐☐ Circinus - "The Compass"
- ☐☐ Columba - "The Dove"
- ☐☐ Coma Berenices - "Berenice's Hair"
- ☐☐ Corona Australis - "The Southern Crown"
- ☐☐ Corona Borealis - "The Northern Crown"
- ☐☐ Corvus - "The Raven"
- ☐☐ Crater - "The Cup"
- ☑☐ Crux - "The Southern Cross"
- ☐☐ Cygnus - "The Swan"
- ☐☐ Delphinus - "The Dolphin"
- ☐☐ Dorado - "The Dolphin fish"
- ☐☐ Draco - "The Dragon"
- ☐☐ Equuleus - "The Little Horse"
- ☐☐ Eridanus - "The Celestial River"
- ☐☐ Fornax - "The Furnace"
- ☐☐ Gemini - "The Twins"
- ☐☐ Grus - "The Crane"
- ☐☐ Hercules - "The Strong Man"
- ☐☐ Horologium - "The Pendulum Clock"
- ☐☐ Hydra - "The Water Serpent"
- ☐☐ Hydrus - "The Water Snake"
- ☐☐ Indus - "The Indian"
- ☐☐ Lacerta - "The Lizard"
- ☐☐ Leo - "The Lion"
- ☐☐ Leo Minor - "The Little Lion"
- ☐☐ Lepus - "The Hare"
- ☐☐ Libra - "The Scales"
- ☐☐ Lupus - "The Wolf"
- ☐☐ Lynx - "The Lynx"

- ☐☐ Lyra - "The Harp"
- ☐☐ Mensa - "The Table Mountain"
- ☐☐ Microscopium - "The Microscope"
- ☐☐ Monoceros - "The Unicorn"
- ☐☐ Musca - "The Fly"
- ☐☐ Norma - "The Level"
- ☐☐ Octans - "The Octant"
- ☐☐ Ophiuchus - "The Serpent Holder"
- ☐☐ Orion - "The Hunter"
- ☐☐ Pavo - "The Peacock"
- ☐☐ Pegasus - "The Winged Horse"
- ☐☐ Perseus - "The Greek Hero"
- ☐☐ Phoenix - "The Firebird"
- ☐☐ Pictor - "The Painter"s Easel"
- ☐☐ Pisces - "The Fishes"
- ☐☐ Piscis Austrinus - "The Southern Fish"
- ☐☐ Puppis - "The Stern of the Argo Navis"
- ☐☐ Pyxis - "The Compass"
- ☐☐ Reticulum - "The Reticle"
- ☐☐ Sagitta - "The Arrow"
- ☐☐ Sagittarius - "The Archer"
- ☑☐ Scorpius - "The Scorpion"
- ☐☐ Sculptor - "The Sculptor"
- ☐☐ Scutum - "The Shield"
- ☐☐ Serpens - "The Serpent"
- ☐☐ Sextans - "The Sextant"
- ☐☐ Taurus - "The Bull"
- ☐☐ Telescopium - "The Telescope"
- ☐☐ Triangulum - "The Triangle"
- ☐☐ Triangulum Australe - "The Southern Triangle"
- ☐☐ Tucana - "The Toucan"
- ☐☐ Ursa Major - "The Big Bear"
- ☐☐ Ursa Minor - "The Small Bear"
- ☐☐ Vela - "The Sails of the Argo Navis"
- ☐☐ Virgo - "The Young Maiden"
- ☐☐ Volans - "The Flying Fish"
- ☐☐ Vulpecula - "The Little Fox"
- ☐☐ See all the asterism in the skies
- ☐☐ Arrowchain
- ☐☐ Backwards 5
- ☐☐ Broken Engagement Ring
- ☐☐ Button hook
- ☐☐ Chi 1, 2, 3
- ☐☐ Davis' Dog
- ☐☐ Delphinus Minor
- ☐☐ Eiffel Tower
- ☐☐ Engagement Ring
- ☐☐ Essertoo String
- ☐☐ Gas Pump Handle
- ☐☐ HD 4798 Group
- ☐☐ Horseshoe
- ☐☐ Kemble's Cascade
- ☐☐ Kemble's Kite
- ☐☐ Klingon Battlecruiser
- ☐☐ Lambda-Lambda
- ☐☐ Leiter 4
- ☐☐ Little Orion
- ☐☐ Lucky 7
- ☐☐ Markov 1
- ☐☐ Meerschaum Pipe
- ☐☐ Mini-Cassiopeia
- ☐☐ Mini-Coathanger
- ☐☐ Nagler 1
- ☐☐ Napoleon's Hat
- ☐☐ Night Owl
- ☐☐ Orion's Belt
- ☐☐ Pakan's 3
- ☐☐ Poskus 1
- ☐☐ Red Necked Emu
- ☐☐ Renou 18
- ☐☐ Rinnan's run
- ☐☐ Ruby Ring
- ☐☐ Smiley Face
- ☐☐ Spermatozoon
- ☐☐ STAR 11
- ☐☐ Stargate

- ☐☐ Stephan's Test
- ☐☐ The Airplane
- ☑☐ The Big Dipper
- ☐☐ The Coathanger
- ☐☐ The Cosmic Question Mark
- ☐☐ The Fairy Ring
- ☐☐ The Flying Minnow
- ☐☐ The Golf Putter
- ☐☐ The Home Plate
- ☐☐ The Little Dipper
- ☐☐ The Mini-Cross
- ☐☐ The Queen's Kite
- ☐☐ The Sailboat Cluster
- ☐☐ The Shark Jaws
- ☐☐ The Spade
- ☐☐ The Toadstool
- ☐☐ Theta Delphinus Group
- ☐☐ TPK 1
- ☐☐ Triangle
- ☐☐ Triangulum Minor
- ☐☐ Unicorn's Horn
- ☐☐ Vultus Irrisorie
- ☐☐ Webb's Wreath
- ☐☐ Zig Zag

Chapter 38: Bridges/Dams and Famous Roads of the World

"Bridges become frames for looking at the world around us."

Bruce Jackson

A bridge is a structure built to span physical obstacles such as a body of water, valley, or road, for the purpose of providing passage over the obstacle. There are many different architectural designs that all serve unique purposes and apply to different situations. A lot of us use bridges on a daily basis to get from one point to another. No matter where you live in the world there is always a bridge that is iconic, such as Sydney has the Harbour Bridge or San Francisco in USA has the San Francisco Bridge. Bridges around the world are used for cars, buses, trains: all forms of transport for a lot of bridges to get us to where we need to be faster.

Although most cities have thousands of streets, one or two streets always become better known than any other. Whether it's because of their shopping opportunities, centre of nightlife, entertainment hub or their place in history, they're the streets that travellers always visit.

A dam is built to control and store water; they are built strong and solid to contain drinking water for cities and they are there to block the impact of massive waves smashing shorelines. We use dams to take the impact so we don't take the hit from large forces of water crashing through the places we live.

- ☐☐ Albert Bridge, Brisbane
- ☐☐ Alfords Point Bridge, Sydney
- ☐☐ Andrew Nixon Bridge, St. George
- ☑☐ Anzac Bridge, Sydney
- ☐☐ Appian Way, Rome, constructed over 2000 years ago and still in use today
- ☐☐ Avenida 9 de Julio, Buenos Aires, Argentina
- ☐☐ Banpo Bridge, Seoul, South Korea
- ☐☐ Batman Bridge, Launceston
- ☐☐ Bolte Bridge, Melbourne
- ☐☐ Bowen Bridge, Tasmania
- ☑☐ Bridge Stairs, Harbour Bridge

- ☐☐ Bridgewater Bridge, Tasmania
- ☐☐ Burdekin Bridge, near Ayr and Home Hill
- ☐☐ Canton Avenue, Pittsburgh, Penn.
- ☐☐ Captain Cook Bridge, Brisbane
- ☑☐ Captain Cook Bridge, Sydney
- ☐☐ Capulin Volcano Road, Capulin, N.M.
- ☐☐ Centenary Bridge, Brisbane
- ☐☐ Chalk Hills Dam
- ☐☐ Chengyang Bridge, China
- ☐☐ Craig Goch Dam, Elan Valley, Wales
- ☐☐ Cross the Cane Bridge in the Village Kabua, Republic of the Congo
- ☐☐ Da Vinci Bridge
- ☐☐ Dalton Highway, Livengood, Alaska
- ☐☐ Desmond Trannore Bridge, Gordonvale
- ☐☐ Devil's Bridge, Sedona, Arizona
- ☐☐ Drive route 66 USA
- ☐☐ Drive the full length of the Pacific Highway
- ☐☐ Drive the Great Ocean Road
- ☐☐ Eleanor Schonell Bridge, Brisbane
- ☐☐ Evergreen Point Floating Bridge
- ☐☐ Foamhenge, Natural Bridge, Virginia
- ☐☐ Forest Bridge, Monteverde, Costa Rica
- ☐☐ Gateshead Millennium Bridge
- ☐☐ Gateway Bridge, Brisbane
- ☑☐ Gladesville Bridge, Sydney
- ☐☐ Go Between Bridge, Brisbane
- ☐☐ Goldern Route
- ☐☐ Goodwill Bridge, Brisbane
- ☐☐ Gotthard Pass in Switzerland
- ☐☐ Grafton Bridge, New South Wales
- ☐☐ Grand Coulee Dam
- ☐☐ Guoliang Tunnel, Hunan, China
- ☐☐ Guri Dam
- ☐☐ Hampden Bridge, Kangaroo Valley
- ☐☐ Hana Highway, Maui, Hawaii
- ☐☐ Hangzhou Bay Bridge
- ☐☐ Hartbeespoort Dam
- ☐☐ Helix Bridge, Singapore
- ☐☐ Henderson Waves
- ☐☐ Highway 1, Iceland
- ☑☐ Historic Lennox Bridge, Blue Mountains
- ☐☐ Hobart Bridge, Hobart
- ☐☐ Hoover Dam
- ☐☐ Houghton Highway, Brisbane
- ☐☐ Inguri Dam
- ☑☐ Iron Cove Bridge, Sydney
- ☐☐ Itaipu Dam
- ☐☐ Jack Pesch Bridge, Brisbane
- ☐☐ Jubilee Bridge, Innisfail
- ☐☐ Juscelino Kubitschek Bridge
- ☐☐ Karakoram Highway, Gilgit-Baltistan, Pakistan
- ☐☐ Krasnoyarsk Dam
- ☐☐ Kurilpa Bridge, Brisbane
- ☐☐ Langkawi Sky Bridge
- ☐☐ Lombard Street, San Francisco, Calif.
- ☐☐ Lop Nor Silk Road
- ☐☐ Mcgees Bridge, Hobart
- ☐☐ Merivale Bridge, Brisbane
- ☐☐ Millau Viaduct, France
- ☐☐ Modern Bamboo Bridge
- ☐☐ Monumental Axis, Brasilia, Brazil
- ☑☐ Mooney Mooney Bridge, Central Coast
- ☐☐ Moses Bridge, Netherlands

- ☐☐ Narrows Bridge, Perth
- ☐☐ New Cornelia Mine Tailings Dam
- ☐☐ Nob Hill, San Francisco, USA
- ☐☐ Northbridge Bridge, Northbridge
- ☐☐ Nowra Bridge, Nowra
- ☐☐ Octavio Frias de Oliveira Bridge
- ☐☐ Oresund Bridge
- ☐☐ Pamban Bridge, Rameswaram, Tamil Nadu, India
- ☐☐ Passo dello Stelvio, Lombardy, Italy
- ☐☐ Pont Gustave-Flaubert
- ☐☐ Puente de la Mujer
- ☑☐ Pyrmont Bridge, Sydney
- ☐☐ Pythonbrug
- ☐☐ Quarter Mile Bridge, Victoria
- ☐☐ Redridge Steel Dam
- ☐☐ Richmond Bridge, Tasmania
- ☐☐ Robert-Bourassa Dam
- ☐☐ Rolling Bridge
- ☐☐ Roosevelt Dam
- ☑☐ Roseville Bridge, Sydney
- ☐☐ Ross Bridge, Tasmania
- ☐☐ San Boldo Pass, Veneto, Italy
- ☐☐ Sand Dams
- ☐☐ Santee Cooper Dam System
- ☐☐ Sayano-Shushenskaya Dam
- ☐☐ Sea Bridge, Malta
- ☑☐ Sea Cliff Bridge, Coalcliff
- ☐☐ See Brooklyn Bridge, USA
- ☐☐ See the Golden Gate Bridge, San Francisco, California
- ☐☐ Seven-Mile Bridge, Florida Keys, USA
- ☐☐ Slauerhoffbrug
- ☑☐ Spit Bridge, Sydney
- ☐☐ Story Bridge, Brisbane
- ☐☐ Sundial Bridge
- ☑☐ Sydney Harbour Bridge, Sydney
- ☐☐ Syncrude Tailings Dam
- ☑☐ Tarban Creek Bridge, New South Wales
- ☐☐ Tasman Bridge, Hobart
- ☐☐ Tateyama Kurobe Alpine Route, Toyama, Japan
- ☐☐ Ted Smout Memorial Bridge, Brisbane
- ☐☐ The Atlanterhavsveien, Møre OG Romsdal, Norway
- ☐☐ The Atlantic Road in Norway, built high enough for the waves to crash through
- ☐☐ The Bridge of Immortals, Huanghsan, China
- ☐☐ The Cherohala Skyway, Robbinsville, N.C.
- ☑☐ The Entrance Bridge, The Entrance
- ☐☐ The High Five Interchange, Dallas, Texas
- ☐☐ The Langkawi sky-bridge is located at Gunung Mat Cincang on the island of Langkawi, Malaysia
- ☐☐ The Magic Roundabout, Swindon, England
- ☐☐ The Neal Bridge
- ☐☐ The Norway Sky Bridge
- ☐☐ The Shahara Bridge in Yemen
- ☐☐ The Tallest Arch Dam in Russia
- ☐☐ Theogefiro (God's bridge), Zitsa, Greece
- ☐☐ Three Gorges Dam: Sandouping, China-Yangtze River
- ☐☐ Tibbitt to Contwoyto Winter Road, Northwest Territories, Canada
- ☐☐ Timber Dams
- ☑☐ Tom Uglys Bridge, Sydney

- ☐☐ Travel along the highest road in the world
- ☐☐ Travel down the Extraterrestrial Highway, Nevada
- ☐☐ Trollstigen, Rauma, Norway
- ☐☐ Verzasca Dam
- ☐☐ Victoria Bridge, Brisbane
- ☐☐ Walter Taylor Bridge, Brisbane
- ☑☐ West Gate Bridge, Melbourne
- ☐☐ Whispering Wall at the Barossa Valley Dam
- ☐☐ William Jolly Bridge, Brisbane
- ☐☐ Wisteria Bridge, Kyoto, Japan
- ☐☐ World's largest beaver dam
- ☐☐ Yungas Road, La Paz, Bolivia

Chapter 39: Australia's Big Statues

"Every block of stone has a statue inside it and it is the task of the sculptor to discover it."

Michelangelo

The big things of Australia are a loosely related set of large structures, some of which are novelty architecture and some are sculptures. Most big things began as tourist traps found along major roads between destinations. They are sometimes used as an excuse for a great road trip with family and friends, where many or all big things are visited and used as a backdrop to a group photograph.

Many of the big things have been heritage-listed; there are at least 100 or so big statues located around Australia, most of which are found along the eastern coast of Australia.

- ☐☐ Black Caviar's Bronze Statue in Nagambie, Victoria
- ☑☐ Dog on the Tuckerbox, located at Snake Gully, five miles from Gundagai, New South Wales
- ☐☐ The Big Apple, Stanthorpe, Queensland
- ☐☐ The Big Avocado, Byron Bay, N.S.W
- ☑☐ The Big Banana, Coffs Harbour, N.S.W
- ☐☐ The Big Barramundi, Daintree, Queensland
- ☐☐ The Big Bottle, Mangrove Mountain, N.S.W
- ☐☐ The Big Bowl of Fruit, Bilpin, N.S.W
- ☐☐ The Big Bull, Rockhampton, Queensland
- ☐☐ The Big Bull, Wauchope, N.S.W
- ☐☐ The Big Cheese, Bodalla, N.S.W
- ☐☐ The Big Cigar, Churchill, Victoria
- ☐☐ The Big Cow, Nambour, Queensland
- ☐☐ The Big Crocodile, Wyndham, Western Australia
- ☐☐ The Big Gold Panner, Bathurst, N.S.W
- ☐☐ The Big Golden Guitar, Tamworth, N.S.W
- ☐☐ The Big Lizzie, Red Cliffs, Victoria
- ☐☐ The Big Lobster, Kingston, South Australia

- ☐☐ The Big Macadamia, Nambour, Queensland
- ☐☐ The Big Mandarin, Mundubbera Mundubbera, Queensland
- ☑☐ The Big Merino, Goulburn, N.S.W
- ☐☐ The Big Milkshake Container, Kyabram, Victoria
- ☑☐ The Big Ned Kelly, Glen Rowan, Victoria
- ☐☐ The Big Orange, Berri, South Australia
- ☐☐ The Big Orange, Gayndah, Queensland
- ☐☐ The Big Orange, Tenterfield, N.S.W
- ☑☐ The Big Oyster, Taree, N.S.W
- ☐☐ The Big Peanut, Tolga, Queensland
- ☐☐ The Big Penguin, Penguin, Tasmania
- ☐☐ The Big Pineapple, Nambour, Queensland
- ☐☐ The Big Potato, Robertson, N.S.W
- ☑☐ The Big Prawn, Ballina, N.S.W
- ☐☐ The Big Ram, Wagin, Western Australia
- ☐☐ The Big Rock, Barrington Tops, N.S.W
- ☐☐ The Big Rocking Horse, Gumeracha, South Australia
- ☐☐ The Big Roo, Border Village
- ☐☐ The Big Tree Goanna, Crystal Brook, South Australia
- ☐☐ The Big Tree, Pemberton, Western Australia
- ☐☐ The Big Trout, Adaminaby, N.S.W
- ☐☐ The Big Winch, Coober Pedy, South Australia
- ☑☐ The Big Windmill, Coff's Harbour, N.S.W
- ☐☐ The Big Wool Bales, Hamilton, Victoria
- ☐☐ The Giant Gumboot, Tully, North Queensland,
- ☑☐ The Giant Murray Cod, Swan Hill, Victoria
- ☐☐ The Giant Mushroom, Belconnen, ACT
- ☐☐ The Giant Owl, Belconnen, ACT
- ☐☐ The Big Ant
- ☐☐ The Big Axe
- ☐☐ The Big Ayers Rock
- ☐☐ The Big Beer Can
- ☐☐ The Big Bench
- ☐☐ The Big Blue Heeler
- ☐☐ The Big Bowl
- ☐☐ The Big Bunch of Bananas
- ☐☐ The Big Bicycle
- ☐☐ The Big Chook
- ☐☐ The Big Flower
- ☐☐ The Big Gold Pick and Pan
- ☐☐ The Big Knight
- ☐☐ The Big Hammer
- ☐☐ The Big Kookaburra
- ☐☐ The Big Lamb
- ☐☐ The Big Miner's Lamp
- ☐☐ The Big Mosquito
- ☐☐ The Big Playable Guitar
- ☐☐ The Big Rabbit Trap
- ☐☐ The Big Rocket
- ☐☐ The Big Rubik's Cube
- ☐☐ The Big Slurpee
- ☐☐ The Big Soldier
- ☐☐ The Big Spider
- ☐☐ The World's Biggest Sundial
- ☐☐ The Big Tennis Racquet

- ☐☐ The Big Turtle
- ☐☐ The Big Wine Bottle
- ☐☐ The Big Wine Cask
- ☐☐ The Big Boxing Crocodile
- ☐☐ The Big Aboriginal Hunter
- ☐☐ The Big Stockwhip
- ☐☐ The Big Barrel
- ☐☐ The Big Bolt and Nut
- ☐☐ The Big Boot/Shoe
- ☐☐ The Big Brolga
- ☐☐ The Big Cassowary
- ☐☐ The Big (Mud) Crab
- ☐☐ The Big Deck Chair
- ☐☐ The Big Dugong
- ☐☐ The Big Dinosaur
- ☐☐ The Big Easel
- ☐☐ The Big Golf Ball
- ☐☐ The Big Golden Gumboot
- ☐☐ The Big Gun
- ☐☐ The Big Hard Rock Guitar
- ☐☐ The Big Macadamia Nut
- ☐☐ The Big Mandarin
- ☐☐ The Big Mango
- ☐☐ The Big Marlin
- ☐☐ The Big Meat Ant
- ☐☐ The Big Miner
- ☐☐ The Big Mower
- ☐☐ The Big Paperclip
- ☐☐ The Big Pelican
- ☐☐ The Big Pick, Shovel and Sieve
- ☐☐ The Big Pie
- ☐☐ The Big Red Elephant
- ☐☐ The Big Pumpkin
- ☐☐ The Big Red back
- ☐☐ The Big Rig
- ☐☐ The Big Rum Bottle
- ☐☐ The Big Sapphire
- ☐☐ The Big Sapphire Ring
- ☐☐ The Big Sausage King
- ☐☐ The Big Shell
- ☐☐ The Big Spanner
- ☐☐ The Big Strawberry
- ☐☐ The Big Stubby
- ☐☐ The Big Whale
- ☐☐ The Big Dice
- ☐☐ The Big Galah
- ☐☐ The Big Kangaroo
- ☐☐ The Big Penguin
- ☐☐ The Big Rock Lobster
- ☐☐ The Big Spud
- ☐☐ The Big Tasmanian Devil
- ☐☐ The Big Wickets
- ☐☐ The Big Abalone
- ☐☐ The Big Cigar
- ☐☐ The Big Coffee Maker
- ☐☐ The Big Koala
- ☐☐ The Big Happy Hens
- ☐☐ The Big Tap
- ☐☐ The Big Wave
- ☐☐ The Big Watermelon
- ☐☐ The Big Wool Bales
- ☐☐ The Giant Worm
- ☐☐ The Giant Pocket Watch
- ☐☐ The Public Purse
- ☐☐ The Leeuwin Way Whale
- ☐☐ The Big Wheelbarrow
- ☐☐ The World's Tallest Bin
- ☐☐ The Cow on the Corner
- ☐☐ The Big Magic Mushroom
- ☐☐ The Big Camera
- ☐☐ The Big Bobtail
- ☐☐ The Big Platypus

Chapter 40:
Visit the Seven Continents

"Once a year, go someplace you've never been before."

Dalai Lama

Visiting all seven continents is no easy task. What is it about our love of exploration that leads us into the unknown? Is it the old adage that the grass is always greener on the other side? Or is it just the thirst for adventure, accomplishment and finding out what we cannot see or have yet to discover and experience?

Lots of consistent travellers strive to reach the seven continents on their bucket lists; if there were any more we would strive to achieve those as well. Each continent has its own unique appeal from landscape, culture to even food cuisines. We strive for the exploration in all of us to unlock the full potential of exploring the unknown.

- ☐☐ Antarctica
- ☐☐ Africa
- ☑☐ Asia
- ☑☐ Europe
- ☐☐ North America
- ☑☐ Oceania
- ☐☐ South America
- ☐☐ Visit all seven continents

Chapter 41: Visit All States/Territories and External Territories of Australia

"Traveling – it leaves you speechless, then turns you into a storyteller."

Ibn Battuta

The states and mainland territories of the Commonwealth of Australia combine to make up the world's sixth-largest country by total area. Australia comprises six states and various territories; the Australian mainland is made up of five states and three territories (including small, somewhat anomalous Jervis Bay Territory), with the sixth state being located on the island of Tasmania to the south of the mainland. In addition, there are six island territories, known as external territories.

Australia also claims part of Antarctica as the Australian Antarctic Territory. It's a must see for myself to view all of my home country. I want to view all of Australia in whole and see all of the unique landmarks in each place around Australia: the Great Barrier Reef Queensland, Pinnacles of Western Australia, the Harbour Bridge Sydney, the 12 Apostles Victoria, the Cradle Mountain Tasmania, Ayers Rock Northern Territory, South Australia's Barossa Valley Vineyards and Australian Capital Territory's Parliament House.

- ☑☐ Visit Australian Capital Territory
- ☑☐ Visit New South Wales
- ☐☐ Visit Northern Territory
- ☑☐ Visit Queensland
- ☐☐ Visit South Australia
- ☐☐ Visit Tasmania
- ☑☐ Visit Victoria
- ☐☐ Visit Western Australia
- ☐☐ Australian Antarctic Territory
- ☐☐ Christmas Island
- ☐☐ Cocos Island
- ☐☐ Macquarie Island
- ☐☐ Norfolk Island

Sport

blacktownsun.com.au

Big run on Lance's bucket list

By Nick Soon

WAREHOUSE stockman Lance Garbutt, 28, Doonside, who is competing in the *Sydney Morning Herald* Sun Run on February 1, will inspire many people.

He has gone from weighing 200kg and drinking 30-40 litres of soft drink a week to 140kg in two and half years and completed his first ultra marathon (50km) early this month.

After giving up soft drinks, Lance made a bucket list for himself with about 5000 things to complete.

From abseiling, parasailing, to bridge climbing, Garbutt has ticked about 800 things off his list.

Garbutt said his fiance, Laura encouraged him to change his lifestyle after learning that his dad is diabetic.

He did this by spending about two hours a day in a gym for five days a week and participating in running and walking events during the weekend.

"I feel good after giving up soft drinks and during exercises in the gym and running in the weekend," he said.

"It made me do a bucket list of things I want to do to enjoy living my life.

"I want to further reduce my weight to 110-115kg as I am about two metres tall and want to do more things including skydiving, driving a V8 Supercar and dancing."

Garbutt said by the time he completed his bucket list he would be able to participate in every running events in Sydney and then every running events in Australia.

Entries are now open: visit www.sunrun.com.au or www.coleclassic.com for more details.

"I feel good after giving up soft drinks"

Inspiration: Lance Garbutt's aim. Picture: Gene Ramirez

Chapter 42:
Visit All States of America

"Investment in travel is an investment in yourself."

Matthew Karsten

The United States is a vast and varied country, ranging from snow-topped mountains to blistering beaches. In each of its fifty states, there are many different wonders and experiences. Some states have more than others. A few of the most famous landmarks known to many include Mount Rushmore, Statue of Liberty, Grand Canyon and the Rocky Mountains. There are many famous national parks, the most famous being Yosemite – not just a great valley, but a beautiful landscape of glaciers and persistence of beautiful animal wildlife and tranquillity. Yellowstone itself is the location of the Old Faithful geyser.

Many other famous locations of America consist of the Walk of Fame, the Hollywood sign, the Vegas Strip – great place for bucks' or hens' nights out – and its natural wonders of the Mississippi River running right across America and ending in New Orleans. My interests in visiting America were brought about by the culture and lifestyle – from the beautiful landscapes to the busy lights of the beautiful cities with massive skyscrapers and landmarks. There are wonderful theme parks throughout America such as Disneyland, Six Flags and many more, to bring back the kid lifestyle in all of us. It's never too late to enjoy life.

- ☐☐ Visit Alabama
- ☐☐ Visit Alaska
- ☐☐ Visit Arizona
- ☐☐ Visit Arkansas
- ☐☐ Visit California
- ☐☐ Visit Colorado
- ☐☐ Visit Connecticut
- ☐☐ Visit Delaware
- ☐☐ Visit Florida
- ☐☐ Visit Hawaiian Islands
- ☐☐ Visit Idaho
- ☐☐ Visit Illinois
- ☐☐ Visit Indiana
- ☐☐ Visit Iowa
- ☐☐ Visit Kansas
- ☐☐ Visit Kentucky
- ☐☐ Visit Louisiana
- ☐☐ Visit Maine
- ☐☐ Visit Maryland
- ☐☐ Visit Massachusetts

- ☐☐ Visit Michigan
- ☐☐ Visit Minnesota
- ☐☐ Visit Mississippi
- ☐☐ Visit Missouri
- ☐☐ Visit Montana
- ☐☐ Visit Nebraska
- ☐☐ Visit Nevada
- ☐☐ Visit New Hampshire
- ☐☐ Visit New Jersey
- ☐☐ Visit New Mexico
- ☐☐ Visit New York
- ☐☐ Visit North Carolina
- ☐☐ Visit North Dakota
- ☐☐ Visit Ohio
- ☐☐ Visit Oklahoma
- ☐☐ Visit Oregon
- ☐☐ Visit Pennsylvania
- ☐☐ Visit Rhode Island
- ☐☐ Visit South Carolina
- ☐☐ Visit South Dakota
- ☐☐ Visit Tennessee
- ☐☐ Visit Texas
- ☐☐ Visit the State of Georgia
- ☐☐ Visit Utah
- ☐☐ Visit Vermont
- ☐☐ Visit Virginia
- ☐☐ Visit Washington
- ☐☐ Visit West Virginia
- ☐☐ Visit Wisconsin
- ☐☐ Visit Wyoming
- ☐☐ Visit all 50 states of the United States

Chapter 43: Countries of the World To Visit

"The most beautiful thing in the world is, of course, the world itself."

Wallace Stevens

Countries of the world: there is always the simple discussion of how many countries there are in the world. Some say 190-196, others say there are 229 and all the way up to 250. No matter how you look at it, the world is a marvellous place filled with many wonderful countries. My list of the countries of the world consists of a total of 219 countries, and I have ticked off very few. My goal is to tick as many countries off as I can from my bucket list. It is a massive goal and achievement for anyone wishing to travel the world with only six from 219 countries ticked off my bucket list. I still strive to tick off many of the remaining 213 countries of the world.

- ☑☐ Visit five countries
- ☐☐ Visit 10 countries
- ☐☐ Visit 15 countries
- ☐☐ Visit 20 countries
- ☐☐ Visit 30 countries
- ☐☐ Visit 40 countries
- ☐☐ Visit 50 countries
- ☐☐ Visit Federated States of Micronesia
- ☐☐ Visit Saint Vincent and the Grenadines
- ☐☐ Visit Afghanistan
- ☐☐ Visit Albania
- ☐☐ Visit Algeria
- ☐☐ Visit Andorra
- ☐☐ Visit Angola
- ☐☐ Visit Anguilla
- ☐☐ Visit Antarctica
- ☐☐ Visit Antigua and Barbuda
- ☐☐ Visit Argentina
- ☐☐ Visit Armenia
- ☑☐ Visit Australia
- ☐☐ Visit Austria
- ☐☐ Visit Azerbaijan
- ☐☐ Visit Bahamas
- ☐☐ Visit Bahrain
- ☐☐ Visit Bangladesh
- ☐☐ Visit Barbados
- ☐☐ Visit Belarus
- ☐☐ Visit Belgium
- ☐☐ Visit Belize
- ☐☐ Visit Benin
- ☐☐ Visit Bermuda
- ☐☐ Visit Bhutan
- ☐☐ Visit Bolivia
- ☐☐ Visit Bosnia and Herzegovina
- ☐☐ Visit Botswana
- ☐☐ Visit Brazil
- ☐☐ Visit Brunei
- ☐☐ Visit Bulgaria

- ☐☐ Visit Burkina Faso
- ☐☐ Visit Burundi
- ☐☐ Visit Cambodia
- ☐☐ Visit Cameroon
- ☐☐ Visit Canada
- ☐☐ Visit Cape Verde
- ☐☐ Visit Cayman Islands
- ☐☐ Visit Central African Republic
- ☐☐ Visit Chad
- ☐☐ Visit Chile and Easter Island
- ☐☐ Visit China
- ☐☐ Visit Colombia
- ☐☐ Visit Comoros and Mayotte
- ☐☐ Visit Cook Islands
- ☐☐ Visit Costa Rica
- ☐☐ Visit Cote d'Ivoire
- ☐☐ Visit Croatia
- ☐☐ Visit Cuba
- ☐☐ Visit Cyprus
- ☐☐ Visit Czech Republic
- ☐☐ Visit Democratic Republic of the Congo
- ☐☐ Visit Denmark
- ☐☐ Visit Djibouti
- ☐☐ Visit Dominica
- ☐☐ Visit Dominican Republic
- ☐☐ Visit East Timor
- ☐☐ Visit Ecuador and the Galapagos Islands
- ☐☐ Visit Egypt
- ☐☐ Visit El Salvador
- ☑☐ Visit England
- ☐☐ Visit Equatorial Guinea
- ☐☐ Visit Eritrea
- ☐☐ Visit Estonia
- ☐☐ Visit Ethiopia
- ☐☐ Visit Falkland Islands
- ☐☐ Visit Fiji
- ☐☐ Visit Finland
- ☑☐ Visit France
- ☐☐ Visit French Guiana
- ☐☐ Visit Gabon
- ☐☐ Visit Gambia
- ☐☐ Visit Georgia
- ☐☐ Visit Germany
- ☐☐ Visit Ghana
- ☐☐ Visit Greece
- ☐☐ Visit Greenland
- ☐☐ Visit Grenada
- ☐☐ Visit Guadeloupe
- ☐☐ Visit Guam and Northern Marianas
- ☐☐ Visit Guatemala
- ☐☐ Visit Guinea
- ☐☐ Visit Guinea-Bissau
- ☐☐ Visit Guyana
- ☐☐ Visit Haiti
- ☐☐ Visit Hawaii
- ☐☐ Visit Honduras
- ☐☐ Visit Hong Kong
- ☐☐ Visit Hungary
- ☐☐ Visit Iceland
- ☐☐ Visit India
- ☐☐ Visit Indonesia
- ☐☐ Visit Iran
- ☐☐ Visit Iraq
- ☐☐ Visit Ireland
- ☐☐ Visit Israel
- ☐☐ Visit Italy
- ☐☐ Visit Jamaica
- ☐☐ Visit Japan
- ☐☐ Visit Jordan
- ☐☐ Visit Kazakhstan
- ☐☐ Visit Kenya
- ☐☐ Visit Kiribati
- ☐☐ Visit Kosovo
- ☐☐ Visit Kuwait
- ☐☐ Visit Kyrgyzstan
- ☐☐ Visit Laos
- ☐☐ Visit Latvia
- ☐☐ Visit Lebanon
- ☐☐ Visit Lesotho

- ☐☐ Visit Liberia
- ☐☐ Visit Libya
- ☐☐ Visit Liechtenstein
- ☐☐ Visit Lithuania
- ☐☐ Visit Luxembourg
- ☐☐ Visit Macau
- ☐☐ Visit Macedonia
- ☐☐ Visit Madagascar
- ☐☐ Visit Malawi
- ☐☐ Visit Malaysia
- ☐☐ Visit Maldives
- ☐☐ Visit Mali
- ☐☐ Visit Malta
- ☐☐ Visit Marshall Islands
- ☐☐ Visit Martinique
- ☐☐ Visit Mauritania
- ☐☐ Visit Mauritius
- ☐☐ Visit Mexico
- ☐☐ Visit Moldova
- ☐☐ Visit Monaco
- ☐☐ Visit Mongolia
- ☐☐ Visit Montenegro
- ☐☐ Visit Morocco
- ☐☐ Visit Mozambique
- ☐☐ Visit Myanmar
- ☐☐ Visit Namibia
- ☐☐ Visit Nauru
- ☐☐ Visit Nepal
- ☑☐ Visit Netherlands
- ☐☐ Visit New Caledonia
- ☐☐ Visit New Zealand
- ☐☐ Visit Nicaragua
- ☐☐ Visit Niger
- ☐☐ Visit Nigeria
- ☐☐ Visit North Korea
- ☐☐ Visit Norway
- ☐☐ Visit Oman
- ☐☐ Visit Pakistan
- ☐☐ Visit Palau
- ☐☐ Visit Palestine
- ☐☐ Visit Panama
- ☐☐ Visit Papua New Guinea
- ☐☐ Visit Paraguay
- ☐☐ Visit Peru
- ☑☐ Visit Philippines
- ☐☐ Visit Pitcairn Islands
- ☐☐ Visit Poland
- ☐☐ Visit Portugal
- ☐☐ Visit Puerto Rico
- ☐☐ Visit Qatar
- ☐☐ Visit Republic of the Congo
- ☐☐ Visit Romania
- ☐☐ Visit Russian Federation
- ☐☐ Visit Rwanda
- ☐☐ Visit Saint Kitts and Nevis
- ☐☐ Visit Saint Lucia
- ☐☐ Visit Samoan Islands
- ☐☐ Visit San Marino
- ☐☐ Visit Sao Tome and Principe
- ☐☐ Visit Saudi Arabia
- ☑☐ Visit Scotland
- ☐☐ Visit Senegal
- ☐☐ Visit Serbia
- ☐☐ Visit Seychelles
- ☐☐ Visit Sierra Leone
- ☐☐ Visit Singapore
- ☐☐ Visit Slovakia
- ☐☐ Visit Slovenia
- ☐☐ Visit Solomon Islands
- ☐☐ Visit Somalia
- ☐☐ Visit South Africa
- ☐☐ Visit South Korea
- ☐☐ Visit Spain
- ☐☐ Visit Sri Lanka
- ☐☐ Visit Sudan
- ☐☐ Visit Suriname
- ☐☐ Visit Swaziland
- ☐☐ Visit Sweden
- ☐☐ Visit Switzerland
- ☐☐ Visit Syria
- ☐☐ Visit Tahiti and French Polynesia

- ☐☐ Visit Taiwan
- ☐☐ Visit Tajikistan
- ☐☐ Visit Tanzania
- ☐☐ Visit Thailand
- ☐☐ Visit Tibet
- ☐☐ Visit Togo
- ☐☐ Visit Tonga
- ☐☐ Visit Trinidad and Tobago
- ☐☐ Visit Tunisia
- ☐☐ Visit Turkey
- ☐☐ Visit Turkmenistan
- ☐☐ Visit Turks and Caicos
- ☐☐ Visit Tuvalu
- ☐☐ Visit Uganda
- ☐☐ Visit Ukraine
- ☐☐ Visit United Arab Emirates (UAE)
- ☐☐ Visit United States of America (USA)
- ☐☐ Visit Uruguay
- ☐☐ Visit Uzbekistan
- ☐☐ Visit Vanuatu
- ☐☐ Visit Vatican City
- ☐☐ Visit Venezuela
- ☐☐ Visit Vietnam
- ☐☐ Visit Virgin Islands
- ☐☐ Visit Wales
- ☐☐ Visit Yemen
- ☐☐ Visit Zambia
- ☐☐ Visit Zimbabwe
- ☐☐ Spin a globe, pick a place at random, and just GO
- ☐☐ Throw a dart at a map and travel wherever it lands
- ☑☐ Travel somewhere solo
- ☑☐ Travel somewhere with family
- ☐☐ Travel somewhere with friends
- ☐☐ Visit a country of every letter of the alphabet (a - z)

Chapter 44:
List of Sports To Participate In Around the World

"To me, it doesn't matter how good you are. Sport is all about playing and competing. Whatever you do in cricket and in sport, enjoy it, be positive and try to win."

Ian Botham

Sports are known all around the world. A lot of us just enjoy the thrill of watching them over the television screen and a few of us like to give sports a go hoping we can make it to the big leagues and give everything a chance. You don't have to be the greatest athlete in the world to give sports a go. You can play sports with a group of workmates, friends, family and, in some cases, you can play a sport solo. Sports help us use our energy and empowers and helps us believe in ourselves – proving to ourselves we can accomplish it if we set our mind to it.

Sports are the key to our goal of healthy lifestyles. No matter if people think you're no good at the sport, if you truly believe in yourself that is all that matters. Enjoy yourself and never care what others think. The main thing is you're the only person you are trying to be better than and with improving yourself you improve confidence, wellbeing, and empower your life – and help others believe in themselves as well.

- ☐☐ American football
- ☐☐ Aquatics
- ☐☐ Archery
- ☐☐ Automobile racing
- ☑☐ Badminton
- ☐☐ Base jumping
- ☑☐ Baseball
- ☑☐ Basketball
- ☑☐ Beach volleyball
- ☐☐ Biathlon
- ☐☐ Bobsleigh
- ☐☐ Bocce ball
- ☐☐ Body building
- ☑☐ Boomerang
- ☑☐ Bowling
- ☑☐ Boxing
- ☑☐ Canoeing
- ☑☐ Caving
- ☐☐ Cheerleading
- ☐☐ Classical dance

- ☑ Cricket
- ☑ Cross country running
- ☐ Cross country skiing
- ☐ Curling
- ☐ Cycling
- ☑ Darts
- ☐ Decathlon
- ☐ Diving
- ☐ Dog sledding
- ☐ Dog training
- ☐ Down hill skiing
- ☐ Equestrianism
- ☐ Falconry
- ☑ Fencing
- ☐ Figure skating
- ☑ Fishing
- ☑ Flag football
- ☑ Foosball
- ☑ Football
- ☑ Golf
- ☑ Gymnastics
- ☑ Hand ball
- ☐ Hang gliding
- ☑ High jump
- ☑ Hiking
- ☑ Hockey
- ☑ Horseshoes
- ☐ Hot air ballooning
- ☑ Ice skating
- ☐ Inline skating
- ☐ Jai alai
- ☐ Judo
- ☑ Karate
- ☑ Kayaking
- ☐ Knee boarding
- ☐ Lacrosse
- ☐ Land sailing
- ☐ Log rolling
- ☑ Long jump
- ☐ Luge
- ☐ Modern dance
- ☐ Modern pentathlon
- ☐ Motorcycle racing
- ☐ Mountain biking
- ☐ Mountaineering
- ☑ Netball
- ☑ Paint ball
- ☐ Para gliding
- ☐ Parachuting
- ☐ Petanque
- ☑ Pool playing
- ☑ Power walking
- ☐ Quad biking
- ☐ Racquetball
- ☐ Remote control boating
- ☐ River rafting
- ☑ Rock climbing
- ☐ Rodeo riding
- ☐ Roller skating
- ☐ Rowing
- ☐ Rugby
- ☐ Sailing
- ☐ Scuba diving
- ☐ Shooting
- ☑ Shotput
- ☐ Shuffleboard
- ☐ Skateboarding
- ☐ Skeet shooting
- ☑ Snooker
- ☐ Snow biking
- ☐ Snow boarding
- ☐ Snow shoeing
- ☐ Snow sledding
- ☑ Soccer
- ☐ Sombo
- ☐ Speed skating
- ☐ Sport fishing
- ☑ Sprint running
- ☑ Squash
- ☐ Stunt plane flying
- ☐ Sumo wrestling
- ☐ Surfing

- ☑☐ Swimming
- ☐☐ Synchronised swimming
- ☑☐ Table tennis
- ☐☐ Taekwondo
- ☐☐ Tchoukball
- ☑☐ Tennis
- ☑☐ Track and field
- ☐☐ Trampolining
- ☐☐ Triathlon
- ☑☐ Tug of war
- ☑☐ Volleyball
- ☐☐ Water polo
- ☐☐ Water skiing
- ☑☐ Weight lifting
- ☑☐ White water rafting
- ☐☐ Wind surfing
- ☐☐ Wrestling
- ☐☐ Wushu
- ☐☐ Yachting
- ☐☐ Yoga

Chapter 45: Video Games

"Every age has its storytelling form, and video gaming is a huge part of our culture. You can ignore or embrace video games and imbue them with the best artistic quality. People are enthralled with video games in the same way as other people love the cinema or theatre."

Andy Serkis

The story behind the video games: we all love a time-out from time to time, just to put our feet up, relax and play a computer game. But many times we do it far more often than we should, where a lot of us turn into obsessed gamers – addicted to video games and spending most of our lives behind a computer screen, oblivious to what is happening in the world around us. I'm guilty of the love of video games myself, but trying to limit the amount of on games and learning things to improve my knowledge of the world instead. Don't get me wrong; I still love to play a video game from time to time, especially with my niece and nephews. I teach them things I have learned from being a gamer for so many years. I help them realise there is more potential though than just a computer screen.

- ☐☐ Be the best in the world for a video game
- ☑☐ Beat 100 video games
- ☐☐ Compete in a gaming competition
- ☐☐ Complete all Elite Quests all characters
- ☐☐ Complete all slays, rares, explores all characters
- ☑☐ Complete Mahjong Titans - Cat
- ☑☐ Complete Mahjong Titans - Crab
- ☐☐ Complete Mahjong Titans - Dragon
- ☑☐ Complete Mahjong Titans - Fortress
- ☑☐ Complete Mahjong Titans - Spider
- ☐☐ Complete Mahjong Titans - Turtle
- ☐☐ Have my guild reach level 100
- ☐☐ Reach all characters to level 25, 3rd Life
- ☐☐ Reach level 29, 3rd life on all my characters DDO
- ☑☐ Win as a team in laser tag
- ☑☐ Win in a claw machine game
- ☑☐ Win with most kill count in laser tag

- ☐☐ Play all The 1000 Best Arcade Games Collection
- ☐☐ 1000 Miglia: Great 1000 Miles Rally
- ☐☐ 1941 - Counter Attack
- ☐☐ 1942
- ☐☐ 1943: The Battle of Midway
- ☐☐ 1944: The Loop Master
- ☐☐ 19XX: The War Against Destiny
- ☐☐ 2 On 2 Open Ice Challenge
- ☐☐ 720 Degrees
- ☐☐ 88 Games
- ☐☐ 9-Ball Shootout
- ☐☐ A.B. Cop
- ☐☐ Acrobatic Dog-Fight
- ☐☐ Action Hollywood
- ☐☐ Aero Fighters
- ☐☐ Aero Fighters 2/Sonic Wings 2
- ☐☐ Aero Fighters 3/Sonic Wings 3
- ☐☐ Aero Fighters Special
- ☐☐ After Burner II
- ☐☐ Air Buster: Trouble Specialty Raid Unit
- ☐☐ Air Rescue
- ☐☐ Airwolf
- ☐☐ Ajax
- ☐☐ Alex Kidd: The Lost Stars
- ☐☐ Alien Storm
- ☐☐ Alien Syndrome
- ☐☐ Alien vs. Predator
- ☐☐ Alien3: The Gun
- ☐☐ Aliens
- ☐☐ Alpine Racer
- ☐☐ Alpine Racer 2
- ☐☐ Alpine Ski
- ☐☐ Altered Beast
- ☐☐ Amazing Maze
- ☐☐ Ambush
- ☐☐ Amidar
- ☐☐ Angel Kids
- ☐☐ APB - All Points Bulletin
- ☐☐ Aqua Jack
- ☐☐ Arabian
- ☐☐ Arabian Magic
- ☑☐ Arcade Classics
- ☐☐ Arch Rivals
- ☐☐ Arkanoid - Revenge of DOH
- ☐☐ Arkanoid
- ☐☐ Arkanoid Returns
- ☐☐ Arlington Horse Racing
- ☐☐ Arm Wrestling
- ☐☐ Armed Formation
- ☐☐ Armored Warriors
- ☐☐ Art of Fighting
- ☐☐ Art of Fighting 2
- ☐☐ Art of Fighting 3
- ☐☐ Ashura Blaster
- ☑☐ Asterix
- ☑☐ Asteroids
- ☑☐ Asteroids Deluxe
- ☑☐ Astro Blaster
- ☐☐ Athena
- ☐☐ Atomic Robo-kid
- ☐☐ Aurail
- ☐☐ B.C. Kid/Bonk's Adventure
- ☐☐ Back Street Soccer
- ☐☐ Bad Dudes vs. Dragonninja
- ☐☐ Bad Lands
- ☐☐ Bagman
- ☐☐ Baluba-louk no Densetsu
- ☐☐ Bang Bang Ball
- ☐☐ Bang!
- ☐☐ Bank Panic
- ☐☐ Batman
- ☐☐ Battlantis
- ☐☐ Battle Cruiser M-12
- ☐☐ Battle Flip Shot
- ☐☐ Battle Garegga
- ☐☐ Battle K-Road
- ☐☐ Battle Lane! Vol. 5
- ☐☐ Battle Shark
- ☑☐ Battle Toads

- ☐☐ Battle Zone
- ☐☐ Beast Busters
- ☐☐ Beezer
- ☐☐ Bells & Whistles
- ☐☐ Berzerk
- ☐☐ Bio-hazard Battle
- ☐☐ Biomechanical Toy
- ☐☐ Bionic Commando
- ☐☐ Black Tiger
- ☐☐ Blasted
- ☐☐ Blaster
- ☐☐ Blasteroids
- ☐☐ Blaze On
- ☐☐ Blazer
- ☐☐ Block Block
- ☐☐ Block Carnival/Thunder & Lightning 2
- ☐☐ Block Out
- ☐☐ Blomby Car
- ☐☐ Blood Bros.
- ☐☐ Blue's Journey/Raguy
- ☐☐ Boggy '84
- ☐☐ Bomb Bee
- ☐☐ Bomb Jack
- ☐☐ Bomber Man World/New Dyna Blaster - Global Quest
- ☐☐ Bombjack Twin
- ☐☐ Bonze Adventure
- ☐☐ Boogie Wings
- ☐☐ Boomer Rang'r/Genesis
- ☐☐ Boot Hill
- ☑☐ Boulder Dash
- ☑☐ Boulder Dash/Boulder Dash Part 2
- ☐☐ Bowl-O-Rama
- ☐☐ Boxer
- ☐☐ Break Thru
- ☐☐ Bubble Bobble
- ☐☐ Bubble Bobble II
- ☐☐ Bubble Memories: The Story of Bubble Bobble III
- ☐☐ Buck Rogers: Planet of Zoom
- ☐☐ Buggy Challenge
- ☐☐ Burger Time
- ☐☐ Burnin' Rubber
- ☐☐ Burning Force
- ☐☐ Butasan
- ☐☐ Cabal
- ☐☐ Cachat
- ☐☐ Cadillacs and Dinosaurs
- ☐☐ Caliber 50
- ☐☐ Calipso
- ☐☐ Cameltry
- ☐☐ Capcom Bowling
- ☐☐ Captain America and the Avengers
- ☐☐ Captain Commando
- ☐☐ Captain Tomaday
- ☐☐ Carnival
- ☐☐ Carrier Air Wing
- ☐☐ Cavelon
- ☐☐ Caveman Ninja
- ☑☐ Centipede
- ☐☐ Chack'n Pop
- ☐☐ Championship Bowling
- ☐☐ Championship Sprint
- ☐☐ Chaos Heat
- ☐☐ Charlie Ninja
- ☐☐ Chase H.Q.
- ☐☐ Check Man
- ☐☐ Checkmate
- ☐☐ Chequered Flag
- ☐☐ Cheyenne
- ☐☐ Chinese Hero
- ☐☐ Choplifter
- ☐☐ Chopper I
- ☐☐ Circus/Acrobat TV
- ☐☐ Circus Charlie
- ☐☐ City Connection
- ☐☐ Clay Pigeon
- ☐☐ Clowns
- ☐☐ Cobra-Command

- ☐☐ Colony 7
- ☐☐ Combat School
- ☐☐ Commando
- ☐☐ Complex X
- ☐☐ Congo Bongo
- ☐☐ Continental Circus
- ☐☐ Contra
- ☐☐ Cool Pool
- ☐☐ Cosmic Cop
- ☐☐ Cosmo Gang the Video
- ☐☐ Cotton
- ☐☐ Cotton 2
- ☐☐ Cotton Boomerang
- ☐☐ Crack Down
- ☐☐ Crazy Balloon
- ☐☐ Crazy Rally
- ☐☐ Crime City
- ☐☐ Critter Crusher
- ☐☐ Crossed Swords
- ☐☐ Crowns Golf
- ☐☐ Cruis'n USA
- ☐☐ Cruis'n World
- ☐☐ Crypt Killer
- ☐☐ Crystal Castles
- ☐☐ Cybattler
- ☐☐ Darius
- ☐☐ Darius Gaiden - Silver Hawk
- ☐☐ Darius II
- ☐☐ Dark Seal
- ☐☐ D-Con
- ☐☐ Dead Angle
- ☐☐ Dead Connection
- ☐☐ Dead Or Alive ++
- ☐☐ Defender
- ☐☐ Demolition Derby
- ☐☐ Demon's World/Horror Story
- ☐☐ Depthcharge
- ☐☐ Destroyer
- ☐☐ Devastators
- ☐☐ Diamond Run
- ☐☐ Die Hard Arcade
- ☐☐ Diet Go Go
- ☐☐ Dig Dug
- ☐☐ Dig Dug II
- ☐☐ Discs of Tron
- ☐☐ DJ Boy
- ☐☐ Do! Run Run
- ☐☐ DoDonPachi
- ☐☐ Domino Man
- ☐☐ Don Doko Don
- ☑☐ Donkey Kong
- ☑☐ Donkey Kong 3
- ☑☐ Donkey Kong Junior
- ☐☐ DonPachi
- ☐☐ Dorachan
- ☐☐ Dorodon
- ☑☐ Double Dragon
- ☑☐ Double Dragon 3 - The Rosetta Stone
- ☑☐ Double Dragon II - The Revenge
- ☐☐ Double Dribble
- ☐☐ Dr. Micro
- ☐☐ Dr. Toppel's Adventure
- ☐☐ Dragon Ball Z V.R.V.S.
- ☐☐ Dragon Blaze
- ☐☐ Dragon Breed
- ☐☐ Dragonball Z
- ☐☐ Dragonball Z 2 - Super Battle
- ☐☐ Dream Soccer '94
- ☐☐ Drift Out
- ☐☐ Drift Out '94 - The Hard Order
- ☐☐ Driving Force
- ☐☐ Dungeon Magic
- ☐☐ Dungeons & Dragons: Shadow over Mystara
- ☐☐ Dungeons & Dragons: Tower of Doom
- ☐☐ Dyna Gear
- ☐☐ Dynablaster/Bomber Man
- ☐☐ Dynamite Duke
- ☐☐ Dynamite Dux

- ☐☐ Dynasty Wars
- ☐☐ Eight Forces
- ☐☐ Elevator Action
- ☐☐ Elevator Action Returns
- ☐☐ Embargo
- ☐☐ Empire City: 1931
- ☐☐ Enduro Racer
- ☐☐ Enforce
- ☐☐ Escape from the Planet of the Robot Monsters
- ☐☐ ESP Ra.De.
- ☐☐ Evil Stone
- ☐☐ Evolution Soccer
- ☐☐ Exciting Soccer
- ☐☐ Exerion
- ☐☐ Express Raider
- ☐☐ Exterminator
- ☐☐ Extreme Downhill
- ☐☐ Exvania
- ☐☐ Exzisus
- ☐☐ Eyes
- ☐☐ Fantasy Zone
- ☐☐ Fatal Fury - King of Fighters
- ☐☐ Fatal Fury 2/Garou Densetsu 2
- ☐☐ Fatal Fury 3 - Road to the Final Victory
- ☐☐ Fatal Fury Special
- ☐☐ Fever SOS
- ☐☐ Field Goal
- ☐☐ Fighting Hawk
- ☐☐ Fighting Roller
- ☐☐ Final Fight
- ☐☐ Final Lap
- ☐☐ Fire One
- ☐☐ Fire Trap
- ☐☐ Flicky
- ☐☐ Fly-Boy
- ☐☐ Flying Shark
- ☐☐ Force Break
- ☐☐ Formation Z
- ☐☐ Forty-Love
- ☑☐ Frogger
- ☐☐ Funky Jet
- ☐☐ Future Spy
- ☐☐ Galactic Storm
- ☐☐ Galaga
- ☐☐ Galaga '88
- ☐☐ Galaxian
- ☐☐ Galaxy Force 2
- ☐☐ Galaxy Gunners
- ☐☐ Gang Busters
- ☐☐ Gaplus
- ☐☐ Gauntlet
- ☐☐ Gauntlet II
- ☐☐ G-Darius Ver.2
- ☐☐ Gee Bee
- ☐☐ Gemini Wing
- ☐☐ Ghostmuncher Galaxian
- ☐☐ Ghosts'n Goblins
- ☐☐ Ghoul Panic
- ☐☐ Ghouls'n Ghosts
- ☐☐ GI Joe
- ☐☐ Giga Wing
- ☐☐ Gladiator 1984
- ☐☐ G-LOC Air Battle
- ☐☐ Go Go! Mile Smile
- ☐☐ Goalie Ghost
- ☐☐ Gokujyou Parodius
- ☐☐ Golden Axe - The Duel
- ☐☐ Golden Axe
- ☐☐ Golden Axe: The Revenge of Death Adder
- ☐☐ Golgo 13
- ☐☐ Gorf
- ☐☐ Gradius
- ☐☐ Gradius 4: Fukkatsu
- ☐☐ Gradius III
- ☐☐ Grand Prix Star
- ☐☐ Grand Striker 2
- ☐☐ Gravitar
- ☐☐ Green Beret
- ☐☐ Gridlee

- ☐☐ Grobda
- ☐☐ Guerrilla War
- ☐☐ Gun & Frontier
- ☐☐ Gun Master
- ☐☐ Gun.Smoke
- ☐☐ Gunbird
- ☐☐ Gunbird 2
- ☐☐ Gunforce - Battle Fire Engulfed Terror Island
- ☐☐ Gunforce 2
- ☐☐ Gunlock
- ☐☐ Guwange
- ☐☐ Guzzler
- ☐☐ Gyrodine
- ☐☐ Gyruss
- ☐☐ Halley's Comet
- ☐☐ Hammerin' Harry
- ☐☐ Hang-On
- ☐☐ Hang-On Jr.
- ☐☐ Hard Drivin'
- ☐☐ Hard Times
- ☐☐ Head On
- ☐☐ Head On 2
- ☐☐ Heavy Barrel
- ☐☐ Hidden Catch
- ☐☐ Hidden Catch 2
- ☐☐ Hidden Catch 3
- ☐☐ High Voltage
- ☐☐ Hole Land
- ☐☐ Hook
- ☐☐ Hopping Mappy
- ☐☐ Horizon
- ☐☐ Hot Shots Tennis
- ☐☐ Hotdog Storm
- ☐☐ Hydra
- ☐☐ Hyper Crash
- ☐☐ Hyper Duel
- ☐☐ Hyper Sports
- ☐☐ Hyper Street Fighter 2: The Anniversary Edition
- ☐☐ Ikari III - The Rescue
- ☐☐ Ikari Warriors
- ☐☐ In The Hunt
- ☐☐ Indiana Jones and the Temple of Doom
- ☐☐ Inferno
- ☐☐ Insector X
- ☐☐ Iron Horse
- ☐☐ Ironman Ivan Stewart's Super Off-Road
- ☐☐ Ironman Ivan Stewart's Super Off-Road Track-Pak
- ☐☐ Ixion
- ☐☐ J. J. Squawkers
- ☐☐ Jack Rabbit
- ☐☐ Jackal
- ☐☐ Joe & Mac Returns
- ☐☐ Joust
- ☐☐ Jr. Pac-Man
- ☐☐ Judge Dredd
- ☐☐ Jump Shot
- ☐☐ Jumping Cross
- ☐☐ Jumping Jack
- ☐☐ Jungle King
- ☐☐ Jungler
- ☐☐ Juno First
- ☐☐ Jurassic Park
- ☐☐ Kamikaze Cabbie
- ☐☐ Kangaroo
- ☐☐ Karate Champ
- ☐☐ Karnov
- ☐☐ Kick Start Wheelie King
- ☐☐ Kicker
- ☐☐ Kid Niki - Radical Ninja
- ☑☐ Killer Instinct
- ☑☐ Killer Instinct 2
- ☐☐ King of the Monsters
- ☐☐ King of the Monsters 2 - The Next Thing
- ☐☐ Kitten Kaboodle
- ☐☐ Klax
- ☐☐ Knights of the Round

- ☐☐ Knuckle Bash
- ☐☐ Koutetsu Yousai Strahl
- ☐☐ Krazy Bowl
- ☐☐ Kung-Fu Master
- ☐☐ Lady Bug
- ☐☐ Laser Ghost
- ☐☐ Lasso
- ☐☐ Last Blade/Bakumatsu Roman
- ☐☐ Last Blade 2/Bakumatsu Roman
- ☐☐ Legend of Hero Tonma
- ☐☐ Legendary Wings
- ☑☐ Lemmings
- ☐☐ Lethal Crash Race
- ☐☐ Lethal Enforcers
- ☐☐ Lethal Enforcers II: Gun Fighters
- ☐☐ Lethal Justice
- ☐☐ Lethal Thunder
- ☐☐ Libble Rabble
- ☐☐ Liberator
- ☐☐ Line of Fire/Bakudan Yarou
- ☐☐ Liquid Kids
- ☐☐ Lock-On
- ☐☐ Loco-Motion
- ☐☐ Lode Runner - The Dig Fight
- ☐☐ Lode Runner
- ☐☐ Lode Runner II - The Bungeling Strikes Back
- ☐☐ Lode Runner III The Golden Labyrinth
- ☐☐ Lode Runner IV - Teikoku Karano Dasshutsu
- ☐☐ Logic Pro
- ☐☐ Logic Pro 2
- ☐☐ Looping
- ☐☐ Lucky & Wild
- ☐☐ Lunar Lander
- ☐☐ M.I.A. - Missing in Action
- ☐☐ Macross Plus
- ☐☐ Mad Crasher
- ☐☐ Mad Gear
- ☐☐ Mad Motor
- ☐☐ Mad Planets
- ☐☐ Mad Shark
- ☐☐ Mag Max
- ☐☐ Magic Sword - Heroic Fantasy
- ☐☐ Magical Cat Adventure
- ☐☐ Magical Crystals
- ☐☐ Magician Lord
- ☐☐ Mahou Daisakusen
- ☐☐ Major Havoc
- ☐☐ Mappy
- ☐☐ Marble Madness
- ☑☐ Mario Bros.
- ☑☐ Marvel Land
- ☑☐ Marvel Super Heroes
- ☑☐ Marvel Super Heroes vs. Street Fighter
- ☑☐ Marvel vs. Capcom: Clash of Super Heroes
- ☐☐ Marvin's Maze
- ☐☐ Match It
- ☐☐ Match It II
- ☐☐ Mazinger Z
- ☐☐ Mechanized Attack
- ☐☐ Mega Man - The Power Battle
- ☐☐ Mega Man 2: The Power Fighters
- ☐☐ Mega Twins
- ☐☐ Mega Zone
- ☐☐ Megadon
- ☐☐ Meikyu Jima
- ☐☐ Mercs
- ☐☐ Metal Clash
- ☐☐ Metal Hawk
- ☐☐ Metal Slug - Super Vehicle-001
- ☐☐ Metal Slug 2 - Super Vehicle-001/II
- ☐☐ Metal Slug 3
- ☐☐ Metal Slug 4
- ☐☐ Metal Slug 5

- ☐☐ Metal Slug X - Super Vehicle-001
- ☐☐ Metro-Cross
- ☐☐ Michael Jackson's Moonwalker
- ☐☐ Midnight Resistance
- ☐☐ Mighty! Pang
- ☐☐ Mille Miglia 2: Great 1000 Miles Rally
- ☐☐ Mini Golf
- ☐☐ Mirai Ninja
- ☐☐ Missile Command
- ☐☐ Mobil Suit Gundam Final Shooting
- ☐☐ Mobile Suit Gundam
- ☐☐ Mobile Suit Gundam EX Revue
- ☐☐ Money Money
- ☐☐ Monster Bash
- ☐☐ Moon Cresta
- ☐☐ Moon Patrol
- ☐☐ Moon Shuttle
- ☑☐ Mortal Kombat
- ☑☐ Mortal Kombat 2
- ☑☐ Mortal Kombat 3
- ☑☐ Mortal Kombat 4
- ☐☐ Motos
- ☐☐ Mouse Trap
- ☐☐ Mouser
- ☐☐ Mr. Do!
- ☐☐ Mr. Do's Castle
- ☐☐ Mr. Do's Wild Ride
- ☐☐ Mr. Goemon
- ☐☐ Mr. TNT
- ☐☐ Ms. Pac-Man
- ☐☐ Mustache Boy
- ☐☐ Mystic Riders
- ☐☐ NAM-1975
- ☑☐ Namco Classics Collection Vol.1
- ☑☐ Namco Classics Collection Vol.2
- ☐☐ Narc
- ☐☐ NBA Hangtime
- ☐☐ NBA Jam
- ☐☐ NBA Jam TE
- ☐☐ Neck-n-Neck
- ☐☐ Nemesis
- ☐☐ Nemo
- ☐☐ Neo Bomberman
- ☐☐ Neo Drift Out - New Technology
- ☐☐ Neo Turf Masters/Big Tournament Golf
- ☐☐ New Hidden Catch/New Tul Lin Gu Lim Chat Ki '98
- ☐☐ New Rally X
- ☐☐ New York! New York!
- ☐☐ Nibbler
- ☐☐ Night Stocker
- ☐☐ Night Striker
- ☐☐ Ninja Combat
- ☐☐ Ninja Commando
- ☐☐ Ninja Emaki
- ☐☐ Ninja Mission
- ☐☐ Ninja Spirit
- ☐☐ Ninja-Kid II/NinjaKun Ashura no Shou
- ☐☐ Onna Sansirou - Typhoon Gal
- ☐☐ Operation Thunderbolt
- ☐☐ Operation Wolf
- ☐☐ Operation Wolf 3
- ☐☐ Ordyne
- ☐☐ Osman
- ☑☐ Out Run
- ☐☐ Out Zone
- ☐☐ Outfoxies
- ☐☐ OutRunners
- ☐☐ P.O.W. - Prisoners of War
- ☐☐ P-47 - The Phantom Fighter
- ☐☐ P-47 Aces
- ☐☐ Pac & Pal
- ☑☐ Pac-Land
- ☑☐ Pac-Man
- ☑☐ Pac-Man Plus
- ☑☐ Pac-Mania

☐☐ Pandora's Palace	☐☐ Puyo Puyo
☐☐ Pang	☐☐ Puyo Puyo 2
☐☐ Pang Pom's	☐☐ Puyo Puyo Sun
☐☐ Pang! 3	☐☐ Puzz Loop
☑☐ Paperboy	☐☐ Puzz Loop 2
☐☐ Parodius DA!	☐☐ Puzzle Bobble
☐☐ Peggle	☐☐ Puzzle Bobble 2
☐☐ Pengo	☐☐ Puzzle Bobble 3
☐☐ Penguin-Kun Wars	☐☐ Puzzle Bobble 4
☐☐ Phoenix	☐☐ Puzzle Uo Poko
☐☐ Pinball Action	☐☐ Q*bert
☐☐ Pipe Dream	☐☐ QB-3
☐☐ Pirates	☐☐ Qix
☑☐ Pitfall II	☐☐ Quantum
☐☐ Pleiads	☐☐ R.C. Pro-Am
☐☐ Plus Alpha	☐☐ R2D Tank
☐☐ Pnickies	☐☐ Race Drivin'
☐☐ Pocket Gal	☐☐ Rack + Roll
☐☐ Pocket Gal Deluxe	☐☐ Radar Zone
☑☐ Point Blank	☐☐ Radiant Silvergun
☑☐ Point Blank 2	☐☐ Radikal Bikers
☑☐ Pole Position	☐☐ Raiden
☑☐ Pole Position II	☐☐ Raiden Fighters
☐☐ Police Trainer	☐☐ Raiden Fighters 2
☐☐ Ponpoko	☐☐ Raiden Fighters Jet
☐☐ Pop Flamer	☐☐ Raiders
☐☐ Popeye	☐☐ Rainbow Islands
☐☐ Popper	☐☐ Rally Bike/Dash Yarou
☐☐ Pound for Pound	☐☐ Rally X
☐☐ Power Drift	☐☐ Rambo III
☐☐ Power Play	☐☐ Rampage
☐☐ Power Spikes	☐☐ Rampage: World Tour
☐☐ Power Spikes II	☐☐ Rampart
☐☐ Power Surge	☐☐ Rastan
☐☐ Primal Rage	☐☐ Ray Storm
☐☐ Progear	☐☐ Red Baron
☐☐ Psychic 5	☐☐ Red Robin
☐☐ Psycho-Nics Oscar	☐☐ Regulus
☐☐ PuckMan	☐☐ Reikai Doushi
☐☐ Pulsar	☐☐ Renegade
☐☐ Punch-Out!!	☐☐ Renju Kizoku

- ☐☐ Rescue
- ☐☐ Return of the Invaders
- ☐☐ Return of the Jedi
- ☐☐ Revolution X
- ☐☐ Rezon
- ☐☐ Ribbit!
- ☐☐ Ridge Racer
- ☐☐ Riding Fight
- ☐☐ Rip Cord
- ☐☐ River Patrol
- ☐☐ Road Blasters
- ☐☐ Road Fighter
- ☐☐ Road Runner
- ☐☐ Robo Army
- ☑☐ Robocop
- ☑☐ Robocop 2
- ☐☐ Robotron
- ☐☐ Roc'n Rope
- ☐☐ Rod-Land
- ☐☐ Roller Jammer
- ☐☐ Rollergames
- ☐☐ Rolling Thunder
- ☐☐ Rolling Thunder 2
- ☐☐ Route 16
- ☐☐ R-Type
- ☐☐ R-Type II
- ☐☐ R-Type Leo
- ☐☐ Run and Gun
- ☐☐ Rygar
- ☐☐ Ryu Jin
- ☐☐ S.P.Y. - Special Project Y
- ☐☐ S.S. Mission
- ☐☐ S.T.U.N. Runner
- ☐☐ Saboten Bombers
- ☐☐ Salamander
- ☐☐ Salamander 2
- ☐☐ Samurai Aces
- ☐☐ Samurai Shodown/Samurai Spirits
- ☐☐ Samurai Shodown II/Shin Samurai Spirits
- ☐☐ Samurai Shodown III/Samurai Spirits
- ☐☐ Samurai Shodown IV - Amakusa's Revenge
- ☐☐ Samurai Shodown V/Samurai Spirits Zero
- ☐☐ Samurai Shodown V Special
- ☐☐ SAR - Search and Rescue
- ☐☐ Sauro
- ☐☐ Scooter Shooter
- ☐☐ Scramble
- ☐☐ Scramble Spirits
- ☐☐ Screw Loose
- ☐☐ SD Gundam Neo Battling
- ☐☐ Sea Fighter Poseidon
- ☐☐ Sea Wolf
- ☐☐ Seawolf II
- ☐☐ SegaSonic The Hedgehog
- ☐☐ Seicross
- ☐☐ Sengoku
- ☐☐ Sengoku 2
- ☐☐ Sengoku 3
- ☐☐ Senjyo
- ☐☐ Sexy Parodius
- ☐☐ Shackled
- ☐☐ Shadow Dancer
- ☐☐ Shadow Force
- ☐☐ Shanghai - The Great Wall/ Shanghai Triple Threat
- ☐☐ Shanghai
- ☐☐ Shanghai II
- ☐☐ Shanghai III
- ☐☐ Shanghai Matekibuyuu
- ☐☐ Shinobi
- ☐☐ Shinobi III
- ☐☐ Shippu Mahou Daisakusen
- ☐☐ Shock Troopers - 2nd Squad
- ☐☐ Shock Troopers
- ☐☐ Shocking
- ☐☐ Shoot Out
- ☐☐ Shot Rider

- ☐☐ Showdown
- ☐☐ Shuffleshot
- ☐☐ Side Arms - Hyper Dyne
- ☐☐ Side Pocket
- ☐☐ Silk Worm
- ☐☐ Sinistar
- ☐☐ Skull & Crossbones
- ☐☐ Sky Diver
- ☐☐ Sky Fox
- ☐☐ Sky Kid
- ☐☐ Sky Raider
- ☐☐ Slap Fight
- ☐☐ Slap Shot
- ☐☐ Slither
- ☐☐ Sly Spy
- ☐☐ Smash T.V.
- ☐☐ Snow Bros. - Nick & Tom
- ☐☐ Snow Bros. 2 - With New Elves
- ☐☐ Sol Divide - The Sword of Darkness
- ☐☐ Solar Fox
- ☐☐ Solomon's Key
- ☐☐ Solvalou
- ☐☐ Son of Phoenix
- ☐☐ Son Son
- ☑☐ Sonic The Hedgehog
- ☑☐ Sonic The Hedgehog 2
- ☐☐ Soul Calibur
- ☐☐ Space Bomber
- ☐☐ Space Duel
- ☐☐ Space Dungeon
- ☐☐ Space Guerrilla
- ☐☐ Space Gun
- ☐☐ Space Harrier
- ☑☐ Space Invaders/Space Invaders M
- ☑☐ Space Invaders '95: The Attack of Lunar Loonies
- ☑☐ Space Invaders DX
- ☑☐ Space Invaders II
- ☐☐ Space Panic
- ☐☐ Space Raider
- ☐☐ Space Zap
- ☐☐ Spatter
- ☐☐ Speak & Rescue
- ☐☐ Spectar
- ☐☐ Speed Coin
- ☐☐ Speed Spin
- ☐☐ Speed Up
- ☐☐ Spelunker
- ☑☐ Spider-Man: The Videogame
- ☐☐ Spin Master/Miracle Adventure
- ☐☐ Spinal Breakers
- ☐☐ Splendor Blast
- ☐☐ SportTime Table Hockey
- ☐☐ Sprint 4
- ☐☐ Sprint 8
- ☐☐ Spy Hunter
- ☐☐ Squash
- ☐☐ Star Trek
- ☐☐ Star Wars
- ☐☐ Starblade
- ☐☐ Stargate
- ☐☐ Starship 1
- ☐☐ Steel Force
- ☐☐ Steel Gunner
- ☐☐ Steel Gunner 2
- ☐☐ Steel Talons
- ☐☐ Stocker
- ☐☐ Straight Flush
- ☑☐ Street Fighter
- ☑☐ Street Fighter Alpha 2
- ☑☐ Street Fighter Alpha 3
- ☑☐ Street Fighter Alpha: Warriors' Dreams
- ☑☐ Street Fighter EX
- ☑☐ Street Fighter EX 2
- ☑☐ Street Fighter EX 2 Plus
- ☑☐ Street Fighter EX Plus
- ☑☐ Street Fighter II - Champion Edition

- ☑☐ Street Fighter II - The World Warrior
- ☑☐ Street Fighter III - 2nd Impact: Giant Attack
- ☑☐ Street Fighter III - 3rd Strike: Fight for the Future
- ☑☐ Street Fighter III: New Generation
- ☑☐ Street Fighter Zero 2 Alpha
- ☑☐ Street Fighter: The Movie
- ☐☐ Street Heat - Cardinal Amusements
- ☐☐ Street Hoop/Street Slam/Dunk Dream
- ☐☐ Street Smart
- ☐☐ Strider
- ☐☐ Strider 2
- ☐☐ Strike Force
- ☐☐ Strikers 1945
- ☐☐ Strikers 1945 II
- ☐☐ Strikers 1945 III
- ☐☐ Strikers 1945 Plus
- ☐☐ Subroc-3D
- ☐☐ Sunset Riders
- ☐☐ Super Burger Time
- ☐☐ Super Contra
- ☐☐ Super Cross II
- ☐☐ Super Dodge Ball
- ☐☐ Super Gem Fighter Mini Mix
- ☐☐ Super Glob
- ☐☐ Super Hang-On
- ☐☐ Super Locomotive
- ☑☐ Super Mario Bros.
- ☑☐ Super Mario Bros. 2
- ☑☐ Super Mario Bros. 3
- ☐☐ Super Monaco GP
- ☑☐ Super Pac-Man
- ☐☐ Super Pang
- ☑☐ Super Pinball Action
- ☑☐ Super Punch-Out!!
- ☐☐ Super Puzzle Bobble
- ☐☐ Super Puzzle Fighter II Turbo
- ☐☐ Super Qix
- ☐☐ Super Sidekicks
- ☐☐ Super Sidekicks 2 - The World Championship
- ☐☐ Super Sidekicks 3 - The Next Glory
- ☐☐ Super Space Invaders '91
- ☐☐ Super Spacefortress Macross
- ☐☐ Super Spacefortress Macross II
- ☑☐ Super Street Fighter II: The New Challengers
- ☐☐ Super Trio
- ☐☐ Super Visual Football: European Sega Cup
- ☐☐ Superbike
- ☐☐ Superman
- ☐☐ Super-X
- ☐☐ Surprise Attack
- ☐☐ Suzuka 8 Hours
- ☐☐ Suzuka 8 Hours 2
- ☐☐ SWAT
- ☐☐ SWAT Police
- ☐☐ Swimmer
- ☐☐ T.N.K III
- ☐☐ Tac/Scan
- ☐☐ Tailgunner
- ☐☐ Talbot
- ☐☐ Tank Battalion
- ☐☐ Tank Busters
- ☐☐ Tank Force
- ☐☐ Tapper
- ☐☐ Targ
- ☐☐ Tazz-Mania
- ☑☐ Teenage Mutant Ninja Turtles - Turtles in Time
- ☑☐ Teenage Mutant Ninja Turtles
- ☐☐ Teeter Torture
- ☐☐ Tehkan World Cup
- ☑☐ Tekken
- ☑☐ Tekken 2

- ☑☐ Tekken 3
- ☑☐ Tekken Tag Tournament
- ☐☐ Tempest
- ☐☐ Terminator 2 - Judgment Day
- ☑☐ Tetris
- ☑☐ Tetris Plus
- ☑☐ Tetris Plus 2
- ☐☐ Tetris Absolute The Grand Master 2
- ☐☐ Tetris The Grand Master
- ☐☐ The Combatribes
- ☐☐ The Deep
- ☐☐ The Electric Yo-Yo
- ☐☐ The Empire Strikes Back
- ☐☐ The FairyLand Story
- ☐☐ The Irritating Maze
- ☐☐ The King of Dragons
- ☐☐ The King of Fighters '94
- ☐☐ The Legend of Kage
- ☐☐ The Main Event
- ☐☐ The NewZealand Story
- ☐☐ The Pit
- ☐☐ The Punisher
- ☐☐ The Real Ghostbusters
- ☐☐ The Simpsons
- ☐☐ The Speed Rumbler
- ☐☐ The Super Spy
- ☐☐ The Tin Star
- ☐☐ Thrash Rally
- ☐☐ Three Wonders
- ☐☐ Thunder Ceptor
- ☐☐ Thunder Cross II
- ☐☐ Thunder Dragon
- ☐☐ Thunder Dragon 2
- ☐☐ Thundercade/Twin Formation
- ☐☐ ThunderJaws
- ☐☐ Tiger Heli
- ☐☐ Tiger Road
- ☐☐ Timber
- ☐☐ Time Limit
- ☐☐ Time Pilot
- ☐☐ Time Pilot '84
- ☐☐ Tinkle Pit
- ☐☐ T-MEK
- ☐☐ Toki
- ☐☐ Tondemo Crisis
- ☐☐ Toobin'
- ☐☐ Top Hunter - Roddy & Cathy
- ☐☐ Top Roller
- ☐☐ Top Speed
- ☐☐ Total Carnage
- ☐☐ Tower of Druaga
- ☐☐ Toypop
- ☑☐ Track & Field
- ☐☐ Tranquillizer Gun
- ☐☐ Traverse USA/Zippy Race
- ☐☐ Triple Hunt
- ☐☐ Trivial Pursuit
- ☐☐ Trog
- ☐☐ Tron
- ☐☐ Tropical Angel
- ☐☐ Truxton/Tatsujin
- ☐☐ Tube Panic
- ☐☐ Tumble Pop
- ☐☐ Tunnel Hunt
- ☐☐ Turbo
- ☐☐ Turbo Force
- ☐☐ Turbo Out Run
- ☐☐ Turkey Shoot
- ☐☐ Tutankham
- ☐☐ Twin Bee Yahhoo!
- ☐☐ Twin Cobra
- ☐☐ Twin Cobra II
- ☐☐ Twin Eagle - Revenge Joe's Brother
- ☐☐ Twin Hawk
- ☐☐ Twin Qix
- ☐☐ U.N. Defense Force: Earth Joker
- ☐☐ U.N. Squadron
- ☐☐ Ultimate 11 - The SNK Football Championship

- [x] Ultimate Mortal Kombat 3
- [ ] Ultimate Tennis
- [ ] Ultra Balloon
- [ ] Under Fire
- [ ] Up'n Down
- [ ] US AAF Mustang
- [ ] Varth - Operation Thunderstorm
- [ ] Vasara
- [ ] Vasara 2
- [ ] Vastar
- [ ] Vendetta
- [ ] Video Hustler
- [ ] Vindicators
- [ ] Vindicators Part II
- [ ] Violent Storm
- [ ] Virtua Fighter
- [ ] Virtua Racing
- [ ] Volfied
- [ ] Vs. Balloon Fight
- [ ] Vs. Battle City
- [ ] Vs. Clu Clu Land
- [ ] Vs. Dr. Mario
- [ ] Vs. Duck Hunt
- [ ] Vs. Excitebike
- [ ] Vs. Gradius
- [ ] Vs. Hogan's Alley
- [ ] Vs. Ice Climber
- [ ] Vs. Mach Rider
- [ ] Vs. Mighty Bomb Jack
- [ ] Vs. Raid on Bungeling Bay
- [ ] Vs. Slalom
- [ ] Vs. Star Luster
- [ ] Vs. Super Mario Bros.
- [ ] Wai Wai Jockey Gate-In!
- [ ] Wall Street
- [ ] Wardner
- [ ] Warp & Warp
- [ ] Warrior Blade - Rastan Saga Episode III
- [ ] Warriors of Fate
- [ ] Water Match
- [ ] Water Ski
- [ ] WEC Le Mans 24
- [ ] Welltris
- [ ] Wild Gunman (PlayChoice-10)
- [ ] Wild West C.O.W.-Boys of Moo Mesa
- [ ] Willow
- [ ] Wily Tower
- [ ] Windjammers/Flying Power Disc
- [ ] Wizard of Wor
- [ ] Wolf Pack
- [x] Wonder Boy
- [x] Wonder Boy III - Monster Lair
- [x] Wonder Boy in Monster Land
- [ ] Wonder Momo
- [ ] World Rally
- [x] WWF WrestleFest
- [x] WWF: Wrestlemania
- [ ] X the Ball
- [ ] Xain'd Sleena
- [ ] Xenophobe
- [ ] Xevious
- [x] X-Men
- [x] X-Men vs. Street Fighter
- [x] X-Men: Children of the Atom
- [ ] Xybots
- [ ] Yam! Yam!
- [ ] Yie Ar Kung-Fu
- [ ] Youjyuden
- [ ] Zaxxon
- [ ] Zero Point
- [ ] Zero Point 2
- [ ] Zing Zing Zip
- [ ] Zombie Raid
- [ ] Zzyzzyxx

Chapter 46:
Visit Famous Beaches, Lakes, Rivers and Waterfalls

"The point is that when I see a sunset or a waterfall or something, for a split second it's so great, because for a little bit I'm out of my brain, and it's got nothing to do with me. I'm not trying to figure it out, you know what I mean? And I wonder if I can somehow find a way to maintain that mind stillness."

Chris Evans

This is a brief introduction to my visits to different beaches around the world and some of their features I have found fascinating. During my travels and marathon runs, I have visited many outstanding beaches: an example of this would be Sydney's City to Surf which starts in the city and culminates running through north Bondi and down to a brilliant view of the beach. These views are both captivating and inspiring with the vast amounts of water and towering waves smashing and pounding on to the beach and rocky areas.

Lakes and rivers I have visited seem so peaceful and tranquil, giving you a relaxed feeling. However, seasonal differences add vast changes to lakes – some drying up altogether during the dry season. Many have different coloured water. Flooded rivers contribute to this with mineral content. When visiting some of the waterfalls, they leave you almost out of breath with the water falling down with enormous power.

- ☐☐ Adventure Bay
- ☐☐ Agnes Water
- ☐☐ Angel Falls, Venezuela
- ☐☐ Australia's amazing Bioluminescent Lake
- ☑☐ Avalon Beach
- ☑☐ Avoca Beach
- ☑☐ Apollo Bay
- ☑☐ Blanket Bay
- ☑☐ Balmoral Beach
- ☐☐ Batemans Bay
- ☐☐ Barefoot Beach Preserve County Park, Bonita Springs, Florida
- ☐☐ Beach Walker Park, Kiawah Island, South Carolina
- ☑☐ Bilgola Beach
- ☐☐ Binalong Bay

- ☐☐ Blue Lake
- ☐☐ Bluestone Bay
- ☐☐ Blyde River Canyon
- ☑☐ Bondi Beach
- ☐☐ Boydtown
- ☐☐ Brahmaputra River, Tibet
- ☐☐ Bramston Beach
- ☐☐ Bridgewater Bay
- ☐☐ Bridport
- ☑☐ Brighton Beach
- ☐☐ British Admiral Beach
- ☑☐ Bronte Beach
- ☐☐ Bucasia
- ☐☐ Cable Beach
- ☐☐ Cape Florida State Park, Key Biscayne, Florida
- ☐☐ Cape Hatteras, North Carolina
- ☐☐ Cape Hillsborough
- ☐☐ Cape Leveque
- ☐☐ Cape Peron
- ☐☐ Casuarina Beach
- ☐☐ Catherine Hill Bay
- ☐☐ Chili Beach
- ☐☐ Coast Guard Beach, Eastham, Cape Cod, Massachusetts
- ☑☐ Collaroy Beach
- ☑☐ Coogee Beach
- ☐☐ Cosy Corner
- ☐☐ Cottesloe
- ☐☐ Crescent Head
- ☑☐ Curl Curl Beach
- ☐☐ Cylinders Beach
- ☑☐ Dee Why Beach
- ☐☐ Diggers Beach
- ☐☐ Eagle Bay
- ☐☐ Eagles Nest
- ☐☐ East Woody Beach
- ☐☐ Eco Beach
- ☐☐ Eighty Mile Beach
- ☐☐ Eimeo
- ☐☐ Elephant Rocks
- ☐☐ Emily Bay
- ☐☐ Es Calo des Moro, Spain
- ☐☐ Fingal Bay
- ☐☐ Fish River Canyon, Namibia
- ☐☐ Fitzroy Falls
- ☐☐ Four Mile Beach
- ☐☐ Frangipani Beach
- ☑☐ Freshwater Beach
- ☐☐ Frozen Baikal Lake and the Ice Cracks, Russia
- ☐☐ Frozen Minnehaha Falls
- ☐☐ Gibsons Steps
- ☐☐ Glass Beach, Fort Bragg, California
- ☐☐ Glenelg
- ☐☐ Godfreys Beach
- ☐☐ Gordon Falls
- ☐☐ Gorgeous and unique waterfall in a forest in Romania
- ☐☐ Govett Leap Falls
- ☐☐ Green Patch
- ☐☐ Halong Bay, Vietnam
- ☐☐ Hamoa Beach, Maui, Hawaii
- ☐☐ Havasu Falls, Arizona, USA
- ☐☐ Hidden beach, Marieta Islands, Mexico
- ☐☐ Horizontal Falls Jet - Boat Kimberley - NT Adventure
- ☐☐ Horseshoe Bay
- ☐☐ Huskisson Beach
- ☐☐ Hyams Beach
- ☐☐ Iguazu Falls
- ☐☐ Ipanema Beach
- ☐☐ Jervis Bay
- ☐☐ Johanna Beach
- ☐☐ Kahanamoku Beach, Honolulu, Hawaii
- ☐☐ Kalbarri
- ☑☐ Katoomba Falls
- ☐☐ Kitty Miller Bay
- ☐☐ Lake Baikal, Russia

- ☑☐ Lake Boga
- ☐☐ Lake Brienz
- ☐☐ Lake Eyre Salt Lakes
- ☐☐ Lake Louise, Canada
- ☐☐ Lake Lucerne, Switzerland
- ☐☐ Lake Lucerne
- ☐☐ Lake Nakuru, Kenya
- ☐☐ Lake Taupo
- ☐☐ Lake Tekapo
- ☐☐ Lake Thun
- ☐☐ Lake Titicaca
- ☐☐ Lake Zurich
- ☐☐ Lipson Cove
- ☐☐ Little Beach
- ☐☐ Long Beach
- ☐☐ Long Beach Nature Tours, Tofino, Canada
- ☑☐ Long Reef Beach
- ☐☐ Lorne
- ☐☐ Lucky Bay
- ☐☐ Main Beach, East Hampton, New York
- ☐☐ Maligne Lake, Canada
- ☐☐ Mandalay Beach
- ☑☐ Manly Beach
- ☐☐ Marina Bay Sands, Singapore
- ☑☐ Maroubra Beach
- ☐☐ Marrawah Beach
- ☐☐ Marvel Lake, Canada
- ☐☐ Meelup
- ☐☐ Merdayerrah Sandpatch
- ☐☐ Miami Beach, Florida
- ☐☐ Mission Beach
- ☐☐ Misty River, Indonesia
- ☐☐ Mitchell Falls, Western Australia
- ☐☐ Mon Repos
- ☑☐ Mona Vale Beach
- ☐☐ Montezuma Falls
- ☐☐ Multnomah Falls, Oregon
- ☐☐ Myall Beach
- ☐☐ Nam Tok Thilawsu Waterfalls, Um Phang, Thailand
- ☐☐ Nananu i ra Fiji Beach
- ☑☐ Narrabeen Beach
- ☐☐ Neds Beach
- ☐☐ Nielsen Park
- ☐☐ Ninety Mile Beach
- ☐☐ Norries Head
- ☐☐ Ocean Beach
- ☐☐ Onuk Island, Balabac Palawan, Philippines
- ☑☐ Palm Beach
- ☐☐ Palm Cove
- ☐☐ Pangong Tso Lake, India-China
- ☐☐ Peaceful Bay
- ☐☐ Pebble Shore Lake in Glacier National Park, Montana, United States
- ☐☐ Perlubie Beach
- ☐☐ Picnic Bay Beach
- ☐☐ Pink Lake, Esperance, Western Australia
- ☐☐ Pirates Bay
- ☑☐ Plantation Beach
- ☐☐ Plitvice Lakes, Croatia
- ☐☐ Pondalowie Bay
- ☐☐ Pongua Falls, Vietnam
- ☐☐ Port Noralunga
- ☐☐ Port Phillips Bay
- ☐☐ Puerto Princesa Subterranean River, Palawan, Philippines
- ☐☐ Rainbow Bay
- ☐☐ Rainbow Beach
- ☐☐ Ramona Falls Oregon
- ☐☐ Red Sand Beach, Hana, Maui, Hawaii
- ☐☐ Redbill, Diamond Island
- ☐☐ Refuge Cove
- ☐☐ Resort Beach
- ☐☐ Rhine Falls
- ☐☐ Rivers Fiji

- ☐☐ Ruby Falls, Chattanooga, Tennessee
- ☐☐ Saliara Beach, Thassos Island, Greece
- ☐☐ Sandy Cape
- ☐☐ Seal Rocks
- ☐☐ Second Beach
- ☐☐ Second Valley
- ☐☐ Secret Beach
- ☐☐ See Devil's Kettle Falls
- ☐☐ See Turkey's Strange Coloured Waterfall
- ☐☐ Seljalandsfoss Waterfall, Iceland
- ☐☐ Seven Mile Beach
- ☐☐ Seventy Five Mile Beach
- ☐☐ Shark Bay
- ☐☐ Shell Beach
- ☑☐ Shelley Beach
- ☐☐ Shifen Waterfall, Taiwan
- ☐☐ Shipwreck Bay
- ☐☐ Silica Beach
- ☐☐ Smith's Beach
- ☐☐ Snellings Beach
- ☐☐ Sorrento Back Beach, Australia
- ☐☐ South Broulee
- ☐☐ St. Croix Lake, Les Gorges du Verdon, Provence, France
- ☐☐ St. George Island State Park, Florida
- ☐☐ Starfish Beach, Grand Cayman
- ☐☐ Sunset Island, Lake Superior, Canada
- ☑☐ Surfers Paradise
- ☐☐ Tangalooma
- ☐☐ Tea Tree Beach
- ☐☐ The Basin
- ☐☐ The Blue Dragon River, Odeleite, Portugal
- ☐☐ The Blue Eye Spring (Syri I Kalter), Albana
- ☐☐ The Coorong
- ☐☐ The Emerald Pool and Waterfall, Baja California, Mexico
- ☐☐ The Nile River System
- ☐☐ The Ocean Blue, Navagio Bay, Greece
- ☐☐ The Pearl Waterfall, Jiuzhaigou Valley, China
- ☐☐ The Red Beach, Liaohe River Delta
- ☐☐ The River of Five Colors, Cano Cristales, Colombia
- ☐☐ The Strand
- ☐☐ Tidal River
- ☐☐ Tortuga Bay
- ☐☐ Trigg
- ☐☐ Trousers Beach
- ☐☐ Tucker's Rock Beach
- ☑☐ Turramurra Beach
- ☐☐ Uluru Waterfalls, Australia
- ☐☐ Vaal River
- ☐☐ Vanuatu, Mele Cascades
- ☐☐ Venice Beach, California
- ☐☐ Very dreamy Lake Camecuaro, Michoacan, Mexico
- ☐☐ Victoria Falls
- ☐☐ Victoria Falls, Zambia/Zimbabwe
- ☑☐ Visit Loch Ness, Scotland
- ☐☐ Visit Niagra Falls, New York
- ☐☐ Visit Spencer Lake, Spencer Glaciers - row out to glaciers by boat see close up
- ☑☐ Visit the Heart of the Murray River, Swan Hill, Victoria
- ☐☐ Waimanalo Bay State Park, Oahu, Hawaii
- ☐☐ Waratah Bay
- ☐☐ Wategos Beach

- ☐☐ Waterfall inside a sea cave on the Na Pali Coast
- ☐☐ Waterfall Island, Alto Parana, Paraguay
- ☐☐ Waterfall Walkway in Thailand
- ☐☐ Waterfall Walkway, St. Beatus Caves, Switzerland
- ☐☐ Waterfalls of Gods, Iceland
- ☐☐ Western River Cove
- ☑☐ Whale Beach
- ☐☐ White Beach in Boracay, Philippines
- ☐☐ Whitehaven Beach
- ☐☐ William Bay, Western Australia
- ☐☐ Wineglass Bay
- ☐☐ Wingan Inlet
- ☑☐ Wreck Beach
- ☐☐ Yamdron Tso Lake, Tibet
- ☐☐ Zaragoza Falls, Pyrenees, Spain

Chapter 47:
Books Collection and Goals

"Every story I create, creates me. I write to create myself."

Octavia E. Butler

Have you ever had a collection of books you like to keep? It may be a Stephen King collection or another famous author. It may even be something geographically orientated like a collection I love to read, Lonely Planet books about countries around the world. A nice book to cosy up to at night or build your mind and help you realise the beautiful world around us. Either way, we all read at least one book in our life, most of us will do so at school where we are learning writer techniques while we read. Have you ever dreamed of writing that own book of yours? I am living that dream and seeing my own writing and all my time in print in a book. It takes so much time to place in writing and a lot to think about, but when you have a dream that you want to succeed and be published to help others in the world enjoy their life, you just have to take that leap of faith and just work on it any chance you can. Dreams are possible if you set your mind to them.

- ☐☐ Attend a poetry slam
- ☑☐ Be able to find an image within a design
- ☐☐ Be *Time* magazine's person of the year
- ☐☐ Hit best sellers list
- ☐☐ Lonely Planet Book - Amsterdam
- ☐☐ Lonely Planet Book - Antarctica
- ☑☐ Lonely Planet Book - Australia
- ☐☐ Lonely Planet Book - Brazil
- ☑☐ Lonely Planet Book - Canada
- ☐☐ Lonely Planet Book - Chile/ Easter Islands
- ☑☐ Lonely Planet Book - China
- ☑☐ Lonely Planet Book - Costa Rica
- ☐☐ Lonely Planet Book - Denmark
- ☐☐ Lonely Planet Book - Ecuador/ Galapagos Islands
- ☑☐ Lonely Planet Book - Egypt
- ☑☐ Lonely Planet Book - England
- ☐☐ Lonely Planet Book - Fiji
- ☑☐ Lonely Planet Book - France
- ☑☐ Lonely Planet Book - Germany
- ☑☐ Lonely Planet Book - Greece
- ☑☐ Lonely Planet Book - Hawai'i
- ☑☐ Lonely Planet Book - India
- ☑☐ Lonely Planet Book - Ireland
- ☑☐ Lonely Planet Book - Italy
- ☑☐ Lonely Planet Book - Japan
- ☐☐ Lonely Planet Book - Mexico

- ☑☐ Lonely Planet Book - New Zealand
- ☐☐ Lonely Planet Book - Norway
- ☑☐ Lonely Planet Book - Peru
- ☐☐ Lonely Planet Book - Philippines
- ☑☐ Lonely Planet Book - Scotland
- ☑☐ Lonely Planet Book - Singapore and Malaysia
- ☐☐ Lonely Planet Book - South Africa
- ☑☐ Lonely Planet Book - Spain
- ☑☐ Lonely Planet Book - Switzerland
- ☑☐ Lonely Planet Book - Thailand
- ☑☐ Lonely Planet Book - Turkey
- ☑☐ Lonely Planet Book - USA
- ☐☐ Lonely Planet Book - Wales
- ☐☐ Make my own cook book for personal use
- ☐☐ Have my book published
- ☑☐ Read a novel book
- ☐☐ Read the whole bible
- ☐☐ Sell a million copies of my book
- ☐☐ Sell a million copies of my eBook
- ☐☐ Sell the movie rights to my novel
- ☑☐ Visit a book signing
- ☐☐ Visit all 101 Beaches in the book *101 Best Australian Beaches*
- ☑☐ Write a biography
- ☑☐ Write a book
- ☑☐ Write a travel book
- ☑☐ Write the story of my life

Chapter 48:
Express Yourself, Creativity, Learning Skills and Education

"A creative man is motivated by the desire to achieve, not by the desire to beat others."

Ayn Rand

Expressing ourselves is a way we love to create, enjoy learning new things, learning new skills and developing skills we already know to improve our own knowledge. It expands our mind and gets us thinking more and developing our knowledge of the world. What we learn today may help someone in the future; it may seem a simple training course today but when the time comes and you're the only person around, that skill could be a life saver. Just by taking that simple course in First Aid or basic knowledge to help your children in their school days with questions they ask you, like where is this country or how to say hello in another language, we always strive to learn new skills and new things day to day. From our families and friends, the news or discovery/geographic channels – each helps us develop our knowledge of the world around us.

"Eye bombing is the act of setting googly eyes on inanimate things in the public space."

- ☐☐ Basic quilt making course
- ☐☐ Basic tapestry course
- ☐☐ Build a blanket and pillow fort with my kids
- ☐☐ Build a fence
- ☐☐ Build a gingerbread house
- ☑☐ Build a Lego robot and have it work thru a computer program
- ☐☐ Build a mosaic
- ☑☐ Build a sandcastle
- ☐☐ Build a treehouse
- ☐☐ Build a village around a model train layout
- ☐☐ Build an igloo
- ☐☐ Build an innukshuk
- ☑☐ Build my own PC
- ☑☐ Build something
- ☑☐ Build a build-a-bear
- ☐☐ Candle making
- ☑☐ Ceramics class
- ☐☐ Clay hand building class

- ☑☐ Communicate with someone who doesn't speak the same language as you
- ☐☐ Create a bumper sticker
- ☐☐ Create a melted crayon art piece
- ☐☐ Create my own perfume
- ☐☐ Create something using charcoal
- ☐☐ Create something using oil pastels
- ☐☐ Create something using watercolors
- ☑☐ Design and make my own t-shirt
- ☐☐ Dip a rose into dye
- ☐☐ Do some batiking
- ☑☐ Draw an artistic drawing
- ☑☐ Draw the Harbour Bridge
- ☐☐ Get a degree
- ☐☐ Glass blowing
- ☐☐ Have a canvas of a memorial moment
- ☐☐ Have a drawing turned into real cuddle toys at Child's Own Studio
- ☐☐ Have my portrait painted
- ☑☐ Join a toastmasters group and learn public speaking techniques
- ☑☐ Learn a foreign language
- ☑☐ Learn a magic trick
- ☑☐ Learn bartending
- ☐☐ Learn calligraphy
- ☑☐ Learn first aid
- ☐☐ Learn flower arrangements
- ☐☐ Learn how to do a vlog
- ☑☐ Learn how to make cocktails
- ☑☐ Learn how to ride a bicycle
- ☐☐ Learn how to ride a motorcycle
- ☐☐ Learn how to sword fight
- ☑☐ Learn how to tie a tie
- ☐☐ Learn how to do two lasso tricks
- ☐☐ Learn how to throw stars
- ☐☐ Learn how to toss pizza dough
- ☐☐ Learn how to use photoshop
- ☑☐ Learn how to weld
- ☐☐ Learn Morse code
- ☐☐ Learn pottery making
- ☐☐ Learn sign language
- ☐☐ Learn the alphabet in sign language
- ☑☐ Learn the basics of car maintenance
- ☐☐ Learn to beat box
- ☑☐ Learn to cook
- ☑☐ Learn to juggle
- ☑☐ Learn to knit
- ☐☐ Learn to paint
- ☑☐ Learn to sail
- ☐☐ Learn to say hello in 50 different languages
- ☑☐ Learn to sculpt
- ☐☐ Learn to sew
- ☑☐ Learn to type fast
- ☑☐ Learn to write with my left hand
- ☐☐ Learn to yodel
- ☐☐ Make a baking soda volcano eruption
- ☐☐ Make a balloon animal
- ☐☐ Make a bead bracelet
- ☐☐ Make a blue sulphur crystal
- ☐☐ Make a bola
- ☐☐ Make a dream catcher
- ☐☐ Make a giant rubber band ball
- ☐☐ Make a handmade greeting card
- ☐☐ Make a homemade wind chime
- ☐☐ Make a model air plane

- ☐☐ Make a model car
- ☐☐ Make a piece of jewelry
- ☐☐ Make a pinata
- ☐☐ Make a real prosthetic mask or face piece
- ☐☐ Make a sand painting
- ☐☐ Make crop circles
- ☐☐ Make fire without matches
- ☐☐ Make personalised stamps
- ☐☐ Make something from blacksmithing
- ☐☐ Make something out of leather
- ☑☐ Make something out of Plaster of Paris
- ☐☐ Make your own coloured sand vases
- ☐☐ Paint a canvas
- ☐☐ Sand mosaics
- ☐☐ Specialty soap making class
- ☐☐ Sports + exercise nutrition course
- ☑☐ Start scrapbooking album
- ☐☐ Stone sculpture class
- ☐☐ Take a course at a university/college
- ☐☐ Take a massage class
- ☐☐ Take an aptitude test
- ☐☐ Take photography class
- ☑☐ Take the IQ test
- ☑☐ Wine basic training

Chapter 49: Charities

"All of the charities we're involved with have touched me in one way or another on a personal level. There are about eight or nine charities that I support."

Ferguson Jenkins

Our inner kind hearts desire to help people in need, and a lot of us love being the person there to help. From discovering cures, or being a part of helping charities to overcome diseases and problems, or helping the homeless off the streets. We like to do our part to help humanity. Even a small donation to a charity can go a very long way, so don't think your one or two dollar coin won't help much. If everyone donated a couple of dollars to a charity, the world would be a better place and we would be finding cures from problems around the world which many of us either suffer from ourselves or we know someone who has been through it or is going through it at the moment, and want to be there to help.

- ☐☐ Australia's Biggest Morning Tea
- ☐☐ Create a Christmas jar
- ☑☐ Donate canned goods or clothing to the needy
- ☑☐ Donate in a wishing well for charity
- ☑☐ Donate money to charity at least once
- ☐☐ Dye my hair blue for depression
- ☑☐ Ice bucket challenge
- ☐☐ National Bandana Day
- ☐☐ Organise a fundraising event
- ☐☐ Raise one million dollars for a charity
- ☑☐ Raise money for a charity
- ☐☐ Sleep on the streets for charity night
- ☐☐ World's Greatest Shave

Chapter 50:
Dancing Lifestyle

"Life is like dancing. If we have a big floor, many people will dance. Some will get angry when the rhythm changes. But life is changing all the time."

Miguel Angel Ruiz

Almost all of us were born with the saying: "I have two left feet when it comes to dancing." Dancing is easy to learn and we all have our own unique dance movements and styles. There are special classes to help us perfect our dancing, such as calligraphy dancing and culture dancing, Irish dancing or tango dancing. There are many styles of dancing. No matter the type of dancing you relate with, there will always be music to go along with the moves you're creating. Watching the movies *Footloose* or *Dirty Dancing* help us believe that anything is possible if we believe in ourselves. Technique is hard to master, but moving to the rhythm takes it to another level of expertise.

- ☐☐ Be in a dance video clip
- ☑☐ Be in a mosh pit
- ☐☐ Choreograph a dance and have it performed
- ☑☐ Compete and win in a dance off
- ☑☐ Dance on stage
- ☐☐ Dance with fire
- ☐☐ Experience a rave party
- ☑☐ Experience Zumba class
- ☐☐ Learn arial dancing
- ☐☐ Learn ballet dance
- ☐☐ Learn ballroom dancing
- ☐☐ Learn belly dancing
- ☐☐ Learn Bharata Natyam, Southern India
- ☐☐ Learn Bollywood dancing
- ☐☐ Learn breakdancing moves
- ☐☐ Learn Capoeira, Brazilian dance
- ☐☐ Learn celestial dance, Cambodian
- ☐☐ Learn Fandango dance
- ☐☐ Learn Flamenco dance
- ☐☐ Learn Flamenco dancing, Spain
- ☐☐ Learn hip hop dancing
- ☐☐ Learn Irish step dance
- ☐☐ Learn Kabuki dance, Japan
- ☐☐ Learn Kathak, Northern India
- ☐☐ Learn Kekak Trance Dance
- ☐☐ Learn krumping
- ☐☐ Learn Polka dance
- ☐☐ Learn Russian Cossacks
- ☐☐ Learn Shaolin Monk dance
- ☐☐ Learn square dancing
- ☐☐ Learn the cha-cha-cha
- ☐☐ Learn the Foxtrot

- ☐☐ Learn the Jitterbug dance
- ☐☐ Learn the Lion dance
- ☐☐ Learn the Merengue dance
- ☐☐ Learn the Rhumba dance
- ☐☐ Learn the swing dance
- ☐☐ Learn the tap dance
- ☑☐ Learn the waltz
- ☐☐ Learn tinikling
- ☐☐ Learn to salsa dance
- ☐☐ Learn to tango
- ☑☐ Stay up all night dancing and go work the next day
- ☐☐ Take a pole dancing class
- ☐☐ Take dancing lessons
- ☐☐ The "Whirling Dervishes," Turkey

Chapter 51: Martial Art Skills

"In martial arts, every time you graduate, move to another level, you don't forget everything you've done. You build on it, but it's always there."

Melody Beattie

Martial arts are a tradition of combat practices which are practised for a variety of reasons consisting of the following: self-defence, competition, physical health and fitness, entertainment, as well as mental, physical, and spiritual development. We empower our coordination and fitness and it helps train our body and mind to focus, and we feel the personal achievement when rewarded with class or levels of coloured belts of progression to determine our strength and abilities. Every type of martial art is unique; everyone has their special techniques, some using arms/hands only, others use the full body and some legs only. No matter what martial art you want to join, you will be proud of the achievements you make. Self-defence is always a useful lesson to be learned in life because you never know when something is going to happen – from a person trying to steal your wallet or handbag, or an attempt to rip your car keys and knock you to the road. It's always a good thing to have the mind set on how you should react to the situations in life – not having to go in full panic mode sitting on the ground in tears while they take off and are laughing that you didn't do anything to protect yourself. The world is full of insecurity so this benefits in helping us learn self-protection skills.

- ☑☐ Break a wooden board with my hand
- ☐☐ Get black belt in a martial art
- ☐☐ Get blue belt in a martial art
- ☐☐ Get brown belt in a martial art
- ☐☐ Get green belt in a martial art
- ☐☐ Get orange belt in a martial art
- ☐☐ Get red belt in a martial art
- ☐☐ Get yellow belt in a martial art
- ☑☐ Learn a martial art
- ☑☐ Take a class in boxing
- ☐☐ Take a class in jiu-jitsu
- ☐☐ Take a class in judo
- ☑☐ Take a class in karate
- ☐☐ Take a class in kickboxing
- ☐☐ Take a class in kung fu
- ☐☐ Take a class in taekwondo
- ☑☐ Take a class in Muay Thai
- ☐☐ Visit the Home of Shaolin - China "Home of Martial Arts"

Chapter 52: Aircraft Flying Experiences

"Some guys travel with expensive Louis Vuitton luggage but it gets all scratched up under the plane. I'd rather not spend too much money on something that's just going to get messed up."

James Harden

We all love the thrill of looking forward to flying and getting away from the daily stresses of life. We look forward to those holidays overseas exploring places we have never been or to visit our family and friends from another country or another state. The hard choice for all of us is with which airplane company should we fly? We consider all possibilities, from cost for tickets, comfort on the plane, service the flight attendants provide, the popularity of the company you wish to fly with and what section of the plane should we fly in. A lot of people fly economy but we always dream of at least once in our lives to fly up front in first class for the extra-special treatment and a great night sleep while we fly. Some planes are international brand flights and others are specific flights for domestic only. Another way to fly is by helicopter. No matter how we get to our destination, we all love every minute of the getaway experience from all the daily stresses in our life and enjoy the experience.

- ☐☐ Buy a round-the-world air ticket
- ☐☐ Fly first class
- ☐☐ Fly in a helicopter
- ☐☐ Fly in a helicopter over glaciers, Alaska
- ☐☐ Fly in a helicopter overlooking Hawaii
- ☐☐ Fly with Adria Airways
- ☐☐ Fly with Aegean Airlines
- ☑☐ Fly with Aer Lingus
- ☐☐ Fly with Aeroflot Russian Airlines
- ☐☐ Fly with Aerolineas Argentinas
- ☐☐ Fly with Aeromexico
- ☐☐ Fly with Air Algerie
- ☐☐ Fly with Air Arabia
- ☐☐ Fly with Air Astana
- ☐☐ Fly with Air Austral
- ☐☐ Fly with Air Bagan
- ☐☐ Fly with Air Baltic
- ☐☐ Fly with Air Berlin
- ☐☐ Fly with Air Canada
- ☐☐ Fly with Air Caraibes
- ☐☐ Fly with Air China
- ☐☐ Fly with Air Dolomiti

- ☐☐ Fly with Air Europa
- ☐☐ Fly with Air France
- ☐☐ Fly with Air India
- ☐☐ Fly with Air Italy
- ☐☐ Fly with Air Koryo
- ☐☐ Fly with Air Macau
- ☐☐ Fly with Air Malta
- ☐☐ Fly with Air Mauritius
- ☐☐ Fly with Air Namibia
- ☐☐ Fly with Air New Zealand
- ☐☐ Fly with Air Niugini
- ☐☐ Fly with Air Nostrum
- ☐☐ Fly with Air Seychelles
- ☐☐ Fly with Air Tahiti Nui
- ☐☐ Fly with Air Transat
- ☐☐ Fly with AirAsia
- ☐☐ Fly with AirAsia X
- ☐☐ Fly with Aircalin
- ☐☐ Fly with Alaska Airlines
- ☐☐ Fly with Alitalia
- ☐☐ Fly with Allegiant Air
- ☐☐ Fly with American Airlines
- ☐☐ Fly with ANA All Nippon Airways
- ☐☐ Fly with Arik Air
- ☐☐ Fly with Arkefly
- ☐☐ Fly with Asiana Airlines
- ☐☐ Fly with Austrian Airlines
- ☐☐ Fly with Avianca
- ☐☐ Fly with Azerbaijan Airlines
- ☐☐ Fly with Bahamasair
- ☐☐ Fly with Bangkok Airways
- ☐☐ Fly with Biman Bangladesh
- ☐☐ Fly with British Airways
- ☐☐ Fly with Brussels Airlines
- ☐☐ Fly with Bulgaria Air
- ☐☐ Fly with Caribbean Airlines
- ☐☐ Fly with Cathay Pacific Airways
- ☐☐ Fly with Cebu Pacific
- ☐☐ Fly with China Airlines
- ☐☐ Fly with China Eastern Airlines
- ☐☐ Fly with China Southern Airlines
- ☐☐ Fly with China United Airlines
- ☐☐ Fly with CityJet
- ☐☐ Fly with Condor Airlines
- ☐☐ Fly with Copa Airlines
- ☐☐ Fly with Croatia Airlines
- ☐☐ Fly with Cubana Airlines
- ☐☐ Fly with Cyprus Airways
- ☐☐ Fly with Czech Airlines
- ☐☐ Fly with Delta Air Lines
- ☐☐ Fly with Dragonair
- ☐☐ Fly with easyJet
- ☐☐ Fly with Edelweiss Air
- ☐☐ Fly with Egyptair
- ☐☐ Fly with El Al Israel Airlines
- ☐☐ Fly with Emirates
- ☐☐ Fly with Estonian Air
- ☐☐ Fly with Ethiopian Airlines
- ☑☐ Fly with Etihad Airways
- ☐☐ Fly with EVA Airways
- ☐☐ Fly with Far Eastern Air Transport
- ☐☐ Fly with Fiji Airways
- ☐☐ Fly with Finnair
- ☐☐ Fly with FlyBe
- ☐☐ Fly with Frontier Airlines
- ☐☐ Fly with Gambia Bird Airlines
- ☐☐ Fly with Garuda Indonesia
- ☐☐ Fly with Germanwings
- ☐☐ Fly with GOL Linhas Aereas
- ☐☐ Fly with Gulf Air
- ☐☐ Fly with Hainan Airlines
- ☐☐ Fly with Hawaiian Airlines
- ☐☐ Fly with Iberia
- ☐☐ Fly with Icelandair
- ☐☐ Fly with Interjet
- ☐☐ Fly with Iran Air
- ☐☐ Fly with Japan Airlines
- ☐☐ Fly with JAT Airways
- ☐☐ Fly with Jazeera Airways

- ☐☐ Fly with Jet Airways
- ☐☐ Fly with Jet2.com
- ☐☐ Fly with JetBlue Airways
- ☐☐ Fly with JetStar Airways
- ☐☐ Fly with Jetstar Asia Airways
- ☐☐ Fly with Juneyao Airlines
- ☐☐ Fly with Kenya Airways
- ☐☐ Fly with KLM Royal Dutch Airlines
- ☐☐ Fly with Korean Air
- ☐☐ Fly with Kuwait Airways
- ☐☐ Fly with LAM Mozambique Airlines
- ☐☐ Fly with LAN Airlines
- ☐☐ Fly with Lion Air
- ☐☐ Fly with LOT Polish Airlines
- ☐☐ Fly with Lufthansa
- ☐☐ Fly with Luxair
- ☐☐ Fly with Mahan Air
- ☐☐ Fly with Malaysia Airlines
- ☐☐ Fly with Meridiana
- ☐☐ Fly with Merpati Nusantara Airlines
- ☐☐ Fly with MIAT Mongolian Airlines
- ☐☐ Fly with Middle East Airlines
- ☐☐ Fly with Moldavian Airlines
- ☐☐ Fly with Monarch Airlines
- ☐☐ Fly with Myanmar Airways International
- ☐☐ Fly with Nepal Airlines
- ☐☐ Fly with NIKI
- ☐☐ Fly with Nok Air
- ☐☐ Fly with Norwegian
- ☐☐ Fly with Okay Airways
- ☐☐ Fly with Olympic Air
- ☐☐ Fly with Oman Air
- ☐☐ Fly with Onur Air
- ☐☐ Fly with Pakistan International
- ☐☐ Fly with Pegasus Airlines
- ☑☐ Fly with Philippine Airlines
- ☐☐ Fly with Porter Airlines
- ☐☐ Fly with Qantas Airways
- ☐☐ Fly with Qatar Airways
- ☐☐ Fly with Rossiya Airlines
- ☐☐ Fly with Royal Air Maroc
- ☐☐ Fly with Royal Brunei Airlines
- ☐☐ Fly with Royal Jordanian Airlines
- ☐☐ Fly with Ryanair
- ☐☐ Fly with S7 Siberia Airlines
- ☐☐ Fly with SAS Scandinavian Airlines
- ☐☐ Fly with SATA Air Azores
- ☐☐ Fly with Saudia Arabian Airlines
- ☐☐ Fly with Scoot
- ☐☐ Fly with Shandong Airlines
- ☐☐ Fly with Shanghai Airlines
- ☐☐ Fly with Shenzhen Airlines
- ☐☐ Fly with Sichuan Airlines
- ☐☐ Fly with Silk Air
- ☐☐ Fly with Singapore Airlines
- ☐☐ Fly with SmartWings
- ☐☐ Fly with South African Airways
- ☐☐ Fly with Southwest Airlines
- ☐☐ Fly with Spirit Airlines
- ☐☐ Fly with Spring Airlines
- ☐☐ Fly with SriLankan Airlines
- ☐☐ Fly with Sudan Airways
- ☐☐ Fly with Swiss International Air Lines
- ☐☐ Fly with Syrianair
- ☐☐ Fly with TAAG Angola Airlines
- ☐☐ Fly with TACA
- ☐☐ Fly with TACV Cabo Verde Airlines
- ☐☐ Fly with Tajik Air
- ☐☐ Fly with TAM Airlines
- ☐☐ Fly with TAP Air Portugal
- ☐☐ Fly with Tarom
- ☐☐ Fly with Thai Airways

- ☐☐ Fly with Thomas Cook Airlines
- ☐☐ Fly with Tianjin Airlines
- ☐☐ Fly with Tiger Airways
- ☐☐ Fly with Tigerair Mandala
- ☐☐ Fly with Transaero Airlines
- ☐☐ Fly with Transavia Airlines
- ☐☐ Fly with Turkish Airlines
- ☐☐ Fly with Turkmenistan Airlines
- ☐☐ Fly with Ukraine Int'l Airlines
- ☐☐ Fly with United Airlines
- ☐☐ Fly with US Airways
- ☐☐ Fly with Uzbekistan Airways
- ☐☐ Fly with Vietnam Airlines
- ☐☐ Fly with Virgin America
- ☐☐ Fly with Virgin Atlantic Airways
- ☑☐ Fly with Virgin Australia
- ☐☐ Fly with Vueling Airlines
- ☐☐ Fly with Westjet
- ☐☐ Fly with Wizz Air
- ☐☐ Fly with WOW air
- ☐☐ Fly with Xiamen Airlines
- ☐☐ Fly with Yemenia

Chapter 53:
Dress Up Experiences

"My dad used to say, 'Just because you dress up in a coat and tie, it doesn't influence your intelligence.'"

Tiger Woods

Everyone loves to dress up and have a fun time. Whether it's a party occasion to dress up for or running a fun run, dressing up for the fun of it and putting a smile on other people's faces when they see your costumes. Sometimes you just need to loosen up and relax and act like a kid again, and dress up in your favourite Disney character, Looney Tune or even a character from computer games like Mario. There are plenty to choose from and many reasons to wear different costumes. Halloween is a special day each year dedicated to dress-up party occasions. Why not live like a kid again and dress up in fancy dress and make a fun, spectacular occasion just to enjoy something different than coming as yourself?

- ☐☐ Be a team mascot for a day
- ☐☐ Dress in a kilt
- ☐☐ Dress in another culture's traditional clothing
- ☐☐ Dress up as a bumblebee
- ☐☐ Dress up as a dinosaur
- ☐☐ Dress up as a disney character
- ☐☐ Dress up as a Star Wars character
- ☐☐ Dress up as Easter Bunny
- ☑☐ Dress up as Grim Reaper
- ☐☐ Dress up as knight in shining armour
- ☑☐ Dress up as Santa Claus
- ☑☐ Dress up for Halloween
- ☐☐ Jump out of a giant cake
- ☐☐ Dress up in a onesie
- ☐☐ Dress as a smurf
- ☐☐ Dress as an astronaut
- ☐☐ Dress as Mario
- ☐☐ Dress as Luigi
- ☐☐ Dress as Toad
- ☐☐ Dress as Donkey Kong
- ☐☐ Dress as Bowser
- ☐☐ Dress as Harry Potter
- ☐☐ Dress as Yoshi
- ☐☐ Dress as Wario
- ☐☐ Dress as Superman
- ☐☐ Dress as Batman
- ☐☐ Dress as a ninja
- ☐☐ Dress as the Joker
- ☐☐ Dress as Ninja Turtle
- ☐☐ Dress as Hulk
- ☐☐ Dress as Captain America
- ☐☐ Dress as Iron Man
- ☐☐ Dress as Cat in the Hat

- ☐☐ Dress as Koopa Troopa
- ☐☐ Dress as Wolverine
- ☐☐ Dress as Woody
- ☐☐ Dress as Buzz Lightyear
- ☐☐ Dress as Shrek
- ☐☐ Dress as the Incredibles
- ☐☐ Dress as Peter Pan
- ☐☐ Dress as Homer Simpson
- ☐☐ Dress as Captain Hook
- ☐☐ Dress as Where's Wally
- ☐☐ Dress as Mickey Mouse
- ☐☐ Dress as Donald Duck
- ☐☐ Dress as Goofy
- ☐☐ Dress as Aladdin
- ☐☐ Dress as Robin
- ☐☐ Dress as Gingerbread Man
- ☐☐ Dress as the Stig
- ☐☐ Dress as Oompa Loompa
- ☐☐ Dress as Freddy Krueger
- ☐☐ Dress as Scream
- ☐☐ Dress as a Pokemon
- ☐☐ Dress as Edward Scissorhands
- ☐☐ Dress as a ghost
- ☐☐ Dress as Chucky
- ☐☐ Dress as a clown
- ☐☐ Dress as an Avatar
- ☐☐ Dress as a werewolf
- ☐☐ Dress as Dracula
- ☐☐ Dress as a mummy
- ☐☐ Dress as a gremlin
- ☐☐ Dress as jigsaw
- ☐☐ Dress as Hellboy
- ☐☐ Dress as an alien
- ☐☐ Dress as Ghostbusters
- ☐☐ Dress as the Addams Family
- ☐☐ Dress as Hellraiser
- ☐☐ Dress as Frankenstein
- ☐☐ Dress as Beetlejuice
- ☐☐ Dress as Texas Chainsaw Massacre
- ☐☐ Dress as the Headless Horseman
- ☐☐ Dress as a pirate
- ☐☐ Dress as Jack the Ripper
- ☐☐ Dress as a Lego Man
- ☐☐ Dress as Tweety
- ☐☐ Dress as Bugs Bunny
- ☐☐ Dress as Daffy Duck
- ☐☐ Dress as Tasmanian devil
- ☐☐ Dress as Sylvester
- ☐☐ Dress as Marvin the Martian
- ☐☐ Dress as Porky Pig
- ☐☐ Dress as Elmer Fudd
- ☐☐ Dress as Yosemite Sam
- ☐☐ Dress as Pepé Le Pew
- ☐☐ Dress as Speedy Gonzales
- ☐☐ Dress as Popeye
- ☐☐ Dress in a monkey suit
- ☐☐ Dress as King Boo
- ☐☐ Dress as Waluigi
- ☐☐ Wrestle in a sumo suit

Chapter 54:
Driving Experiences

"Driving will never be away from me - I can't just give it up. It's all I've ever done, and there's something about being in that car."

Jimmie Johnson

A lot of us look forward to the day we get our learner licence, then enjoy the moment even more when we actually get our full licence and sense of freedom to go wherever we want to go without needing a person watching over our shoulders while we drive. Many of us find a model car and stay to the one-brand-type of car all our lives and never change to any other type model. However, my aim is to give every model a go and explore the advantages and disadvantages of every model car there is available. Why not give it a go? Sure, there may be tight fits in some cars, or cars that we totally regret we ever bought because they have been trouble since day one of buying them. But until we give them a go we never truly know the capability of any other model car than the ones we are already driving day to day.

- ☐☐ Drive a 4WD
- ☐☐ Drive a Bentley
- ☐☐ Drive a BMW
- ☐☐ Drive a Bugatti
- ☐☐ Drive a bull dozer
- ☐☐ Drive a Cadillac
- ☐☐ Drive a Caparo
- ☐☐ Drive a Caterham
- ☐☐ Drive a Chevrolet
- ☐☐ Drive a Chrysler
- ☐☐ Drive a Citroen
- ☐☐ Drive a classic car in Havana, Cuba
- ☐☐ Drive a Corvette
- ☐☐ Drive a Dacia
- ☐☐ Drive a Daihatsu
- ☐☐ Drive a Dodge
- ☐☐ Drive a Ferrari
- ☐☐ Drive a Fiat
- ☐☐ Drive a Fisker
- ☐☐ Drive a Ford
- ☑☐ Drive a forklift
- ☑☐ Drive a Holden
- ☐☐ Drive a Honda
- ☐☐ Drive a Hummer
- ☑☐ Drive a Hyundai
- ☐☐ Drive a Jaguar
- ☐☐ Drive a Jeep
- ☐☐ Drive a Kia
- ☐☐ Drive a Koenigsegg
- ☐☐ Drive a Landrover
- ☑☐ Drive a Lexus

- ☐☐ Drive a Lotus
- ☐☐ Drive a Maserati
- ☐☐ Drive a Maybach
- ☐☐ Drive a Mazda
- ☐☐ Drive a Mcclaren
- ☐☐ Drive a Mercedes Benz
- ☐☐ Drive an MG
- ☐☐ Drive a Mini
- ☑☐ Drive a Mini Bus
- ☑☐ Drive a Mitsubishi
- ☐☐ Drive a Morgan
- ☑☐ Drive a Nissan
- ☐☐ Drive a Noble
- ☐☐ Drive a Pagani
- ☐☐ Drive a Peugeot
- ☐☐ Drive a Porshe
- ☐☐ Drive a Proton
- ☐☐ Drive a Renault
- ☐☐ Drive a Rolls Royce
- ☐☐ Drive an RV
- ☑☐ Drive a Saab
- ☑☐ Drive a scissor lift
- ☐☐ Drive a Seat
- ☐☐ Drive a Skoda
- ☐☐ Drive a Smart Car
- ☐☐ Drive a Subaru
- ☐☐ Drive a Suzuki
- ☐☐ Drive a tank
- ☐☐ Drive a Tata
- ☑☐ Drive a Toyota
- ☑☐ Drive a tractor
- ☐☐ Drive a truck
- ☐☐ Drive a Vauxhall
- ☐☐ Drive a Volvo
- ☐☐ Drive a VW
- ☐☐ Drive an Abarth
- ☐☐ Drive an Alfa Romeo
- ☐☐ Drive an Aston Martin
- ☐☐ Drive an Audi
- ☐☐ Drive an Infiniti
- ☐☐ Drive an order picker (LO)
- ☑☐ Get car license
- ☐☐ Learn to drive stick (manual)
- ☑☐ Peg the speedometer
- ☑☐ Ride monorail
- ☑☐ Teach someone how to drive a car

Chapter 55: Visit the Seas and Oceans of the World

"Man cannot discover new oceans unless he has the courage to lose sight of the shore."

Andre Gide

My first introduction to the large oceans of the world was on a visit to Thuroul Beach which is near Wollongong, New South Wales, Australia. I wanted to follow my brothers and go further and further out into the ocean, but my parents had different ideas to keep me safe. I remember my brother was on a sandbank that collapsed and was saved by the life guards and a surf board, so I was taught to respect the oceans and their undertow pulling you in with a great deal of power. My first, of course, ocean I visited was the Pacific and my fascination grew with the large power it had. When I was nine years old, I went with my parents to Holland and caught the ferry across the North Sea from Hull to Rotterdam. I remember the Humber bringing in soily brown water into the harbour at Hull.

- ☐☐ See all five oceans
- ☐☐ See the Adriatic Sea
- ☐☐ See the Aegean Sea
- ☐☐ See the Aland Sea
- ☐☐ See the Amakusa Sea
- ☐☐ See the Amundsen Sea
- ☐☐ See the Andaman Sea
- ☐☐ See the Arabian Sea
- ☐☐ See the Arafura Sea
- ☐☐ See the Aral Sea
- ☐☐ See the Arctic Ocean
- ☐☐ See the Atlantic Ocean
- ☐☐ See the Balearic Sea
- ☐☐ See the Bali Sea
- ☐☐ See the Baltic Sea
- ☐☐ See the Banda Sea
- ☐☐ See the Barents Sea
- ☐☐ See the Beaufort Sea
- ☐☐ See the Bellighausen Sea
- ☐☐ See the Bering Sea
- ☐☐ See the Bismark Sea
- ☐☐ See the Black Sea
- ☐☐ See the Bohol Sea
- ☐☐ See the Bothian Sea
- ☐☐ See the Camotes Sea
- ☐☐ See the Caribbean Sea
- ☐☐ See the Caspian Sea
- ☐☐ See the Celebs Sea
- ☐☐ See the Celtic Sea
- ☐☐ See the Ceram Sea

- ☐☐ See the Chuckchi Sea
- ☐☐ See the Coral Sea
- ☐☐ See the Davis Sea
- ☐☐ See the Dead Sea
- ☐☐ See the East China Sea
- ☐☐ See the East Siberian Sea
- ☐☐ See the Flores Sea
- ☐☐ See the Greenland Sea
- ☐☐ See the Halmahera Sea
- ☐☐ See the Harima Sea
- ☐☐ See the Indian Ocean
- ☐☐ See the Inland Sea
- ☐☐ See the Ionian Sea
- ☐☐ See the Irish Sea
- ☐☐ See the Iyo Sea
- ☐☐ See the Japan Sea
- ☐☐ See the Java Sea
- ☐☐ See the Kara Sea
- ☐☐ See the Labrador Sea
- ☐☐ See the Laccidive Sea
- ☐☐ See the Laptev (Nordenskjold) Sea
- ☐☐ See the Ligurian Sea
- ☐☐ See the Lincoln Sea
- ☐☐ See the Mediterranean Sea
- ☐☐ See the Mindanao Sea
- ☐☐ See the Moluccas Sea
- ☑☐ See the North Sea
- ☐☐ See the Norwegian Sea
- ☐☐ See the Okhotsk Sea
- ☑☐ See the Pacific Ocean
- ☐☐ See the Philippine Sea
- ☐☐ See the Queen Victoria Sea
- ☐☐ See the Red Sea
- ☐☐ See the Ross Sea
- ☐☐ See the Sagami Sea
- ☐☐ See the Sargasso Sea
- ☐☐ See the Savu Sea
- ☐☐ See the Scotia Sea
- ☐☐ See the Sea of Azov
- ☐☐ See the Sea of Crete
- ☐☐ See the Sea of Galilee
- ☐☐ See the Sea of Marmara
- ☐☐ See the Sea of the Hebrides
- ☐☐ See the Seta Sea
- ☐☐ See the Sibuyan Sea
- ☐☐ See the Solomon Sea
- ☐☐ See the South China Sea
- ☐☐ See the Southern Ocean
- ☐☐ See the Sulu Sea
- ☐☐ See the Sunda Sea
- ☑☐ See the Tasman Sea
- ☐☐ See the Thracian Sea
- ☐☐ See the Timor Sea
- ☐☐ See the Tyrrhenian Sea
- ☐☐ See the Visayan Sea
- ☐☐ See the Wadden Sea
- ☐☐ See the Wandel or McKinley Sea
- ☐☐ See the Weddel Sea
- ☐☐ See the White Sea
- ☐☐ See the Yatsushiro Sea
- ☐☐ See the Yellow Sea
- ☐☐ The Koro Sea
- ☐☐ The Tranquil Sea, Algarve, Portugal

Chapter 56: Drink Tasting

"The point of drinking in moderation is that sometimes you don't drink in moderation."

Artie Lange

I have never been much of a drinker but it's a part of life for Aussies and many European countries to celebrate with a good drink, so I have had to at least taste the types of drinks. If I was to drink anything I think I would be a spirit drinker preferably, but I prefer the new lifestyle I live by only drinking water – a lot healthier and you don't make a fool of yourself in public places or anything. And above all your mates always need that designated driver to get them home, so I am always happy to get them home safe. It's just my own personal choice in life, but you need to give everything possible in life a go; you never know unless you try it at least.

- ☐☐ Brew my own beer
- ☐☐ Have a drink at a swim up bar
- ☑☐ Pop the cork off a champagne bottle
- ☑☐ Taste a beer
- ☑☐ Taste a bourbon
- ☑☐ Taste a cocktail
- ☑☐ Taste a spirit
- ☑☐ Taste a wine
- ☐☐ Visit the Guinness Brewery

Chapter 57: Markets and Gardens

"Always do your best. What you plant now, you will harvest later."

Og Mandino

Markets offer an extensive range of produce, new and second-hand merchandise. There are both outdoor and covered markets with a range of products from design clothing to toys or even plants and gardening products. We go there to get fresh sea food or fruit and vegetables; there is plenty on offer from our local markets. Also down the road from the well-known Paddy's Markets near Chinatown in Sydney, is the beautiful Chinese Gardens: majestic and wonderfully irresistible rippling waterfalls and plantations thoughout. Architectural towers are throughout the place also, and you are offered the chance to dress in traditional culture clothing if you so wish. Experience the blissful relaxation of walking through the gardens; I'm sure you won't regret it.

- ☐☐ Adelaide Botanic Garden
- ☐☐ Arashiyama Bamboo Grove, Kyoto, Japan
- ☐☐ Berowra Majestic Gardens
- ☐☐ Blackheath Rhododendron Gardens
- ☐☐ Bomarzo: Grove of the Monsters
- ☐☐ Bondi Beach Market
- ☐☐ Bonsai Exotique
- ☐☐ Bundeena Markets by the Sea
- ☐☐ Bush Gardens, Florida, USA
- ☐☐ Butchart Gardens at night, Canada
- ☐☐ Chinatown Night Market, Sydney
- ☑☐ Chinese Gardens
- ☐☐ Crystal Castle and Shambhala Gardens, Byron Bay
- ☐☐ Designer Fashion Markets, Sydney
- ☐☐ Epping Markets, Sydney
- ☐☐ Eveleigh Artisans' Arts & Crafts Market, Sydney
- ☐☐ Eveleigh Farmers' Market, Sydney
- ☐☐ Explore Istanbul's Grand Bazaar
- ☑☐ Fitzroy Gardens
- ☑☐ Flemington Markets
- ☐☐ Floating Market
- ☐☐ Garden of the Sleeping Giant
- ☐☐ Grow a bonsai tree
- ☐☐ Grow a flower from seed to full bloom

- ☐☐ Grow a vegetable garden
- ☑☐ Haggle at an open market
- ☑☐ Herb garden
- ☐☐ Heritage Craft Fair, St. Ives, Sydney
- ☑☐ Hong Kong Bank Oriental Garden
- ☐☐ Jardim Botânico, Curitiba, Paraná, Brazil
- ☐☐ Kawachi Fuji Garden Wisteria Tunnel
- ☐☐ Keukenhof Gardens
- ☐☐ Kings Cross Sunday Market, Sydney
- ☐☐ Kirribilli General, Art & Design & Fashion Markets, Sydney
- ☐☐ Learn zen gardening
- ☑☐ Look inside Monty's Tree in the Blue Mountains
- ☐☐ Lost Gardens of Heligan, England
- ☐☐ Madison Square Gardens, NY
- ☐☐ Mayfield Gardens
- ☐☐ Mosman Village Art & Craft Market, Sydney
- ☐☐ Mount Annan Botanical Gardens
- ☐☐ Mount Tomah Botanical Gardens
- ☑☐ North Sydney Market, Sydney
- ☐☐ Northside Produce Market, Sydney
- ☑☐ Paddington Markets
- ☑☐ Parklea Markets
- ☐☐ Participate in the New South Wales Royal Agricultural Society Easter Show - biggest agricultural show in the southern hemisphere. I compete in flower & garden
- ☑☐ Plant a tree
- ☐☐ Plantasia
- ☑☐ Queen Victoria Markets
- ☐☐ Rio de Janeiro Botanical Garden
- ☑☐ Royal Botanic Gardens, Sydney, Australia
- ☑☐ Royal Botanic Gardens, Melbourne, Australia
- ☐☐ See the Eden Project, Cornwell, United Kingdom
- ☐☐ See the tulip farms, Netherlands
- ☐☐ Spice market in Cairo, Egypt
- ☐☐ Start a compost bin
- ☐☐ Stepping stones in Tenju-An Gardens, Northern Higashiyama, Kyoto, Japan
- ☐☐ Sunflower Valley, Valencia, Spain
- ☐☐ Sunken Alcove Garden in New Zealand
- ☐☐ Sydney Fish Markets
- ☐☐ Tea garden near Mt. Fuji in Japan
- ☐☐ The amazing fairytale flower tunnel. The Kawachi Fuji Gardens, Japan
- ☐☐ The Dazzling Boutique Markets
- ☐☐ The Good Living Growers' Market, Sydney
- ☑☐ The Rocks Markets
- ☐☐ The Storybook Garden, Hunter Valley Gardens
- ☐☐ Thurston Gardens
- ☐☐ Tivoli Gardens
- ☑☐ Treasury Gardens
- ☐☐ Tulip Sunset, Skagit, Washington
- ☐☐ Visit a pumpkin patch
- ☐☐ Visit the Bangkok Train Markets

- ☐☐ William Ricketts Sanctuary in Mount Dandenong, Australia
- ☐☐ Windy Ridge Gardens, Mt Wilson
- ☐☐ Wollongong Botanic Garden
- ☐☐ Woodstock Gardens, Kilkenny, Ireland
- ☐☐ Zappeion, Gardens, Athens, Greece

- ☐☐ Spend a night at the Shangri-La
- ☐☐ Spend a night at the Sheraton
- ☐☐ Spend a night at the Sofitel
- ☐☐ Spend a night at the Travelodge
- ☐☐ Spend a night at the Vibe
- ☐☐ Spend a night at the Waldorf
- ☑☐ Spend a night in hotel in Canberra CBD
- ☑☐ Spend a night in hotel in Melbourne CBD
- ☐☐ Spend a night in hotel in Northern Territory CBD
- ☐☐ Spend a night in hotel in Queensland CBD
- ☐☐ Spend a night in hotel in South Australia CBD
- ☐☐ Spend a night in hotel in Sydney CBD
- ☐☐ Spend a night in hotel in Tasmania CBD
- ☐☐ Spend a night in hotel in Western Australia CBD
- ☐☐ Spend Christmas in another country
- ☐☐ Spend Christmas in New York
- ☑☐ Spend romantic night in a hotel
- ☐☐ Spend some time with an African tribe
- ☐☐ Spend summer solstice at Stone Henge
- ☐☐ Spend the night in the presidential suite anywhere in the world
- ☑☐ Spend weekend away Blue Mountains
- ☐☐ Stay a night at Wadigi Island, Fiji Resort
- ☐☐ Stay at a Ryokan "Traditional Japanese Inn"
- ☐☐ Stay at an ice hotel
- ☐☐ Stay in a five-star hotel
- ☐☐ Stay in a seven-star hotel
- ☐☐ Stay in a treehouse at an Eco-Resort
- ☐☐ Swim Resort in Bali, Indonesia
- ☐☐ The Grand Canyon Caverns, Cavern Motel Room "World's Deepest Hotel Room"
- ☐☐ The Grotto Spa at Tigh-Na-Mara Seaside Spa Resort, Western Canada
- ☐☐ The Mirrorcube
- ☐☐ The Poseidon Resort in Fiji. You can sleep on the ocean floor
- ☐☐ The Springs Resort, Costa Rica
- ☐☐ The Westin Maui Resort Spa, Hawaii
- ☐☐ Tianzi Hotel
- ☐☐ Watch the stars while you sleep. Hotel Kakslauttanen, Finland
- ☐☐ Westin Maui Resort & Spa, Kaanapali Beach, Hawaii

Chapter 59: Castles, Palaces, Towers, Ancient Ruins and Abbeys

"Even Castles made of sand, fall into the sea, eventually."

Jimi Hendrix

The excitement of walking through old castles, ancient ruins, abbeys and palaces has always fascinated a lot of us. Being able to go back in time and experience how life was back in the medieval era – the beauty of the great halls, stonework and beautiful surrounding landscapes throughout the castles – there is much to explore and be fascinated with. I was lucky enough to have such a wonderful experience while visiting Scotland with my fiancée. We slept in two castles and experienced walking through at least another eight others with a unique haunted ghost self-drive tour. It was an experience I will forever remember. Castles are generally more so found throughout European countries of origin.

One of the most memorable towers I experienced was climbing to the top of William Wallace Monument Tower in Scotland. It has over 246 spiral steps and a breathtaking view of Scotland at the top of the tower and great story of history within the building. I was lucky to see the famous Great Sword used by William Wallace and learn the history behind his death itself.

- ☐☐ "Star" castle in the Netherlands
- ☑☐ 102-year-old abandoned ship is now a floating forest in Home Bush Bay Sydney, Australia
- ☐☐ Achilleion - palace
- ☐☐ Agora Tower, Taiwan
- ☑☐ Airth Castle
- ☐☐ Alhambra - palace
- ☐☐ Amalienborg - palace
- ☐☐ Ananta Samakhom Throne Hall
- ☐☐ Ancient keyhole door, Turkey
- ☐☐ Arizona: Ride to Ancient Ruins
- ☑☐ Armadale Castle Isle of Skye Scotland
- ☐☐ Baalbek in Lebanon
- ☐☐ Bahai World Center, Haifa, Israel
- ☐☐ Bantur, Indonesia
- ☐☐ Barrack Tower Botany Bay
- ☐☐ Basilica Cistern in Istanbul

- ☐☐ Biggest clock tower: Abraj Al-Bait Clock Tower, Mecca, Saudi Arabia
- ☐☐ Blarney Castle, Ireland
- ☐☐ Boldogkovaralja Castle, Hungary
- ☐☐ Borreby Castle
- ☑☐ Buckingham Palace
- ☐☐ Bunratty Castle, Ireland
- ☐☐ Burg Eltz Castle. One of the most beautiful and best preserved castles in Münstermaifeld, Germany
- ☐☐ Burj Khalifa, Dubai
- ☐☐ Caerphilly Castle
- ☐☐ Cairo Tower
- ☐☐ Capital Gate, Abu Dhabi
- ☐☐ Cardiff Castle
- ☐☐ Castle Coch
- ☐☐ Castle in Kylemore, Ireland
- ☐☐ Castle Keukenhof
- ☐☐ Castle Sant'Angelo
- ☐☐ Catherine Palace, outside St. Petersburg, Russia
- ☑☐ Cawdor Castle
- ☐☐ Château De Chillon, Switzerland
- ☐☐ Chichen Itza, Mexico
- ☐☐ Christian VIII's palace
- ☐☐ Clock Tower
- ☐☐ CN Tower
- ☐☐ Cobá, Quintana Roo, Mexico
- ☐☐ Colossi of Memnon
- ☐☐ Colossus of Rhodes
- ☐☐ Crystal Castle, Byron Bay
- ☐☐ Davinci rotating tower, Dubai
- ☐☐ Devils Tower, Wyoming, USA
- ☐☐ Dezhou, China: Energy Grid
- ☐☐ Domus Aurea
- ☐☐ Dracula's Castle, Transylvania, Romania
- ☐☐ Dublin Castle, Ireland
- ☐☐ Dunluce and Slane Castles
- ☑☐ Dunrobbin Castle
- ☑☐ Dunvegan Castle, Isle of Skye
- ☐☐ Edifício Copan, tower
- ☐☐ Edifício Itália, tower
- ☑☐ Edinburgh Castle
- ☐☐ Efes (Ephesus), Turkey - ruins
- ☑☐ Eiffel Tower
- ☑☐ Eilean Castle, Highlands, Scotland
- ☐☐ El Escorial
- ☐☐ Elephant Tower
- ☐☐ Ephesus Ruins, Turkey
- ☑☐ Eureka Sky deck and the edge
- ☐☐ Fernsehturm, Berlin
- ☐☐ Fonmon Castle
- ☐☐ Fountainebleau Chateau, Paris, France
- ☐☐ Frederiksborg Castle in Hillerød, Denmark
- ☐☐ Freedom Tower, NYC
- ☐☐ Galata Tower, Istanbul
- ☐☐ Gaochang, Xinjiang, China
- ☐☐ Gate to the sea, Tintagel, UK
- ☑☐ Glamis Castle
- ☐☐ Grand Palace & Wat Prakeaw
- ☐☐ Heidelberg Castle. The epitome of German Romanticism
- ☐☐ Herculaneum, Italy
- ☐☐ Hierapolis, Turkey
- ☐☐ Himeji Castle, Japan
- ☐☐ Hunyad castle, Transylvania, Romania
- ☐☐ Iran - Persepolis
- ☐☐ Italy - Pompeii and Herculaneum
- ☐☐ Jin Mao Tower, Shanghai
- ☐☐ Jubiläumswarte Lookout Tower, Vienna
- ☐☐ Karnak

- ☐☐ Kensington Palace
- ☐☐ Kerameikos
- ☐☐ King of Light Mauseleum, Shiraz, Iran
- ☐☐ Kissing the Blarney Stone, Blarney Castle, Ireland
- ☐☐ Knossos, Crete, Greece
- ☐☐ Kronborg Castle
- ☐☐ Kruja Castle, Albania
- ☐☐ Kylemore Abbey
- ☑☐ Leeds Castle
- ☑☐ Linlithgow Palace
- ☐☐ Look At Leptis Magna, Libya
- ☐☐ Luxor Temple
- ☐☐ Mad King Ludwig's Linderhof Castle
- ☐☐ Maheno Wreck
- ☐☐ Malahide Castle, Ireland
- ☐☐ Malkata
- ☐☐ Manhattan Skyline, New York
- ☐☐ Margam Country Park
- ☐☐ Mexico - Palenque
- ☐☐ Montezuma Castle National Monument, Arizona
- ☐☐ Morocco - Hassan Tower
- ☐☐ Myra (Demre), Antalya, Turkey
- ☐☐ Neo-gothic castle - Black Sea - Ukraine
- ☐☐ Neolithic Site of Çatalhöyük, Turkey
- ☐☐ Neuschwanstein Castle - Germany's fairytale castle
- ☐☐ Odeon of Herodes Atticus
- ☐☐ Old Summer Palace, China
- ☐☐ Orbit Tower, London
- ☐☐ Osaka Castle, Japan
- ☑☐ Palace of Holyrood
- ☐☐ Palace of Iturbide
- ☑☐ Palace of Versailles
- ☐☐ Palácio do Planalto
- ☐☐ Palais Des Nations
- ☐☐ Palatu Parlamentului, Romania
- ☐☐ Palm Island, Dubai City, Dubai - take a photograph from the sky at awesome shape of Dubai
- ☐☐ Pergamum (Bergama), Izmir, Turkey
- ☐☐ Perge (Perga), Antalya, Turkey
- ☐☐ Place a love lock at the bell tower, Perth, WA
- ☐☐ Potala Palace, Lhasa
- ☐☐ Qutub Minar - tallest brick minaret in the world standing 239 ft. - Delhi, India
- ☐☐ Ramesseum Temple, Egypt
- ☐☐ Rapunzel's Tower, Wales
- ☐☐ Reflecting pool, Hearst Castle, California
- ☐☐ Residenz Munchen (Munich Palace), Germany
- ☐☐ Roman Baths, Bath, England
- ☐☐ Roman Forum
- ☐☐ Royal Copenhagen
- ☐☐ Royal Palace, Amsterdam
- ☐☐ Royal Palace, Norway
- ☐☐ Royal Palace of Madrid
- ☐☐ Ruins of Amphitheatre, Cartagena, Murcia, Spain
- ☐☐ Ruins on Mount Nemrut, Turkey, burial site of kings, date from the first century B.C

- ☐☐ Sacsayhuamán
- ☐☐ Sears Tower, Chicago
- ☑☐ See Rivaelx Abbey, Yorkshire, England
- ☐☐ See the Empire State Building, New York
- ☐☐ See the Petronas Towers, Kuala Lumpur, Malaysia
- ☐☐ See Windsor Castle
- ☐☐ Shanghai World Financial Building
- ☐☐ Slane Castle, Ireland
- ☑☐ Sleep in a castle
- ☑☐ Stirling Castle
- ☐☐ Stoa of Attalos
- ☐☐ Taichung, Taiwan: Floating Observatories
- ☐☐ Tambo Colorado
- ☐☐ Taos Pueblo, Taos, NM
- ☐☐ Tapei 101, Taiwan
- ☐☐ Teotihuacán, Mexico
- ☐☐ The Alhambra in Granada, Spain
- ☐☐ The Ancient City
- ☑☐ The Big Dig Archaeological Dig Site, Rocks, Sydney
- ☐☐ The Great Lighthouse at Alexandria Ruins
- ☐☐ The Hanging Gardens of Babylon
- ☑☐ The Pineapple House, Scotland
- ☐☐ The Royal Palace, Wat Phra Kaew, Thailand
- ☐☐ The Skybridge at Petronas Towers, Kuala Lumpur, Malaysia
- ☐☐ The Statue of Zeus at Olympia
- ☐☐ The Tower of Babel
- ☐☐ Theatre of Dionysus
- ☐☐ Thracian Ruins, Bulgaria
- ☐☐ Tikal Ruins, Guatemala
- ☐☐ Tokyo Tower, Japan
- ☐☐ Torre Jaume I, Barcelona
- ☑☐ Tower of London
- ☐☐ Trango Towers, Pakistan
- ☐☐ Transparent Balcony on 103 floor skyscraper, the Sears Tower in Chicago
- ☐☐ Tsarevets Fortress, Bulgaria
- ☐☐ Tsurugaoka Hachimangu Shrine, Kanagawa Prefecture, Japan
- ☑☐ Tullock Castle
- ☐☐ Tulum, Yucatán, Mexico
- ☐☐ Two International Finance Centre, Hong Kong
- ☐☐ Under Water Stonehenge, Lake Michigan
- ☐☐ Underground Castle Ruins
- ☑☐ Urquhart Castle
- ☐☐ Uzbekistan - The Ark Fortress
- ☐☐ Valley of the Kings
- ☐☐ Vienna Donauturm, Vienna
- ☐☐ Vijayanagar Ruins, India
- ☐☐ Virgin Islands, Blackbeard's Castle
- ☑☐ Visit a castle in Scotland
- ☐☐ Visit Castle at the Fall, Canada
- ☐☐ Visit Skara Brae, a Neolithic settlement located on the Orkney mainland, Scotland
- ☐☐ Visit the Ancient Callanish Stones, Scotland
- ☐☐ Visit the ancient city of Troy, Istanbul, Turkey
- ☐☐ Visit the Bell Tower Perth, WA
- ☐☐ Visit the Oracle at Delphi Archaeological Site
- ☐☐ Visit the Topkapi Palace, Istanbul

- ☐☐ Wales Millennium Centre
- ☑☐ Westminster Abbey
- ☐☐ White Tower of Thessaloniki

Chapter 60: Scenic Tours

"The scenic ideals that surround even our national parks are carriers of a nostalgia for heavenly bliss and eternal calmness."

Robert Smithson

Going on scenic tours is a great and interesting way to meet new people and see new places – exploring the world in a different light rather than doing something alone all the time. It's good to see how other people relate and enjoy the moment, and to have other people's opinions on what they see. Every person will see a situation differently. We all enjoy a tour to explore the world and learn new things, and see places others don't normally see. Scenic tours are the ultimate in luxury touring. Explore exciting and exotic destinations worldwide and enjoy.

- ☐☐ Artesian Country Tours, multiple locations
- ☐☐ Bondi Aboriginal Rock Engravings Tour
- ☑☐ Cruise and Illuminations Tour
- ☐☐ Go on a scenic tour
- ☐☐ Go on backstage tour
- ☐☐ Highway to Hell, Freemantle, WA - AC/DC Tour, Sunday
- ☐☐ Melbourne Crime Tour
- ☐☐ Nura Diya Guided Tours
- ☐☐ Rangito Volcatic Explorer Tour
- ☐☐ Sydney Bike Tours
- ☐☐ Sydney Crime & Passions Walking Tour King Cross
- ☐☐ Sydney Hospital - Guided Historical Private Tours
- ☐☐ Sydney Opera House Guided Tour
- ☐☐ Sydney Quarantine Station Tours
- ☑☐ Tour a lighthouse
- ☐☐ Tour Montparnasse, Paris
- ☐☐ Tour the castle ruins at Paronella Park
- ☐☐ Tour the Titanic wreckage at the bottom of the Atlantic
- ☐☐ Tour the White House, Washington, D.C.
- ☐☐ Underground tour of Sydney
- ☐☐ Zip line with Zip Trek Eco Tours, Whistler, Canada, through a snow-covered rainforest

Chapter 61: Spiritual Guidance

"Just as a candle cannot burn without fire, men cannot live without a spiritual life."

Buddha

Sometimes in our lives we all struggle to look to where we want to go and where we are headed. We get stuck in a rut and don't know where to turn. We try to change, but without guidance we struggle on our own. Some of us get spiritual guidance from the other side, whether it be a palm read, a talk with a clairvoyant or a belief in God. To light our future, we as human beings turn to others for guidance in our own life. Not sure how to react in every situation in life, we turn to those who know and have been there before us. We seek advice on how to deal with the situation with which we are having problems – whether it be relationship difficulties, money issues or weight problems. There are people out there that help us realise we are not alone and that many people go through the same problems as us. It's how we deal with the problems that will make us stronger people and able to handle the situations.

- ☐☐ Have a clairvoyant flower reading
- ☐☐ Have a crystal ball reading by an authentic gypsy
- ☑☐ Have a palm reading
- ☐☐ Have a reading of tea leaves, "tasseomancy"
- ☑☐ Learn to read tarot cards
- ☑☐ Spiritual reading with clairvoyance
- ☑☐ Use a Ouija board

Chapter 62: Churches, Cemeteries, Cathedrals, Tombs, Temples and Ghost Tours

"Infuse your life with action. Don't wait for it to happen. Make it happen. Make your own future. Make your own hope. Make your own love. And whatever your beliefs, honor your creator, not by passively waiting for grace to come down from upon high, but by doing what you can to make grace happen . . . yourself, right now, right down here on Earth."

Bradley Whitford

We all go to a church at least once in our lifetime whether it be a wedding, a weekend commitment to God or, worst-case scenario, someone passes away. We go there to pray, to sing and to worship. Cathedrals and temples are also other forms of places we go to worship and pay our respects. It doesn't matter who we are, we are bound to visit cemeteries when a family member or loved one passes over. We go there to pay our respects and place flowers and other things that have meant something to them throughout their lifetime – like small toys or gift items to resemble things that have meant the world to them in their lives. The rest of us that believe in spirits and the afterlife seek ways to acknowledge people that have passed by. We go on an exploration and learn about how people passed and listen to things moving in rooms or ghostly images in windows or dark streets or even throughout cemeteries. We do that by learning the skills of a Spirit Investigator or joining in groups of ghost tours.

- ☐☐ A place in China called Crescent Moon Lake. It's a body of water surrounded by a desert and a temple
- ☐☐ Abu Simbel Temples, Egypt
- ☐☐ Agra Fort, Agra, India
- ☐☐ Arch and Tomb of Galerius
- ☐☐ Archbasilica of St. John Lateran
- ☐☐ Assistens Graveyard
- ☐☐ Babylon Fortress
- ☐☐ Bagan Temples
- ☐☐ Basílica Del Voto Nacional
- ☐☐ Basilica di Santa Maria Maggiore

- ☐☐ Beechworth Ghost Tours
- ☐☐ Biggest church: The Basilica of Our Lady of Peace, Yamoussoukro, Ivory Coast
- ☐☐ Blue Mountains Mystery Tours
- ☐☐ Borgund Church, Norway
- ☐☐ Borobudur, Indonesia
- ☐☐ Canadian Tomb of the Unknown Solider
- ☐☐ Capilla Obispo
- ☑☐ Catacombs of Paris
- ☐☐ Central Station: Ghost Platforms & Tunnels
- ☐☐ Cologne Cathedral
- ☐☐ Cowra Ghost Tours
- ☐☐ Deir el-Bahari
- ☐☐ Dendera Temple complex
- ☐☐ Destiny Tours
- ☐☐ Enter the Forbidden City, Beijing, China
- ☐☐ Enter the Lunatic Asylum, Ghost Tour, Ararat
- ☐☐ Forgotten Temple of Lysistrata, Greece
- ☐☐ Galata, Istanbul, Blue Mosque
- ☐☐ Ganesha Shrine
- ☐☐ Ghost Platforms & Subterranean Sydney
- ☐☐ Gladesville Mental Hospital
- ☐☐ Gledswood Homestead Lantern Light Ghost Tour
- ☑☐ Go on ghost tour
- ☐☐ Go trick or treating
- ☐☐ Golden Temple
- ☐☐ Gore Hill Memorial Cemetery
- ☐☐ Gore Hill Memorial Cemetery Ghost Tour
- ☐☐ Great Synagogue, Sydney
- ☐☐ Hagia Sophia, Turkey
- ☐☐ Hallgrimskirkja, Reykjavík, Iceland
- ☐☐ Haunted Fremantle Prison
- ☑☐ Haunted Ghost Castle Tour
- ☐☐ Haunting Hawkesbury Tour
- ☐☐ Hyde Park Barracks Ghost Tour
- ☐☐ Jenolan Caves Ghost Tours
- ☐☐ Kiyomizu-dera, Japan
- ☐☐ Kotoku-in, Japan
- ☐☐ La Perouse Jail Ghost Tours
- ☐☐ Lama Temple
- ☐☐ Lantern Ghost Tours
- ☐☐ Lindholm Hoje Viking Cemetery
- ☐☐ Llandaff Cathedral
- ☐☐ Lotus Temple
- ☐☐ Macquarie Park Cemetery
- ☐☐ Macquarie Park Cemetery & Crematorium Tour
- ☐☐ Maitland Gaol
- ☐☐ Meiji - jingo, a Shinto shrine dedicated to Emperor Meiji and Empress Shoken
- ☐☐ Meteora
- ☐☐ Mill Hill Hotel in Bondi Junction
- ☐☐ Ming Tomb
- ☐☐ Mont Saint-Michel, France
- ☐☐ Monte Cristo, Australia's Most Haunted House
- ☐☐ Morelia Cathedral
- ☐☐ Morpeth Ghost and History Tour
- ☐☐ Mosque of Muhammad Ali
- ☑☐ Nan Tien Temple
- ☐☐ New Cathedral of Cuenca
- ☐☐ Norweign Church
- ☑☐ Notre Dame Cathedral, Paris
- ☐☐ Old Government House Ghost Tour
- ☐☐ Pantheon Italy
- ☑☐ Pantheon Paris
- ☐☐ Paro Taktsang Monastery, Bhutan

- ☐☐ Parramatta Orphanage
- ☐☐ Parramatta's Sinister Side Tour
- ☐☐ Past Time Tours
- ☐☐ Picton, Ghost Bridge
- ☐☐ Picton Cemetary Ghost Tour
- ☐☐ Picton Cemetery
- ☐☐ Picton Ghost Hunts Tour
- ☐☐ Po Lin Monastery and Tian Tan Buddha, Hong Kong
- ☐☐ Prince Henry Hospital, Sydney
- ☐☐ Quarantine Station Ghost Tour
- ☐☐ Real Mary Kings Close
- ☐☐ Ribe Cathedral
- ☐☐ Richmond Gaol
- ☐☐ Rolling Hills Asylum, East Bethany, NY, Ghost Tour
- ☐☐ Rookwood Cemetery, Sydney
- ☐☐ Sagrada Familia, Barcelona, Spain
- ☐☐ Saint Basil's Cathedral, Russia
- ☐☐ Saint Catherine's Monastery
- ☐☐ Santa Teresa
- ☐☐ Schönbrunn Palace, Vienna, Austria
- ☑☐ See Canterbury Cathedral
- ☐☐ See the real Amityville house
- ☐☐ See Tutankhamun's Tomb, Valley of the Kings
- ☐☐ Shanghai Jade Buddha Temple
- ☐☐ Shwedagon Pagoda, Myanmar
- ☑☐ Sir Henry Parkes, former Premier of NSW, grave site
- ☑☐ South Head General Cemetery
- ☐☐ Spend a night in a haunted house
- ☐☐ Spend a night in a haunted mansion
- ☐☐ Spooky Sydney by Night, the Ghost Bus Tour
- ☐☐ St. Andrews Cathedral
- ☐☐ St. Bartholomew Church & Cemetery Ghost Tour
- ☐☐ St. Bartholomew church and cemetery
- ☑☐ St. James Church
- ☑☐ St. Mary's Cathedral
- ☑☐ St. Paul's Cathedral
- ☐☐ St. Peter's Basilica, the Vatican, and Rome
- ☐☐ Studley Park
- ☐☐ Sze Yup Temple
- ☐☐ Ta Prohm temple, Cambodia
- ☐☐ Take a midnight stroll through a grave yard
- ☐☐ Temple of Edfu
- ☐☐ Temple of Hephaestus
- ☐☐ Temple of Hera, Olympia
- ☐☐ Temple of Kom Ombo
- ☐☐ Temple of Olympian Zeus, Athens
- ☐☐ Temples & Gardens, Kyoto, Japan
- ☐☐ Temples of Bagan, Myanmar
- ☐☐ The Alamo, San Antonio, Texas
- ☐☐ The Arms of Australian Inn Ghost Tour
- ☑☐ The Baha'i Temple
- ☐☐ The Baptistery of the Cathedral of Pisa, Pisa, Italy
- ☐☐ The Basilica di San Marco, Venice
- ☐☐ The Doric Temple of Aphaia (500BC), Aegina island, Greece*
- ☐☐ The Forgotten Temple of Lysistrata
- ☐☐ The Ggantija Temples on Gozo, Malta. These structures date back to 3500 to 2500 BC
- ☐☐ The Mausoleum at Halicarnassus

- ☐☐ The Mezquita in Cordoba, Spain
- ☐☐ The Mysterious Wat Samphran Temple, Thailand "Dragon Design Looks Awesome"
- ☐☐ The Red Fort
- ☑☐ The Rocks Ghost Tours
- ☐☐ The Temple of Artemis at Ephesus
- ☐☐ The Tiger's Nest is a prominent Himalayan Buddhist sacred site and temple complex, located in the Cliffside of the upper Paro Valley, Bhutan
- ☐☐ Theban Necropolis
- ☐☐ Tomb of Kings, Paphos, Cyprus
- ☐☐ Twilight Monastery, Meteora Greece
- ☐☐ Ulun Danu Temple, Bali
- ☐☐ Valle dei Templi, Agrigento, Sicily
- ☐☐ Visit Salem, Massachusetts
- ☐☐ Visovac Island with Franciscan monastery, Croatia
- ☐☐ Visovats Monastery, Croatia
- ☐☐ Walhalla Ghost Tour
- ☐☐ Wat Arun, The Temple of Dawn
- ☐☐ Wat Rong Khun, Chiang Rai, Thailand
- ☐☐ Waverly Cemetery
- ☐☐ Weird Campbelltown Ghost and History Tour
- ☐☐ Weird Parramatta Ghost and History Tour
- ☐☐ Weird Sydney Ghost and History Tour
- ☐☐ Whispering Bones Tour
- ☐☐ Windsor Cemetery
- ☐☐ Windsor Cemetery ghost tour

Chapter 63: Movies List

"Movies can and do have tremendous influence in shaping young lives in the realm of entertainment towards the ideals and objectives of normal adulthood."

Walt Disney

Movies are a great way to relax after a long stressful day at work, or even going to the movie cinema just to watch a movie with family or friends. There are millions of different movies out there. A few things I really want to say I have done in my life is watch every Disney movie, the inner kid in me, and watch every movie by my favourite actor, Adam Sandler, as well as every horror movie ever made. There is something about horror movies that make you interested and leave you wanting more. We all know when something is about to happen in a horror movie because the music changes and builds suspense for the viewer, but we can't help but crave the thrill of a horror movie and see if it scares us. There is always one person that gets scared and screams throughout a horror movie, but as humans it's a natural instinct that's inside us. We are born to be scared of at least one thing in our lives; no one is invincible even if sometimes some of us think we are.

- ☑☐ 101 Dalmatian's II: Patch's London Adventure
- ☑☐ 101 Dalmatians
- ☑☐ 101 Dalmatians, animated
- ☐☐ 102 Dalmatians
- ☐☐ 20,000 Leagues under the Sea
- ☐☐ 20,000 Leagues under the Sea: Captain Nemo
- ☐☐ A Tiger Walks
- ☐☐ The Adventures of Bullwhip Griffin
- ☐☐ The Adventures of Huck Finn
- ☐☐ Air Bud
- ☐☐ Air Bud 3: World Pup
- ☐☐ Air Bud Spikes Back
- ☐☐ Air Bud: Golden Receiver
- ☐☐ Air Bud: Seventh Inning Fetch
- ☐☐ Air Buddies
- ☑☐ Aladdin
- ☑☐ Aladdin: The Return of Jafar
- ☑☐ Aladdin and the King of Thieves
- ☐☐ Alexander and the Terrible, Horrible, No Good, Very Bad Day
- ☑☐ Alice in Wonderland
- ☑☐ Alice in Wonderland, movie version

- ☐☐ Alley Cats Strike
- ☐☐ Almost Angels
- ☐☐ Amy
- ☐☐ Angels in the Endzone
- ☐☐ Angels in the Infield
- ☐☐ Angels in the Outfield
- ☑☐ Annie
- ☐☐ Apple Dumpling Gang Rides Again
- ☐☐ The Apple Dumpling Gang
- ☐☐ Around the World in 80 Days
- ☐☐ Atlantis: Milo's Return
- ☐☐ Atlantis: The Lost Empire
- ☐☐ Avalon High
- ☐☐ Babes in Toyland
- ☑☐ Balloon Farm
- ☑☐ Bambi
- ☑☐ Bambi II
- ☐☐ The Barefoot Executive
- ☐☐ Basil - The Great Mouse Detective
- ☐☐ The Bears and I
- ☑☐ Beauty and the Beast
- ☐☐ Beauty and the Beast: The Enchanted Christmas
- ☑☐ Bedknobs and Broomsticks
- ☐☐ Benji the Hunted
- ☑☐ Beverly Hills Chihuahua
- ☑☐ Beverly Hills Chihuahua 2
- ☑☐ Beverly Hills Chihuahua 3: Viva La Fiesta!
- ☐☐ The Big Green
- ☐☐ Big Hero 6
- ☐☐ Big Red
- ☐☐ The Biscuit Eater
- ☑☐ The Black Cauldron
- ☐☐ The Black Hole
- ☐☐ Blackbeard's Ghost
- ☐☐ Blank Check
- ☐☐ The Boatniks
- ☑☐ Bolt
- ☐☐ Bon Voyage!
- ☐☐ The Boy Who Talked to Badgers
- ☑☐ Brave
- ☐☐ The Brave Little Toaster
- ☐☐ Bridge to Terabithia
- ☐☐ Brink!
- ☑☐ Brother Bear
- ☑☐ Brother Bear 2
- ☐☐ Buffalo Dreams
- ☑☐ A Bugs Life
- ☐☐ Cadet Kelly
- ☐☐ Camp Rock
- ☐☐ Camp Rock 2: The Final Jam
- ☐☐ Can of Worms
- ☐☐ Candleshoe
- ☑☐ Cars
- ☑☐ Cars 2
- ☐☐ Castaway Cowboy
- ☐☐ The Cat from Outer Space
- ☐☐ Chandar, the Black Leopard of Ceylon
- ☐☐ Charley and the Angel
- ☐☐ Charlie, the Lonesome Cougar
- ☐☐ Cheetah
- ☐☐ The Cheetah Girls
- ☐☐ The Cheetah Girls 2
- ☐☐ The Cheetah Girls: One World 2008
- ☑☐ Chicken Little
- ☐☐ A Christmas Carol
- ☑☐ Chronicles of Narnia: Prince Caspian
- ☑☐ Chronicles of Narnia: The Lion, Witch and the Wardrobe
- ☑☐ Cinderella
- ☐☐ Cinderella, the movie version
- ☑☐ Cinderella II: Dreams Come True
- ☑☐ Cinderella III: A Twist in Time
- ☐☐ College Road Trip

- ☐☐ The Color of Friendship
- ☐☐ The Computer Wore Tennis Shoes
- ☐☐ Condorman
- ☐☐ Confessions of a Teenage Drama Queen
- ☑☐ Cool Runnings
- ☑☐ The Country Bears
- ☐☐ Cow Belles
- ☑☐ D2: The Mighty Ducks
- ☑☐ D3: The Mighty Ducks
- ☐☐ Dad Napped
- ☐☐ Darby O'Gill and the Little People
- ☐☐ That Darn Cat
- ☐☐ Davy Crockett and the River Pirates
- ☐☐ Davy Crockett, King of the Wild Frontier
- ☐☐ Den Brother
- ☐☐ The Devil and Max Devlin
- ☑☐ Dinosaur
- ☐☐ Don't Look Under the Bed
- ☐☐ Double Teamed
- ☐☐ Doug's 1st Movie
- ☐☐ Dragonslayer
- ☐☐ DuckTales: The Movie - Treasure of the Lost Lamp
- ☑☐ Dumbo
- ☐☐ Eddie's Million Dollar Cook-Off
- ☑☐ Eight Below
- ☐☐ Emil and the Detectives
- ☑☐ Emperor's New Groove
- ☑☐ The Emperor's New Groove 2: Kronk's New Groove
- ☑☐ Enchanted
- ☐☐ Endurance
- ☐☐ Escape from the Dark, The Littlest Horse Thieves
- ☐☐ Escape to Witch Mountain
- ☑☐ The Even Stevens Movie
- ☐☐ An Extremely Goofy Movie
- ☑☐ Fantasia
- ☑☐ Fantasia 2000
- ☐☐ A Far Off Place
- ☐☐ Finding Dory
- ☑☐ Finding Nemo
- ☐☐ First Kid
- ☐☐ Flight of the Navigator
- ☑☐ Flubber
- ☐☐ Follow Me, Boys!
- ☑☐ The Fox and the Hound
- ☑☐ The Fox and the Hound 2
- ☑☐ Frankenweenie
- ☐☐ Freaky Friday
- ☐☐ Frenemies
- ☑☐ Frozen
- ☐☐ Full-Court Miracle
- ☑☐ Fun & Fancy Free
- ☐☐ The Game Plan
- ☐☐ Geek Charming
- ☐☐ Genius
- ☑☐ George of the Jungle
- ☑☐ George of the Jungle 2
- ☑☐ Geppetto
- ☐☐ Get a Clue
- ☐☐ G-Force
- ☐☐ Girl vs. Monster
- ☐☐ Glory Road
- ☐☐ The Gnome-Mobile
- ☐☐ Go Figure
- ☑☐ Going to the Mat
- ☐☐ The Good Dinosaur
- ☐☐ Good Luck Charlie, It's Christmas
- ☐☐ A Goofy Movie
- ☐☐ Gotta Kick It Up!
- ☐☐ The Greatest Game Ever Played
- ☐☐ Greyfriars Bobby
- ☐☐ Gus
- ☐☐ Halloweentown

- ☐☐ Halloweentown High
- ☐☐ Halloweentown II: Kalabar's Revenge
- ☐☐ Hannah Montana: The Movie
- ☐☐ The Happiest Millionaire
- ☐☐ Hatching Pete
- ☑☐ The Haunted Mansion
- ☐☐ H-E Double Hockey Sticks
- ☐☐ Heavy Weights
- ☑☐ Herbie Fully Loaded
- ☐☐ Herbie Goes Bananas
- ☐☐ Herbie Goes to Monte Carlo
- ☐☐ Herbie Rides Again
- ☑☐ Hercules
- ☐☐ High School Musical
- ☐☐ High School Musical 2
- ☐☐ High School Musical 3: Senior Year
- ☐☐ The Hill
- ☑☐ Hocus Pocus
- ☑☐ Holes
- ☑☐ Home on the Range
- ☑☐ Homeward Bound II: Lost in San Francisco
- ☑☐ Homeward Bound: The Incredible Journey
- ☑☐ Honey, I Blew Up the Kid
- ☑☐ Honey, I Shrunk the Kids
- ☐☐ The Horse in the Gray Flannel Suit
- ☐☐ Horse Sense
- ☐☐ Hot Lead and Cold Feet
- ☐☐ Hounded
- ☐☐ Howl's Moving Castle
- ☐☐ Ice Princess
- ☐☐ I'll Be Home for Christmas
- ☐☐ In Search of Castaways
- ☐☐ Inside Out
- ☑☐ Inspector Gadget
- ☑☐ Inspector Gadget 2
- ☐☐ Into The Woods
- ☐☐ Invincible
- ☐☐ Iron Will
- ☐☐ The Island at the Top of the World
- ☑☐ James and the Giant Peach
- ☐☐ The Jennie Project
- ☐☐ Jett Jackson: The Movie
- ☑☐ John Carter
- ☐☐ Johnny Kapahala: Back on Board
- ☐☐ Johnny Tremain
- ☐☐ Johnny Tsunami
- ☐☐ The Journey of Natty Gann
- ☐☐ Jump In!
- ☐☐ Jumping Ship
- ☑☐ Jungle 2 Jungle
- ☑☐ The Jungle Book 2
- ☐☐ Jungle Cruise
- ☐☐ A Kid in King Arthur's Court
- ☑☐ The Kid
- ☐☐ Kidnapped
- ☐☐ Kim Possible Movie: So the Drama
- ☐☐ Kim Possible: A Stich in Time
- ☐☐ King of the Grizzlies
- ☐☐ A Knight in Camelot
- ☑☐ Lady and the Tramp
- ☑☐ Lady and the Tramp II: Scamp's Adventure
- ☐☐ The Last Flight of Noah's Ark
- ☐☐ Lemonade Mouth
- ☐☐ Let It Shine
- ☐☐ Life is Ruff
- ☐☐ Lilo & Stitch
- ☐☐ Lilo and Stitch 2: Stitch Has a Glitch
- ☑☐ The Lion King
- ☑☐ The Lion King 1 1/2
- ☑☐ The Lion King II: Simba's Pride
- ☑☐ The Little Mermaid

- ☑☐ The Little Mermaid II: Return to the Sea
- ☑☐ The Little Mermaid III: Ariel's Beginning
- ☐☐ Lizzie McGuire Movie
- ☑☐ Lone Ranger
- ☑☐ The Love Bug
- ☐☐ Love Leads the Way
- ☐☐ Lt. Robin Crusoe, U.S.N.
- ☐☐ Luck of the Irish
- ☐☐ Magic Kingdom, movie
- ☐☐ Mail to the Chief
- ☐☐ Make Mine Music
- ☑☐ Maleficent
- ☐☐ Man of the House
- ☐☐ The Many Adventures of Winnie the Pooh
- ☐☐ Mars Needs Moms
- ☑☐ Mary Poppins
- ☐☐ Max Keeble's Big Move
- ☐☐ McFarland
- ☐☐ Meet the Deedles
- ☑☐ Meet the Robinsons
- ☐☐ Melody Time
- ☐☐ Mickey's Magical Christmas: Snowed in at the House of Mouse
- ☐☐ Mickey's Once Upon a Christmas
- ☐☐ Mickey's Twice Upon a Christmas
- ☐☐ Midnight Madness
- ☑☐ The Mighty Ducks
- ☐☐ Mighty Joe Young
- ☐☐ Million Dollar Arm
- ☑☐ The Million Dollar Duck
- ☐☐ Minutemen
- ☐☐ Miracle
- ☐☐ Miracle in Lane 2
- ☐☐ Miracle of the White Stallions
- ☐☐ Mom's Got a Date with a Vampire
- ☐☐ Monkeys, Go Home!
- ☑☐ Monsters University
- ☑☐ Monsters, Inc
- ☐☐ Moon Pilot
- ☐☐ Motocrossed
- ☐☐ Mr. Magoo
- ☑☐ Mulan
- ☑☐ Mulan II
- ☐☐ The Muppet Christmas Carol
- ☐☐ The Muppet Movie
- ☐☐ Muppet Treasure Island
- ☑☐ The Muppets
- ☐☐ Muppets: Most Wanted
- ☐☐ Mustang
- ☑☐ My Favorite Martian
- ☐☐ My Friends Tigger and Pooh: Super Sleuth Christmas
- ☐☐ Napoleon and Samantha
- ☐☐ National Treasure
- ☐☐ National Treasure 3
- ☑☐ National Treasure: Book of Secrets
- ☐☐ Never a Dull Moment
- ☐☐ Never Cry Wolf
- ☐☐ Newsies
- ☐☐ Night Crossing
- ☑☐ The Nightmare Before Christmas
- ☐☐ No Deposit, No Return
- ☐☐ TheNorth Avenue Irregulars
- ☐☐ Northern Lights
- ☐☐ Now You See Him, Now You Don't
- ☐☐ Now You See It
- ☑☐ The Odd Life of Timothy Green
- ☑☐ Old Dogs
- ☐☐ Old Yeller
- ☑☐ Oliver and Company
- ☐☐ Once Upon a Mattress

- ☐☐ Once Upon a Warrior (Anaganaga O Dheerudu)
- ☐☐ The One and Only, Genuine, Original Family Band
- ☐☐ One Little Indian
- ☑☐ One Magic Christmas
- ☐☐ One of Our Dinosaurs is Missing
- ☑☐ Operation Dumbo Drop
- ☐☐ The Other Me
- ☐☐ The Other Side of Heaven
- ☑☐ Oz: The Great and Powerful
- ☐☐ The Pacifier
- ☑☐ Peter Pan
- ☑☐ Pete's Dragon
- ☐☐ Phantom of the Megaplex
- ☐☐ Phineas & Ferb: Across the 2nd Dimension
- ☐☐ Phineas and Ferb Movie
- ☑☐ Piglet's Big Movie
- ☑☐ Pinocchio
- ☐☐ The Pirate Fairy
- ☑☐ Pirates of the Caribbean: At World's End
- ☑☐ Pirates of the Caribbean: Dead Man's Chest
- ☐☐ Pirates of the Caribbean: Dead Men Tell No Tales
- ☑☐ Pirates of the Caribbean: On Stranger Tides
- ☑☐ Pirates of the Caribbean: The Curse of the Black Pearl
- ☐☐ Pixel Perfect
- ☑☐ Planes
- ☐☐ Planes: Fire Rescue
- ☑☐ Pocahontas
- ☑☐ Pocahontas II: Journey to a New World
- ☐☐ Pollyanna
- ☐☐ Ponyo
- ☐☐ The Poof Point
- ☐☐ Pooh's Heffalump Halloween Movie
- ☐☐ Pooh's Heffalump Movie
- ☐☐ Popeye
- ☐☐ Prince of Persia: Sands of Time
- ☑☐ The Princess and the Frog
- ☐☐ Princess Diaries 2: Royal Engagement
- ☐☐ The Princess Diaries
- ☐☐ Princess Protection Program
- ☐☐ Prom
- ☐☐ The Proud Family Movie
- ☐☐ Quints
- ☐☐ Race to Witch Mountain
- ☐☐ Radio Rebel
- ☐☐ Rascal
- ☑☐ Ratatouille
- ☐☐ Read It and Weep
- ☐☐ Ready to Run
- ☑☐ Recess: School's Out
- ☑☐ Remember the Titans
- ☐☐ The Rescuers
- ☑☐ The Rescuers Down Under
- ☐☐ Return from Witch Mountain
- ☑☐ Return to Halloweentown
- ☑☐ Return to Never Land
- ☐☐ Return to Oz
- ☐☐ Return to Snowy River
- ☐☐ Ride a Wild Pony
- ☐☐ Right on Track
- ☐☐ A Ring of Endless Light
- ☐☐ Rip Girls
- ☐☐ Rob Roy: The Highland Rogue
- ☑☐ Robin Hood
- ☐☐ Rocket Man
- ☑☐ The Rocketeer
- ☐☐ The Rookie
- ☐☐ Rudyard Kipling's the Jungle Book
- ☐☐ Run, Cougar, Run
- ☐☐ Saludos Amigos

- ☑☐ Santa Buddies
- ☑☐ Santa Clause 2: The Mrs. Clause
- ☑☐ Santa Clause 3: The Escape Clause
- ☑☐ The Santa Clause
- ☑☐ Santa Paws 2: The Santa Pups
- ☐☐ Savage Sam
- ☐☐ Saving Mr. Banks
- ☐☐ Scandalous John
- ☐☐ The Scream Team
- ☑☐ The Search for Santa Paws
- ☐☐ The Secret of the Magic Gourd
- ☐☐ The Secret World of Arrietty
- ☐☐ Secretariat
- ☐☐ The Shaggy D.A.
- ☑☐ The Shaggy Dog
- ☐☐ Sharpay's Fabulous Adventure
- ☐☐ Shipwrecked
- ☑☐ Sky High
- ☑☐ Sleeping Beauty
- ☐☐ Smart House
- ☐☐ Smith!
- ☐☐ Smoke
- ☑☐ Snow Buddies
- ☑☐ Snow Dogs
- ☑☐ Snow White and the Seven Dwarfs
- ☐☐ Snowball Express
- ☐☐ So Dear to My Heart
- ☐☐ Sofia the First: Once Upon a Princess
- ☐☐ Something Wicked This Way Comes
- ☐☐ Son of Flubber
- ☐☐ Song of the South
- ☐☐ Sorcerer's Apprentice
- ☑☐ Space Buddies
- ☐☐ Spirited Away
- ☑☐ Spooky Buddies
- ☐☐ Squanto: A Warrior's Tale
- ☐☐ Star Struck
- ☐☐ Stepsister from Planet Weird
- ☐☐ The Straight Story
- ☐☐ The Strongest Man in the World
- ☐☐ Stuck in the Suburbs
- ☐☐ The Suite Life Movie
- ☐☐ Summer Magic
- ☑☐ Super Buddies
- ☐☐ Superdad
- ☑☐ Swiss Family Robinson
- ☐☐ A Tale of Two Critters
- ☑☐ Tall Tale
- ☑☐ Tangled
- ☑☐ Tarzan
- ☑☐ Teacher's Pet
- ☐☐ Teen Beach Movie
- ☐☐ Ten Who Dared
- ☐☐ Tex
- ☐☐ That Darn Cat
- ☐☐ The Absent-Minded Professor
- ☐☐ The Adventures of Ichabod and Mr. Toad
- ☑☐ The AristoCats
- ☐☐ The Fighting Prince of Donegal
- ☐☐ The Great Locomotive Chase
- ☑☐ The Hunchback of Notre Dame
- ☑☐ The Hunchback of Notre Dame 2
- ☐☐ The Incredible Journey
- ☑☐ The Incredibles
- ☑☐ The Jungle Book
- ☑☐ The Legend of Lobo
- ☐☐ The Light in the Forest
- ☐☐ The Littlest Outlaw
- ☐☐ The Misadventures of Merlin Jones
- ☐☐ The Monkey's Uncle
- ☐☐ The Moon Spinners
- ☐☐ The Parent Trap
- ☑☐ The Pooch and the Pauper

- ☐☐ The Reluctant Dragon
- ☑☐ The Shaggy Dog
- ☑☐ The Sign of Zorro
- ☐☐ The Story of Robin Hood and His Merrie Men
- ☐☐ The Sword and the Rose
- ☑☐ The Sword in the Stone
- ☐☐ The Three Caballeros
- ☐☐ The Three Lives of Thomasina
- ☑☐ The Wild
- ☐☐ Third Man on the Mountain
- ☐☐ The Thirteenth Year
- ☐☐ Those Calloways
- ☐☐ The Three Musketeers
- ☐☐ The Three Musketeers animated
- ☐☐ Tiger Cruise
- ☐☐ Tiger Town
- ☐☐ Tigger & Pooh and a Musical Too
- ☐☐ Tink
- ☑☐ Tinker Bell
- ☐☐ Tinker Bell and the Great Fairy Rescue
- ☑☐ Tinker Bell and the Lost Treasure
- ☐☐ Tinker Bell and the Pirate Fairy
- ☑☐ Tinker Bell: Secret of the Wings
- ☐☐ Toby Tyler
- ☐☐ Tom and Huck
- ☐☐ Tomorrowland
- ☐☐ Tonka
- ☐☐ Tower of Terror
- ☑☐ Toy Story
- ☑☐ Toy Story 2
- ☑☐ Toy Story 3
- ☐☐ Toy Story 4
- ☑☐ Treasure Buddies
- ☐☐ Treasure Island
- ☐☐ Treasure of Matecumbe
- ☑☐ Treasure Planet
- ☐☐ Trenchcoat
- ☑☐ TRON
- ☑☐ TRON 3
- ☑☐ TRON Legacy
- ☐☐ Tru Confessions
- ☐☐ Tuck Everlasting
- ☐☐ Twas the Night
- ☐☐ Twitches
- ☐☐ Twitches Too
- ☐☐ The Ugly Dachshund
- ☐☐ The Ultimate Christmas Present
- ☐☐ Under Wraps
- ☐☐ Underdog
- ☐☐ Unidentified Flying Oddball
- ☑☐ Up
- ☐☐ Up, Up, and Away
- ☐☐ Valiant
- ☐☐ Victory Through Air Power
- ☑☐ Wall E
- ☑☐ Watch all series episodes of Seinfield
- ☐☐ Watch every single Disney movie ever made
- ☑☐ Watch the movie "The Bucket List"
- ☐☐ The Watcher in the Woods
- ☐☐ Wendy Wu: Homecoming Warrior
- ☐☐ Westward Ho, the Wagons!
- ☐☐ Where the Toys Come From
- ☑☐ Whispers: An Elephant's Tale
- ☐☐ White Fang
- ☐☐ White Fang 2
- ☐☐ The Wild Country
- ☐☐ Wild Hearts Can't Be Broken
- ☐☐ Winnie the Pooh
- ☐☐ Winnie the Pooh: A Very Merry Christmas
- ☐☐ Winnie the Pooh: Springtime with Roo

- ☐☐ Wizards of Waverly Place: The Movie
- ☐☐ The Wonderful Ice Cream Suit
- ☐☐ The World's Greatest Athlete
- ☑☐ Wreck-It Ralph
- ☐☐ You Lucky Dog
- ☐☐ You Wish!
- ☐☐ The Young Black Stallion
- ☐☐ Zenon: Girl of the 21st Century
- ☐☐ Zenon: The Zequel
- ☐☐ Zenon: Z3
- ☐☐ Zootopia
- ☐☐ Watch all of Stephen King's movies
- ☐☐ 1408
- ☐☐ A Return to Salem's Lot
- ☐☐ A Very Tight Place
- ☐☐ All That You Love Will Be Carried Away
- ☐☐ Apt Pupil
- ☐☐ Autopsy Room Four
- ☐☐ Bag of Bones
- ☐☐ Cain Rose Up
- ☑☐ Carrie
- ☐☐ Cat's Eye
- ☑☐ Children of the Corn
- ☐☐ Chinga
- ☑☐ Christine
- ☐☐ Creepshow
- ☐☐ Creepshow 2
- ☑☐ Cujo
- ☐☐ Desperation
- ☐☐ Disciples of the Crow
- ☐☐ Dolan's Cadillac
- ☐☐ Dolores Claiborne
- ☑☐ Dreamcatcher
- ☐☐ Everything's Eventual
- ☑☐ Firestarter
- ☐☐ Ghosts
- ☐☐ Golden Years
- ☐☐ Gramma
- ☐☐ Graveyard Shift
- ☐☐ Grey Matter
- ☐☐ Hearts in Atlantis
- ☐☐ Here There Be Tygers
- ☐☐ Here There May Be Tygers
- ☐☐ I Know What You Need
- ☐☐ In the Deathroom
- ☑☐ It
- ☐☐ Kingdom Hospital
- ☐☐ Llamadas
- ☐☐ Love Never Dies
- ☐☐ Luckey Quarter
- ☐☐ Maximum Overdrive
- ☐☐ Maxwell Edison
- ☐☐ Message from Jerusalem
- ☑☐ Misery
- ☐☐ Needful Things
- ☐☐ Night Surf
- ☐☐ Nightmares and Dreamscapes: From the Stories of Stephen King
- ☐☐ No Smoking
- ☐☐ One for the Road
- ☐☐ Paranoid
- ☑☐ Pet Sematary
- ☐☐ Popsy
- ☑☐ Quicksilver Highway
- ☐☐ Rainy Season
- ☐☐ Riding the Bullet
- ☐☐ Rose Red
- ☐☐ Salem's Lot
- ☐☐ Secret Window
- ☐☐ Silver Bullet
- ☑☐ Sleepwalkers
- ☐☐ Sometimes They Come Back
- ☐☐ Sorry, Right Number
- ☐☐ Stand By Me
- ☐☐ Storm of the Century
- ☐☐ Strawberry Spring
- ☐☐ Suffer the Little Children
- ☐☐ Survivor Type

- ☐☐ That Feeling, You Can Only Say What It Is In French
- ☐☐ The Boogeyman
- ☐☐ The Cat from Hell
- ☐☐ The Dark Half
- ☐☐ The Dead Zone
- ☐☐ The Diary of Ellen Rimbauer
- ☑☐ The Green Mile
- ☐☐ The Haven
- ☑☐ The Langoliers
- ☐☐ The Last Rung on the Ladder
- ☐☐ The Man in the Black Suit
- ☐☐ The Man Who Loved Flowers
- ☐☐ The Mangler
- ☐☐ The Mist
- ☐☐ The Moving Finger
- ☐☐ The Night Flier
- ☐☐ The Rage: Carrie 2
- ☐☐ The Reaper's Image
- ☐☐ The Running Man
- ☐☐ The Secret Transit Codes of America's Highways
- ☐☐ The Shawshank Redemption
- ☑☐ The Shining
- ☐☐ The Stand
- ☐☐ The Things They Left Behind
- ☑☐ The Tommyknockers
- ☐☐ The Woman in the Room
- ☐☐ Thinner
- ☑☐ Trucks
- ☐☐ Under the Dome
- ☐☐ Willa
- ☐☐ Word Processor of the Gods
- ☐☐ Collect all my favourite actor's movies - Adam Sandler
- ☑☐ Adam Sandler - 50 First Dates
- ☑☐ Adam Sandler - Airheads
- ☑☐ Adam Sandler - Anger Management
- ☑☐ Adam Sandler - Bedtime Stories
- ☑☐ Adam Sandler - Big Daddy
- ☑☐ Adam Sandler - Billy Madison
- ☑☐ Adam Sandler - Blended
- ☐☐ Adam Sandler - Blossoms & Blood
- ☑☐ Adam Sandler - Bulletproof
- ☑☐ Adam Sandler - Click
- ☑☐ Adam Sandler - Eight Crazy Nights
- ☑☐ Adam Sandler - Funny People
- ☐☐ Adam Sandler - Going Overboard
- ☑☐ Adam Sandler - Grown Ups
- ☑☐ Adam Sandler - Grown Ups 2
- ☑☐ Adam Sandler - Happy Gilmore
- ☑☐ Adam Sandler - Hotel Transylvania
- ☑☐ Adam Sandler - I Now Pronounce You Chuck and Larry
- ☑☐ Adam Sandler - Jack and Jill
- ☑☐ Adam Sandler - Just Go With It
- ☑☐ Adam Sandler - Little Nicky
- ☐☐ Adam Sandler - Mixed Nuts
- ☑☐ Adam Sandler - Mr. Deeds
- ☑☐ Adam Sandler - Punch - Drunk Love
- ☑☐ Adam Sandler - Reign Over Me
- ☐☐ Adam Sandler - Shakes the Clown
- ☑☐ Adam Sandler - Spanglish
- ☑☐ Adam Sandler - That's My Boy
- ☐☐ Adam Sandler - The Cobbler
- ☑☐ Adam Sandler - The Longest Yard
- ☑☐ Adam Sandler - The Waterboy
- ☑☐ Adam Sandler - The Wedding Singer
- ☐☐ Adam Sandler - Valet Guys
- ☑☐ Adam Sandler - You Don't Mess With the Zohan

- ☐☐ Act out the "I'm the king of the world" scene from Titanic
- ☑☐ Do a Harry Potter marathon
- ☑☐ Do a Lord of the Rings marathon
- ☑☐ Do a Star Wars marathon
- ☑☐ Go to the movies and get a ticket for the next movie showing
- ☐☐ Lord the Rings 1/2 Day Middle Earth film locations
- ☐☐ Visit the Full House home in San Francisco
- ☐☐ Watch a black and white movie
- ☐☐ Watch all series episodes of Top Gear

Chapter 64: Water Adventures

"It is in the compelling zest of high adventure and of victory, and in creative action, that man finds his supreme joys."

Antoine de Saint-Exupery

Experience the thrill of an adventure-packed summer filled with a water adventure schedule, whether it be in the pool or the beach. A lot of Aussies live for the beach lifestyle – swimming laps of the pool or diving from the podium, sitting back and relaxing with a classic beer, or throwing a fishing line out from a boat with family and mates. We are born to enjoy the water; we love the excitement of the sports that have been created within this lifestyle and we are always thinking up new ideas of what we can create on water. The adrenalin of water sports is outstanding: surfing that beautiful classic wave as it crashes against the shoreline, or scuba diving at that shipwreck we will never see from land. The beauty on top of the water is nothing compared to the marvellous beauty that lives under the ocean. The Great Barrier Reef in Queensland is one of the most recognisable reefs in the world.

- ☐☐ 10 metres high dive board
- ☐☐ 1770 LARC! Tours, multiple locations
- ☐☐ 3 metres high dive board
- ☐☐ 5 metres high dive board
- ☐☐ 7.5 metres high dive board
- ☐☐ Air boat across an alligator-infested swamp
- ☐☐ Aqua aerobics (AQ)
- ☑☐ Assist steering the Tall Ship
- ☐☐ Become scuba diving certified
- ☐☐ Cables Wake Park
- ☐☐ Cage-dive with crocodiles
- ☑☐ Catch a fish
- ☐☐ Catch a marlin
- ☐☐ Catch a trophy fish
- ☐☐ Cliff dive
- ☐☐ Crocodile feeding experience, Darwin
- ☐☐ Cruise the Panama Canal
- ☐☐ Deep sea fishing
- ☐☐ Deep water (DW) exercises
- ☐☐ Dive the renowned 102-year-old wreck of the S.S. Yongala, off the coast off Townsville
- ☐☐ Dive under the ice
- ☐☐ Diving in Alexandria's sunken city, Egypt
- ☐☐ Dolphin Cruise
- ☐☐ Emerald Pool, the Alps, Austria

- ☐☐ Experience clamming
- ☑☐ Experience climbing Crow's Nest on Tall Ship
- ☑☐ Experience going fishing
- ☐☐ Experience logrolling
- ☐☐ Experience rowing a dragon boat
- ☐☐ Experience shrimping
- ☐☐ Experience skooter snorkelling
- ☑☐ Experience Tall Ship
- ☐☐ Explore the ocean in a submarine
- ☐☐ Feed the sharks
- ☐☐ Fishing charters
- ☐☐ Free dive at Dean's Blue Hole, Bahamas
- ☐☐ Get my boating license
- ☐☐ Go bamboo rafting
- ☑☐ Go body boarding
- ☐☐ Go diving in the Red Sea in Egypt
- ☐☐ Go ice fishing
- ☐☐ Go ice swimming, Finland
- ☑☐ Go kayaking
- ☐☐ Go on a Disneyland cruise ship
- ☐☐ Go on a glass bottom boat
- ☐☐ Go on an Alaskan cruise
- ☐☐ Go on cruise ship
- ☐☐ Go reef walking, Fiji
- ☐☐ Go scuba diving
- ☐☐ Go skim boarding
- ☐☐ Go snorkelling
- ☐☐ Go snorkelling in a shipwreck
- ☐☐ Gondola ride, Venetian Resort, Vegas
- ☐☐ Horseback riding in the ocean
- ☑☐ Jet Pack experience
- ☐☐ Jump from a cliff into deep water
- ☑☐ Jump in a pool fully clothed
- ☐☐ Jump into a frozen lake with ice suit on
- ☐☐ Jump off a pier
- ☐☐ Kayak in a pumpkin
- ☐☐ Kayak in Halong Bay, Vietnam
- ☐☐ Learn how to spear fish
- ☑☐ Learn to swim
- ☐☐ Learn to water ski
- ☐☐ Maltese underwater statue of Jesus Christ
- ☐☐ North Carolina: dive a German u-boat
- ☐☐ Ocean jet boat ride, Gold Coast, Queensland, Australia
- ☐☐ Ocean walker experience
- ☐☐ Oklahoma: catch a catfish barehanded
- ☑☐ Oz Jet Boating
- ☐☐ Paddle wheeler, Nepean River
- ☐☐ Participate in red bull flugtag
- ☐☐ Party on a mega yacht
- ☐☐ Phang Nga bay cruises with Ayodhaya
- ☑☐ Putting sails up on a ship
- ☐☐ Recover a pearl from oyster in ocean
- ☑☐ Release a fish I caught
- ☐☐ Ride a gondola in Venice, Italy
- ☐☐ Ride a zap cat
- ☐☐ Ride an aqua bike
- ☐☐ Ride in a hovercraft
- ☐☐ Ride on the Maiden of the Mist, a legend of Niagara Falls
- ☐☐ Rope swing into the water
- ☐☐ Row a viking ship in Norway
- ☐☐ Sail the postman's run up the Hawkesbury, NSW
- ☐☐ Sailing America's Cup yacht racing experience
- ☐☐ Sailing the Milford Sound, New Zealand

- ☐☐ Scuba dive/snorkel on the Great Barrier Reef
- ☐☐ Scuba dive a shipwreck
- ☐☐ Scuba dive an underwater volcano, Halmahera, Indonesia
- ☐☐ Scuba dive at night
- ☐☐ Seward, Alaska, deep sea fishing experience
- ☐☐ Snorkel in the Galapagos Islands
- ☑☐ Stand under a waterfall
- ☐☐ Stand up on a wave
- ☐☐ Stand up paddle boarding
- ☐☐ Substation Curaçao
- ☐☐ Surf experience
- ☑☐ Swim 50 metres, the length of a swimming pool
- ☐☐ Swim in the Dead Sea
- ☐☐ Swimming with the Sharks, Water Slide and Aquarium, Dubai
- ☐☐ Sydney Showboats Cabaret Dinner Cruise
- ☐☐ Take a dip in Iceland's Blue Lagoon
- ☐☐ Take an airboat ride across the Mary River flood plain from Bamurru Plains
- ☐☐ Take an outdoor bath in Budapest
- ☑☐ Thames River Cruise
- ☐☐ The Corinth Canal, Greece
- ☐☐ Try flyboarding
- ☐☐ Try kiteboarding
- ☐☐ Try windsurfing
- ☐☐ Visit the natural rock pools of Pamukkale, Turkey
- ☐☐ Water skiing
- ☐☐ Water zorbing
- ☑☐ White water rafting
- ☑☐ White water stadium
- ☐☐ World's largest pool at San Alfonso del Mar resort in Chile

Chapter 65: Flying Adventures

"If you think, 'I'm jumping out of a plane at 30,000 feet!' you're not going to do it. But if you just jump out, then you'll have an interesting ride."

Luke Treadaway

From the beginning of time man has been fascinated by flight. In today's living, we enjoy the special moments and thrill of the adrenalin flight offers us. Some allow us to experience flight even for a brief moment: to fly like the birds that live around us or soar in a hot air balloon as we look down from above viewing the beautiful landscapes below. More terrifying things, like bungee jumping off a bridge or dam. Crazy stunt flights will get the blood flowing as the pilot performs flips, twists and turns in mid-air – and even a stall to get the heart pumping. We all seek out adrenalin rushes; we strive for them. No matter how we get it, it makes us feel alive.

- ☐☐ Air experience glider flight
- ☐☐ Auckland Bridge Bungi Jump
- ☐☐ Be a human catapult
- ☐☐ Bungee jump
- ☐☐ Cage bungee slingshot
- ☐☐ Do reverse bungee
- ☐☐ Dog flight red baron flight
- ☐☐ Experience slack lining
- ☐☐ Experience weightlessness
- ☐☐ Extreme velocity vertical wind tunnel
- ☐☐ Fly a helicopter
- ☐☐ Fly an airplane
- ☐☐ Fly geyser, Nevada
- ☐☐ Fly in a blimp
- ☐☐ Fly in a wing suit
- ☐☐ Fly over Great Barrier Reef
- ☐☐ Get a pilot's licence
- ☑☐ Get dunked in the water while parasailing
- ☐☐ Go into a zero gravity room
- ☑☐ Go parasailing
- ☐☐ Go sky diving
- ☐☐ Hang glide
- ☐☐ Hot air balloon exploration over the Serengeti, Africa
- ☐☐ Jet fighter flight
- ☐☐ Learn to fly a micro light
- ☐☐ Macau Tower bungee jump
- ☐☐ Macau Tower sky jump
- ☐☐ Paragliding
- ☐☐ Paramotoring
- ☐☐ Ride a hot air balloon
- ☑☐ Ride in an airplane
- ☑☐ Scenic skyway
- ☐☐ Sea flight plane
- ☐☐ Sky dive at night

- ☐☐ Sky jump Auckland Tower
- ☑☐ Swing on a trapeze
- ☐☐ Sydney Thrill Flight
- ☐☐ Take an early-morning hot air balloon flight over the Yarra Valley, Victoria, Australia
- ☐☐ Wing-walking

Chapter 66: Sand Adventures

"It is only in adventure that some people succeed in knowing themselves - in finding themselves."

Andre Gide

Sand offers the chance to be creative: from building sandcastles of different designs, to massive artworks by the most skilled with the art of sand and water mixing carving ability. A lot of us, though, visit the beach throughout the summer months and most the time we come out of the water, lay down on the sand with our beach towels out and relax. The more adventurous of us would love the thrill of quad biking or dune buggy driving around an open sand dune. One such big sand dune to enjoy the thrill is at Port Stephens, New South Wales. Then you also have the people who love a running challenge – running along the open sands to test their true ability. Or even a quiet walk to collect the shells along the beach line that wash ashore. No matter what we do, we are drawn to sand. Although more so in summer, we still end up there throughout the rest of the year, even if only to sit on a beach and view the beautiful sunrise or sunsets.

- ☐☐ Blokarting, Mackay
- ☐☐ Collect seashells on the beach for a day
- ☐☐ Drive along a beach front on the sand
- ☐☐ Drive a dune buggy
- ☑☐ Get buried up to my neck in sand
- ☐☐ Ride a quad bike, sand pits of Port Stephens
- ☐☐ Ride a camel
- ☐☐ Sandboarding
- ☑☐ Sculptures by the sea

Chapter 67: Land Adventures

"Life is either a daring adventure or nothing."

Helen Keller

The land offers so many more adventures than any other type of adventure sports, simply because we have lived all our lives on land and have had more time to create amazing adventures. The thrill of land sports is amazing – from abseiling down rock faces to climbing to the top of the highest buildings in the world for extraordinary views. We build things massive on land: skyscraper buildings, bridges and other architectural designs to make us live better lives and to create more adventure sports. We drive for the power of driving a race car or doing hot laps around a circuit to get our adrenalin pumping. Some of us climb the highest heights to enjoy the land around us. Some of us like the thrill of being in power and going to a shooting range and firing off weapons, like archery or rifles. Maybe even something crazy, like medieval times where we go joust while horseback riding. No matter what we like to do, I assure you there is plenty to offer all around us. We just need to open our eyes and explore our surroundings.

- ☑☐ Three-pointer shot basketball
- ☐☐ 4x4 driving experience
- ☑☐ 9D Action Cinema Experience
- ☐☐ 9D Action Cinema Experience - Bob's racing
- ☐☐ 9D Action Cinema Experience - Canyon Coaster
- ☐☐ 9D Action Cinema Experience - House of Hell
- ☑☐ 9D Action Cinema Experience - Iceberg Adventure
- ☐☐ 9D Action Cinema Experience - Lava Valley
- ☐☐ 9D Action Cinema Experience - Snow Coaster
- ☐☐ 9D Action Cinema Experience - Snow War
- ☐☐ 9D Action Cinema Experience - Triangle
- ☐☐ Abseiling a bridge
- ☑☐ Abseiling a building
- ☑☐ Abseiling a cliff face
- ☐☐ Abseiling a waterfall
- ☐☐ Abseiling ascending a wall
- ☑☐ Abseiling Forward Run, Melbourne "Rap Jumping"
- ☐☐ Auckland Bridge Climb
- ☑☐ Bale hay in England
- ☐☐ Be a contestant on a game show

- ☐☐ Be a kid again and visit the trampoline park
- ☐☐ Be a postman for a day, Coober Pedy 9am Monday and Thursday, South Australia
- ☐☐ Be a street performer for a day
- ☑☐ Be a tourist in your own city
- ☐☐ Be an extra in a film
- ☑☐ Be front row at a concert
- ☐☐ Climb to the top of the Arch in St. Louis, Missouri
- ☐☐ Be set on fire Stunt Academy, Nerang, QLD
- ☐☐ Be the Human Bowling Ball, Zorbing Down a Blow-Up Bowling Ball Lane
- ☐☐ Beach bonfire
- ☐☐ Bell ringing
- ☐☐ Blow something up
- ☐☐ Board down a volcano at Cerro Negro Volcano, Nicaragua, South of Mexico
- ☑☐ Bowl 100 in a game of ten pin bowling
- ☑☐ Bowl 200 in a game of ten pin bowling
- ☐☐ Bowl 300 perfect game in a game of ten pin bowling
- ☑☐ Bowl a turkey ten pin bowling
- ☑☐ Breathe in helium
- ☐☐ Carve a pumpkin
- ☐☐ Catch a home run/foul ball at a baseball game
- ☑☐ Changing of the Guard
- ☐☐ Chase a tornado and capture it on film
- ☐☐ Climb a coconut tree barefoot
- ☐☐ Climb a Solo, Illinos, North America
- ☐☐ Climb a water tower
- ☑☐ Climb Sydney Harbour Bridge
- ☐☐ Climb the top of Ayers Rock, Uluru, NT, Australia
- ☑☐ Climb to the top of a tree
- ☐☐ Climb to the top of an Amazon Rainforest tree with harness attached
- ☐☐ Climb to the top of the Leaning Tower of Pisa, Italy
- ☐☐ Climb to the top of the Arc De Triomphe
- ☐☐ Climb to the top of the Statue of Liberty, New York
- ☑☐ Climb to the top of Sydney Centerpoint Tower
- ☐☐ Climb to the top of Sydney Opera House
- ☐☐ Climb to the top of the Pyramids of Giza, Egypt
- ☐☐ CN Tower Climb
- ☑☐ Compete in a poker tournament
- ☑☐ Construct furniture
- ☐☐ Contribute to the Gum Wall
- ☑☐ Convict Settlers' engravements
- ☑☐ Crack a whip
- ☐☐ Crowd surf
- ☐☐ Crush grapes in a vineyard with my feet
- ☐☐ Defensive Driving School
- ☑☐ Destroy something with a sledgehammer
- ☐☐ DJ crash course
- ☑☐ Do a flip on a trampoline
- ☐☐ Drag racing experience
- ☐☐ Draw funny faces on all the eggs in my fridge
- ☐☐ Drifting experience
- ☐☐ Drive 200+ kph on the German Autobahn
- ☐☐ Drive a convertible with the top down

- ☐☐ Drive a Formula One racing car
- ☐☐ Drive a hot rod
- ☐☐ Drive a monster truck
- ☐☐ Drive a NASCAR car
- ☐☐ Drive a rally car
- ☐☐ Drive a V8 Supercar
- ☑☐ Drive a vintage car
- ☐☐ Drive across Australia, from east to west
- ☐☐ Drive in a country that drives on the "wrong" side of the road
- ☑☐ Drive onto the boat at Wiseman's ferry
- ☑☐ Drive the dirt tracks of Wiseman's ferry
- ☑☐ Drive through Nurragingy Reserve
- ☐☐ Escape from a straight jacket
- ☐☐ Event Cinema's Hot Seat Experience
- ☑☐ Experience a ride in a vintage car
- ☐☐ Experience an earthquake
- ☐☐ Experience axe throwing
- ☐☐ Experience being hypnotised
- ☐☐ Experience blob jumping
- ☑☐ Experience Flight Simulator Darling Harbour
- ☑☐ Experience ice skating
- ☐☐ Experience knife throwing
- ☐☐ Experience laughing gas
- ☐☐ Experience levitation trick done on me
- ☑☐ Experience ride in horse and carriage
- ☐☐ Experience roller blading
- ☑☐ Explore and climb through a bomber aircraft
- ☐☐ F1 racing simulator
- ☑☐ Fast (intake nothing but water) for 72 hours
- ☑☐ Finish a new colouring book
- ☑☐ First class bus coach ride
- ☑☐ Flip a table
- ☑☐ Fly a kite
- ☑☐ Fold A4 piece of paper more than seven times
- ☑☐ Free throw line shot basketball
- ☐☐ Get a piece of art into an exhibition
- ☑☐ Get VIP passes
- ☑☐ Go barefoot for the day
- ☐☐ Go Christmas carolling
- ☐☐ Go geocaching
- ☑☐ Go go-karting
- ☑☐ Go on a road trip
- ☑☐ Go on a roller coaster
- ☐☐ Go on the sky deck in Chicago
- ☐☐ Go on zip line (flying fox)
- ☑☐ Go paintballing
- ☑☐ Go panning for gold
- ☑☐ Go rock-climbing *outdoors*
- ☐☐ Go shopping on Rodeo Drive
- ☑☐ Go through a hedge maze
- ☐☐ Go to a bean bag cinema
- ☑☐ Go to a comedy club
- ☑☐ Go to a foam party
- ☑☐ Go to all the Australian monopoly properties
- ☑☐ Go to cinema alone and watch a movie
- ☐☐ Go zorbing in New Zealand
- ☐☐ Graffiti a wall
- ☐☐ Grand Canyon Skywalk, Arizona
- ☐☐ Gyro-riding
- ☐☐ Hang from Toronto's CN Tower
- ☑☐ Have a huge water balloon fight in summer

- ☐☐ Have a jigsaw puzzle made from a photo I have taken
- ☑☐ Have a look round a navy ship
- ☑☐ Have a look round a submarine
- ☐☐ Have a marble face statue done
- ☑☐ Have a meaningful conversation with a stranger
- ☐☐ Have a paint fight
- ☐☐ Have a portrait of me photographed
- ☐☐ Have a professional driver do a lap with me as a passenger
- ☑☐ Have a water fight
- ☑☐ Hit a home run, baseball
- ☑☐ Hit bull's eye on a dartboard
- ☐☐ Hit the archery bull's eye
- ☐☐ Invent a board game
- ☑☐ Invent something
- ☐☐ Join a flash mob
- ☐☐ Join in a hula celebration
- ☐☐ Joust on horseback with a lance
- ☑☐ Kick a field goal
- ☑☐ Knock out someone in boxing match
- ☐☐ Laser clay pigeon shooting
- ☑☐ Laser skirmish
- ☐☐ Lawn mower racing
- ☐☐ Learn to curl
- ☐☐ Learn to ride a uni bicycle
- ☐☐ Learn to skateboard
- ☐☐ Let go of a floating lantern
- ☐☐ Macau Tower skywalk
- ☐☐ Make a hole in one, golf
- ☐☐ Minjin Jungle Swing, Queensland, Australia
- ☐☐ Montecasino
- ☐☐ Moonlight cinemas
- ☐☐ Neon midnight bowling, put glow sticks in water bottles for outdoor night time fun
- ☐☐ Open air cinema
- ☐☐ Paint a picture good enough to hang on the wall
- ☐☐ Paint eggs for Easter
- ☐☐ Plan a street party
- ☐☐ Plate spinning class
- ☑☐ Play 18 holes of golf
- ☑☐ Play a game of mini golf
- ☐☐ Play a game of polo
- ☐☐ Play a game of soccer in zorbing balls
- ☑☐ Play aqua golf, Penrith
- ☐☐ Play bossaball
- ☑☐ Play catch with a baseball and mitt with someone
- ☑☐ Play with sparklers
- ☐☐ Queue for something for 24 hours
- ☑☐ Repair an appliance
- ☑☐ Research the history of my home town
- ☐☐ Ride a mattress down a staircase
- ☐☐ Ride a mechanical bull
- ☑☐ Ride a red London bus
- ☐☐ Ride a scooter
- ☐☐ Ride a tandem bike
- ☐☐ Ride around the Nurburgring, Germany
- ☐☐ Ride down a laundry chute
- ☐☐ Ride in a chariot
- ☐☐ Ride in a limousine
- ☐☐ Ride on the back of a motorbike
- ☑☐ Ride on the London Eye
- ☑☐ Rock-climbing, indoors
- ☑☐ Save a life
- ☐☐ Score albatross in golf

- ☑☐ Score birdie in golf
- ☑☐ Score bogey in golf
- ☑☐ Score double and triple bogeys in golf
- ☐☐ Score eagle in golf
- ☑☐ Score par in golf
- ☑☐ Score the winning point(s) in a game
- ☐☐ See a moonbow
- ☑☐ See myself as an animation cartoon character
- ☑☐ See the Rainbow Crossing, Oxford Street
- ☑☐ See the Scottish and English border, UK
- ☐☐ See the space shuttle launch
- ☑☐ See the sword William Wallace wielded in battle in Scotland
- ☐☐ Segway tour
- ☐☐ Set off fireworks
- ☐☐ Shoot a bazooka
- ☐☐ Shoot a Crossbow
- ☐☐ Shoot a flamethrower
- ☐☐ Shoot a flaming bow & arrow
- ☑☐ Shoot a gun
- ☐☐ Shoot a machine gun
- ☐☐ Shoot a sling shot
- ☐☐ Shoot guns on a shooting range
- ☑☐ Shoot a basketball in from full way court
- ☑☐ Shoot a basketball in from half way court
- ☐☐ Sing "100 Bottles of Beer on the Wall" all the way to the end
- ☐☐ Sing a karaoke duet
- ☐☐ Sing at a karaoke bar
- ☑☐ Sing karaoke
- ☐☐ Sing the national anthem of Australia for an event
- ☑☐ Sit on top of a roof and enjoy the view
- ☑☐ Skim stones (on water)
- ☐☐ Sky Point Tower Climb
- ☐☐ Sky Tower Observatory Deck
- ☐☐ Sky walking at Mt. Nimbus, Canada
- ☐☐ Sky walking, the Alps, Switzerland
- ☐☐ Skyline Luge Greentown
- ☐☐ Skywalk Auckland Tower
- ☑☐ Slam dunk basketball ring
- ☐☐ Slide down a firehouse pole
- ☑☐ Spin a basketball on my finger
- ☐☐ Stand atop Table Mountain for beautiful views, South Africa
- ☐☐ Stand atop the Shard in London
- ☐☐ Stand at the northernmost tip of Australia
- ☐☐ Stand at the top of one of the pyramids of Egypt
- ☐☐ Stand atop the Eiffel Tower
- ☑☐ Stand in a red phone booth, England
- ☐☐ Stand in and explore a meteor crater
- ☐☐ Stand in centre of Four Corners of USA
- ☐☐ Stand in John Wayne's footprints at the Chinese Theatre
- ☐☐ Stand in the audience in a Top Gear episode
- ☐☐ Stand on the Equator Line in Ecuador
- ☐☐ Stand on the International Date Line
- ☑☐ Stand out in the rain and get drenched
- ☐☐ Stand out of the roof of a limo

- ☐☐ Story Bridge climb
- ☐☐ Stunt driving school
- ☐☐ Stunt man academy
- ☐☐ Super Moto Wheelie Training Real Bike Simulator 30min, Penshurst, Sydney
- ☐☐ Supercar Drive Central Coast
- ☑☐ Swing from a vine
- ☑☐ Swing on a tyre tube
- ☐☐ Take a lie detector test
- ☐☐ Take part in a Rickshaw Run, India
- ☑☐ Throw a boomerang
- ☑☐ Throw a fistful of glitter up into the air
- ☐☐ Throw a hand grenade
- ☑☐ Throw a javelin
- ☐☐ Tie a note to a balloon and let it go
- ☐☐ Tie dye a shirt
- ☐☐ Tree top walk in Estonia
- ☑☐ Try fencing
- ☐☐ Tuk Tuk Experience, Thailand
- ☐☐ Turn off a candle with a bull whip
- ☐☐ Use a blow dart gun
- ☐☐ Use a bow for archery
- ☑☐ Use a fire extinguisher
- ☐☐ Use a paddle to bid at an auction
- ☐☐ Use a potter's wheel
- ☐☐ Use a valet service
- ☑☐ Use a whole roll of gaffa tape in one day
- ☑☐ Use walkie talkies
- ☐☐ V8 racing simulator
- ☐☐ Virtual race center experience
- ☐☐ Walk on a tight rope
- ☐☐ Watch a rocket launch
- ☐☐ Watch a volcano erupt
- ☐☐ Watch Carols in Domain
- ☐☐ Watch fireworks from a boat
- ☑☐ Watch jet fighter fly over Sydney Harbour
- ☑☐ Watch someone fire a cannon
- ☐☐ Watch the ball drop in Times Square
- ☑☐ Watch the sunrise twice in 24hrs without sleeping
- ☑☐ Win a prize at Easter show
- ☑☐ Win a raffle
- ☑☐ Win in a game of snooker

Chapter 68: Snow and Ice Adventures

"One way to get the most out of life is to look upon it as an adventure."

William Feather

Being raised in Sydney, Australia, I have grown up with beaches and beautiful backdrops. Yet it has always fascinated me what the lifestyle would be like where people have their entire lives turned into snow and ice around them – their cars frozen, their lakes frozen and turned into ice skating parks, the different adventure sports that come along with the snow, the feeling of the white flakes running through my hands. One day I will find out what it's like, but it is a must for my bucket list. I want to experience the cold ice and snow and the world's largest snow and ice field before it fades away. Antarctica, a land of ice and snow-covered lands: the lands are so beautiful and make the most wonderful backdrops with wildlife all around. The one place left on Earth that has not yet been truly overtaken by humans and still remains a natural beauty. Also, the massive icebergs that float above the oceans and ice-clogged waters fascinate my mind. I can't wait for my dreams of visiting such lands, hopefully in the near future.

- ☐☐ "The Comet" bobsled at Utah Olympic Park, Park City, UT
- ☐☐ Alta snowfields
- ☐☐ Amazing icebergs in Pleneau Antarctica
- ☐☐ Antarctica wildlife
- ☐☐ Be in a jacuzzi in the snow
- ☐☐ Briksdal glaciers
- ☐☐ Eat fresh snow
- ☐☐ European alps and glaciers
- ☐☐ Experience a white Christmas
- ☐☐ Experience snowshoeing
- ☐☐ Fox Glacier, South Island, New Zealand
- ☐☐ Franz Josef Hot Pools Ice Explorer
- ☐☐ Frozen Sea in Luleå, Sweden
- ☐☐ Glaciers of Perito Moreno, Argentina
- ☐☐ Go bobsledding
- ☐☐ Go for a reindeer sleigh ride
- ☐☐ Go skiing
- ☐☐ Go sledging
- ☐☐ Go snow boarding
- ☐☐ Go snow mobiling
- ☐☐ Ice canyon, Greenland
- ☐☐ Ice climbing adventure
- ☐☐ Ice clogged waters/broken ice
- ☐☐ Ice sculptures

- ☐☐ Land of snow and ice
- ☐☐ Majestic icebergs and mountain reflections
- ☐☐ Make a snow angel
- ☐☐ Make a snowman
- ☐☐ Melting on Greenland ice sheet
- ☐☐ Mush a dog sled
- ☐☐ Outdoor jacuzzi in Matterhorn Mountain
- ☐☐ Perito Moreno Glacier, Patagonia, Argentina
- ☐☐ Reindeer Safari Kakslauttanen
- ☐☐ Ride a sky lift
- ☐☐ See snow
- ☐☐ Snowmobile Safari, Kakslauttanen
- ☐☐ Stand at the North or South Pole
- ☐☐ Stand at the North Pole
- ☐☐ Stand at the South Pole
- ☐☐ Stand on top of an iceberg
- ☐☐ Step foot on a glacier
- ☐☐ Striped iceberg, Antarctica
- ☐☐ Svínafellsjökull glacier in Skaftafell, Iceland
- ☐☐ Taste a snowflake
- ☐☐ The Perito Moreno Glacier
- ☐☐ Throw a snowball
- ☐☐ Touch an iceberg
- ☐☐ Tube rides at snow
- ☐☐ West Coast Glaciers

Chapter 69: Space Adventures

"Aim for the moon. If you miss, you may hit a star."

W. Clement Stone

Space, the galaxy and open adventures beyond the Earth's atmosphere: trying things only others dream to see. Discovering the Earth in a different view from just everyday life walking the streets and exploring the world. It would be truly awesome to sit in a space shuttle looking down over Earth, imagining how big the world is we are living in and seeing for ourselves from above how massive Earth is and how many people live down there. Would you take a plunge and land on another planet or even a moon? It's a once-in-a-lifetime opportunity. If the opportunity presents itself, I recommend taking it for the many interesting stories that can be told to your family of your adventures into outer space.

- ☐☐ Become a space tourist
- ☐☐ Do a space jump?
- ☐☐ Go into space and see earth from up above
- ☐☐ Walk on Mars "another planet"?
- ☐☐ Walk on the moon

Chapter 70:
Train Adventures

"Railway termini are our gates to the glorious and the unknown. Through them we pass out into adventure and sunshine, to them, alas! we return."

E. M. Forster

Trains have made a major impact in our lives since they were invented in 1829, when people were first allowed to ride them. They have changed the way we live our lives. Yes, a lot of us love our freedom of being in a car, but too many of us driving causes bumper-to-bumper driving, especially going into major cities like Sydney. Every morning and every night you are basically moving at a snail's pace, and very few of us that travel into the city would prefer to take the train. That's not what I mean with train adventures, though. Trains can be a great escape from the hustle and bustle of city life where you can explore the open rocky mountains or the desert areas – from Adelaide to Darwin or Alaska's beautiful scenery. They are a lot more than subway rides and metro systems. Man has made special railways for families to enjoy beautiful landscapes around the world. In some places, cog trains take you to the top of mountains to view over cities. China has the world's fastest train, a unique experience some of us have never thought about .

- ☐☐ Albula Railway
- ☐☐ Bernina Railway
- ☑☐ First class train ride
- ☐☐ Go on Ghann Railway Darwin to Adelaide, north to south
- ☐☐ Indian Pacific train ride east to west
- ☑☐ Melbourne tram ride
- ☐☐ Mount Washington's cog train
- ☐☐ Participate in the no pants subway ride
- ☐☐ Pikes Peak Railway
- ☐☐ Puffing Billy Railway
- ☐☐ Ride on top of or hanging on the side of the train in India
- ☐☐ Ride the Rocky Mountaineer
- ☐☐ Ride the subway, New York
- ☐☐ Ride the Trans-Siberian Railway, Russia
- ☑☐ Ride the tube, London
- ☐☐ Ride trams, Sydney
- ☐☐ Ride world's fastest train, Shanghai, China
- ☐☐ Ride San Francisco's cable cars
- ☐☐ Sky train in Japan
- ☐☐ Take a ride on Alaska's railway

- ☐☐ The world's steepest cogwheel railway at Mount Pilatus
- ☐☐ Visit Platform 9 ¾
- ☑☐ Visit Flinders Station, Melbourne

Chapter 71: Iconic Landmarks of the World

"To my mind, the greatest reward and luxury of travel is to be able to experience everyday things as if for the first time, to be in a position in which almost nothing is so familiar it is taken for granted."

Bill Bryson

So many beautiful places to see in the world; however, just a few are iconic. Whether it is a natural wonder or an architectural site, these famous landmarks are definitely among the most recognisable in the world. How many of them have you seen? There are many iconic landmarks all around the world, but most of us know the more publically announced landmarks – the Eiffel Tower, the pyramids or the Hollywood Sign. These iconic landmarks are seen in the media and are more known to people around the world, but there are also many more iconic places all around us. Famous landmarks that one person sees as the landmark they want to view in the lifetime could be a totally different opinion by another person. As humans, we all have our personal way in which we see the world. But I have to tell you, I would love to see all of these iconic places in the world because every one of them is unique in their own special way.

- ☑☐ 12 Apostles, Melbourne, Australia
- ☐☐ Adiyaman, Turkey, Head Designs Statues
- ☐☐ Admirals Arch
- ☐☐ Aghios Demetrios, Athens Greece
- ☐☐ Angkor Wat, Cambodia
- ☑☐ Arc De Triomphe
- ☐☐ Arch of Constantine
- ☑☐ Archibald Fountain, Hyde Park
- ☑☐ Arthurs Seat, Holyrood Park
- ☐☐ Atacama Giant Markings, Desert, Chile
- ☐☐ Aurora Australis, Goats Beach, Tasmania, Australia
- ☐☐ Ballast Point Park, Walama
- ☐☐ Baltra Island
- ☐☐ Bare Island on Botany Bay, Sydney
- ☐☐ Blue City, Jodhpur, India
- ☐☐ Brandenburg Gate (Brandenburger Tor)
- ☑☐ Brighton Beach Colourful Huts
- ☐☐ Cadillac Ranch, Amarillo, Texas
- ☑☐ Canals of Amsterdam
- ☐☐ Cannes, France
- ☐☐ Capitoline Hill

- ☐☐ Cappadocia, Turkey, Fairy Chimneys
- ☐☐ Carhenge, Alliance, Nebraska
- ☐☐ Celebrate the 4th of July in America
- ☐☐ Central Park, New York
- ☑☐ Champs-Elysée
- ☐☐ Chapultepec
- ☐☐ Cinque Terre, Italy
- ☑☐ Convict Cell at Bull's Camp
- ☑☐ Cremone Point
- ☑☐ Darling Harbour
- ☐☐ Deer stones at the foot of Mount Uushig, in Khövsgöl Province, Mongolia
- ☐☐ Dun Chaoin Pier, Ireland
- ☑☐ El Alamein Fountain
- ☐☐ El Camino Del Rey (King's pathway) in Malaga, Spain
- ☐☐ Experience the atmosphere of Tokyo, Japan
- ☐☐ Galleria Vittorio Emanuele II, Milan, Italy
- ☐☐ Gateway Arch, St. Louis
- ☐☐ Gateway of the Sun
- ☐☐ Genovesa Island
- ☐☐ Giant sculptures in Nemrut, Turkey
- ☐☐ Giethoorn, Holland, a roadless village
- ☑☐ Glen Innes standing stones
- ☐☐ Go to John O'Groats
- ☐☐ Go to Lands' End
- ☐☐ Go to Santorini, Greece
- ☐☐ Go to the top of the Seattle Space Needle
- ☐☐ Go to the top of Eiffel Tower
- ☐☐ Go to the top of the Washington Monument, USA
- ☐☐ Goat Island
- ☐☐ Ground Zero Memorial, New York
- ☐☐ Hadrian's Arch at Jerash, Jordan
- ☑☐ Hadrian's Wall, England
- ☐☐ Headington Shark, Headington, Oxfordshire, England
- ☐☐ Heart of Midlothian Royal Mile
- ☐☐ Hollywood Sign, California
- ☐☐ Hollywood Walk of Fame
- ☐☐ Honest Abraham Lincoln, Washington
- ☐☐ Huayna Picchu
- ☐☐ Ibiza
- ☐☐ India Gate
- ☐☐ Itabaca Channel
- ☐☐ Kangaroo Island, Adelaide
- ☐☐ Kanuhuraa, Maldives
- ☐☐ Kindlifresser (Child Eater) Fountain, Bern, Switzerland
- ☐☐ La Portada: Antofagasta, Chile
- ☐☐ Leshan Giant Buddha, China
- ☐☐ Little Mermaid
- ☐☐ Longmen Grottoes, China
- ☐☐ Lord Howe Island
- ☐☐ Lucy the Elephant, Margate, New Jersey
- ☐☐ Machu Picchu
- ☐☐ Madeira, Portugal
- ☐☐ Malta, the medieval walled city of Mdina
- ☐☐ Mamanuca Islands
- ☐☐ Mannekin Pis, Brussels
- ☑☐ Mini Statue of Statue of Liberty, Paris, France
- ☑☐ Mini village Coffs Harbour
- ☐☐ Mongolia, Tov Province, Tsonjin Boldog, a 40m tall statue of Genghis Khan on Horseback Stands
- ☐☐ Moray, Cusco

- ☑☐ Mrs. Macquarie Chair
- ☐☐ Natural Walkway, Maldives
- ☐☐ Nazca Lines
- ☐☐ Newgrange, Ireland
- ☐☐ Northkapp
- ☑☐ Olympic Cauldron at Sydney Olympic Park
- ☐☐ Our Lady of Lebanon
- ☐☐ Palawan, Philippines
- ☐☐ Parque Forestal
- ☐☐ Paul Bunyan, Minnesota
- ☐☐ Pearl Harbour, Hawaii
- ☐☐ Post a Letter on Juliet's Wall, Italy
- ☐☐ Prague, Czech Republic
- ☐☐ Pyramid of Djoser
- ☐☐ Pyramid of Khafre
- ☐☐ Pyramid of Menkaure
- ☐☐ Pyramid of the Sun
- ☐☐ Rice Fields of Philippines
- ☐☐ Robinson Crusoe Island
- ☐☐ Rock houses in Cappadocia, Turkey
- ☐☐ Rodd Island on Port Jackson, Sydney Harbour
- ☐☐ Saint Wenceslas Riding a Dead Horse, Prague
- ☐☐ Scope the Skeleton Coast, Namibia, Africa
- ☐☐ See a totem pole design in person
- ☐☐ See and photograph Cristo Redentor
- ☐☐ See Berlin Wall
- ☐☐ See Jumbo the Elephant in St. Thomas, Ontario, Canada
- ☐☐ See Sphinx
- ☐☐ See the Alice in Wonderland statue in Central Park
- ☐☐ See the Atomium, Brussels, Belgium
- ☑☐ See the Crown Jewels, London, England
- ☐☐ See the Faberge eggs in the Kremlin Armoury
- ☐☐ See the Terracotta Warriors, Xi'an, China
- ☐☐ See the Titanic in a submarine
- ☐☐ See the Trojan horse, Canakkale, Turkey
- ☑☐ See the White Horse of Yorkshire England
- ☐☐ See Timbuktu, Mali
- ☑☐ See White Cliffs of Dover
- ☐☐ Shark Island on Port Jackson, Sydney Harbour
- ☐☐ Statue of Liberty, New York
- ☑☐ Stonehenge, United Kingdom
- ☐☐ Syntagma Square
- ☐☐ Taj Mahal
- ☐☐ Tank Stream Fountain
- ☐☐ The Acropolis in Greece
- ☐☐ The Baths, Virgin Gorda, BVI
- ☐☐ The Burren, Ireland
- ☐☐ The Carpet of Flowers in Brussels, Belgium
- ☐☐ The Chocolate Hills, Philippines
- ☐☐ The Cliffs of Moher
- ☐☐ The Colosseum in Rome
- ☐☐ The Galapagos Archipelago
- ☐☐ The Giant's Causeway, Ireland
- ☐☐ The Great Blue Hole, Belize
- ☐☐ The Initiation Well in Sintra, Portugal
- ☐☐ The Island of Seychelles
- ☐☐ The Kremlin in Russia
- ☐☐ The Leaning Tower of Pisa
- ☐☐ The Lost City of Petra
- ☐☐ The Magic Bus, Alaska
- ☐☐ The Moeraki Boulders, New Zealand

- ☐☐ The Northern Lights (Aurora Borealis)
- ☐☐ The Olgas
- ☐☐ The Parthenon in Greece
- ☐☐ The Pinnacles Western Australia
- ☑☐ The Pool of Reflections, Hyde Park
- ☐☐ The Pyramid of Giza, Egypt
- ☐☐ The Rosetta stone, Egypt's hieroglyphics
- ☑☐ The Shard
- ☐☐ The Statues of Easter Island, Chile
- ☐☐ The Stone Mirror, Turkey
- ☐☐ The World Islands, Dubai
- ☐☐ Times Square, New York
- ☑☐ Trafalgar Square
- ☐☐ Trevi Fountain, Rome
- ☐☐ Tromso
- ☐☐ Tuscany
- ☐☐ United States Capitol, Washington. D.C.
- ☐☐ Uruguay, Mano de Punta Del Este
- ☐☐ Ushiku Daibutsu, Ushiku, Ibaraki Prefecture, Japan, religious statue
- ☐☐ Victoria & Alfred Waterfront
- ☐☐ Visit an Amish Village
- ☐☐ Visit Area 51, Nevada
- ☐☐ Visit llanfairpwllgwyngyllgo-gerychwyrndrobwllllantysili-ogogogoch, United Kingdom, worlds longest town name
- ☐☐ Visit one of the locations with the "Before I die . . ." chalkboards
- ☐☐ Visit the Bermuda Triangle
- ☐☐ Visit the Bone Yards in Las Vegas
- ☐☐ Visit the Colosso Dell'Appennino in Italy
- ☐☐ Visit the Giant Buddha, Hong Kong
- ☐☐ Visit the Great Barrier Reef
- ☐☐ Visit the Holy Land
- ☐☐ Visit the Isle of Man, Irish Sea
- ☐☐ Visit the Mall of America
- ☐☐ Visit the Seven Wonders of the World
- ☐☐ Visit the Sistine Chapel, Vatican City
- ☐☐ Visit Tiananmen Square, Beijing, China
- ☐☐ Visit Tikal, Maya Civilisation
- ☐☐ Visit Vatican City and all of its attractions

Chapter 72: Live Entertainment

"I love watching live shows from different artists from different stages of their lives. I'm always interested in the mastery of the live performance."

Stjepan Hauser

Experience live entertainment throughout the world from music and shows, to festivals and street theatre. A perfect way to see the beautiful lights and sounds on the main stage, and enjoy the chance to dress up and entertain the family. A lot of the time our first live entertainment shows as children is the grand spectacular of the big top circus appearances. We see animals entertaining with tricks and jumping and riding around the stage, and clowns preforming for the laughter of people in the audience. We enjoy live entertainment because it gives us the chance to imagine and be part of the great atmosphere, a lot better than the entertainment just over television. We experience the atmosphere and thrill of the excitement up close: the laughter, the tears, the excitement of the live entertainment.

- ☐☐ Attend a black-tie affair
- ☑☐ Attend a Cirque du Soleil show
- ☐☐ Attend a dinner murder mystery
- ☐☐ Attend a film premiere
- ☑☐ Attend a random free seminar
- ☑☐ Attend an event at ANZ Stadium
- ☐☐ Attend the Eurovision Grand Finals
- ☐☐ Be in the audience for the Footy Show
- ☑☐ Capitol Theatre
- ☐☐ Circus Australis
- ☐☐ Circus Maximus
- ☐☐ Circus OZ
- ☐☐ Cirque Mother Africa
- ☑☐ Disney on Ice live
- ☐☐ Dr. Who experience
- ☐☐ Dracula's Cabaret
- ☐☐ Edinburgh Military Tattoo
- ☑☐ Exhibition Center
- ☐☐ Galactic Circus
- ☐☐ Geisha dances, Kyoto, Japan
- ☐☐ Go to live show of "Deal or No Deal"
- ☐☐ Go to see a play on Broadway
- ☐☐ Go to the Aria Awards
- ☐☐ Go to the Grammy Awards
- ☐☐ Go to the Moulin Rouge
- ☐☐ Grease the musical
- ☐☐ Jesus Christ Superstar the musical
- ☐☐ Lennon Bros Circus

- ☐☐ Live blues
- ☑☐ Live choir
- ☑☐ Live classical orchestra
- ☐☐ Live Jazz (Basement - Circular Quay)
- ☑☐ Live magic show
- ☐☐ Live opera singer
- ☐☐ Matilda the musical
- ☑☐ National Geographic Live! - Coral, Fire and Ice: Underwater Worlds
- ☐☐ Palau de la musica catalana
- ☐☐ Princess Theatre, Melbourne, Melbourne, Australia
- ☑☐ Riverside Theaters, Parramatta
- ☑☐ See 3D movie
- ☑☐ See a futurist
- ☐☐ See a hypnotist
- ☑☐ See a magician deceptionist
- ☑☐ See a magician manipulator
- ☑☐ See a master magician
- ☑☐ See a performance at the Sydney Opera House
- ☐☐ See a ventriloquist
- ☑☐ See a Warrior of the Magic Dark Arts
- ☑☐ See an unusualist
- ☐☐ See Australia's Got Talent live
- ☐☐ See Cosentino - The Magician live
- ☐☐ See David Copperfield Magic Show live
- ☐☐ See Phantom of the Opera
- ☑☐ See the Illusionist 2.0 Live Magic Show
- ☑☐ See Wicked on Broadway
- ☐☐ See X-Factor live
- ☐☐ Silvers Circus
- ☐☐ Sound of Music, musical
- ☐☐ Stardust Circus
- ☑☐ Sydney Convention Centre
- ☑☐ Sydney Entertainment
- ☐☐ The Amphitheatre of El Djem - El Djem is a city in northern Tunisia
- ☐☐ The famous Spanish Riding School, Vienna, Austria
- ☑☐ The Sydney Opera House, Australia
- ☐☐ Theatro Municipal
- ☑☐ Visit Star City Casino
- ☑☐ Visit the Sunrise crew and studio, Martin Place
- ☑☐ Watch a Broadway musical
- ☑☐ Watch a circus
- ☐☐ Watch a fashion show live
- ☑☐ Watch a joust
- ☐☐ Watch a mime performance
- ☑☐ Watch a movie at the drive-in theatre
- ☑☐ Watch a show at Capital Theatre
- ☑☐ Watch a show at Enmore Theatre
- ☐☐ Watch a show at IMAX Theatre
- ☑☐ Watch a show at Metro Theatre
- ☐☐ Watch a show at State Theatre
- ☑☐ Watch a show at Sydney Entertainment Centre
- ☑☐ Watch Disney Lion King live
- ☐☐ Watch Les Miserable
- ☐☐ Watch Matthew Bourne's Swan Lake Ballet and Dance
- ☐☐ Watch Shadow Land Live
- ☐☐ Watch Strictly Ballroom, the musical
- ☐☐ Watch the Blue Man Group live
- ☐☐ Watch the King and Me
- ☐☐ Watch the Rocky Horror Show
- ☐☐ Zurich Opera House

Chapter 73: Personal Lifestyle and Iidiotic Stuff!

"I like the challenge of trying different things and wondering whether it's going to work or whether I'm going to fall flat on my face."

Johnny Depp

Our personal lifestyles: we prefer to keep a lot of it to ourselves, but there are certain things we love to share with others. Whether it be a new hairstyle you just got from the hairdresser, how you spent your weekend, or even that new pair of shoes you have always wanted and finally afforded. A lot of us are shy but, personally, I'm not worried what others think or how they judge me; I am enjoying my life no matter what I do or what I look like. It's my life and I'm enjoying every single moment of it. You will never see me being one of these people on Facebook putting up their status as "I'm Bored." There are too many things to life. Even idiotic things that we muck around with in our life make us different; stupid things we do set us apart from the everyday. Go to work, go on Facebook, sleep, eat: repeating these processes every day is a boring life for anyone. When the world is so large, so beautiful and a whole lot to explore, get out there and enjoy life and don't care if others ever judge you – just live for the moment. People may laugh or think you're great for doing the things you do.

- ☑☐ Unplug for 48 hours
- ☑☐ Accept a dare
- ☑☐ Ask a hairdresser to do "whatever they like"
- ☐☐ Attach a lock of love to a bridge
- ☐☐ Attend a protest march
- ☐☐ Audition for something
- ☐☐ Be a nude model for a life-drawing class
- ☐☐ Be naked in a rainforest
- ☐☐ Be a subject in a research study
- ☐☐ Be handcuffed
- ☑☐ Be in a wedding party
- ☑☐ Be part of the craziness running in the shops on boxing day sales
- ☑☐ Be someone's secret Santa
- ☐☐ Be the voice of an anime character
- ☑☐ Carve initials into a tree

- [ ] ☐ Catch a guitar pick or drum stick at a concert
- [x] ☐ Catch a wedding garter
- [x] ☐ Celebrate my birthday in a foreign country
- [x] ☐ Change a baby's diaper
- [x] ☐ Conquer a fear
- [ ] ☐ Cover someone's car in Post-it notes
- [ ] ☐ Cover the bed in rose petals
- [x] ☐ Crash a party
- [ ] ☐ Cuddle up next to a fire
- [x] ☐ Dance in the rain
- [x] ☐ Decorate a Christmas tree
- [ ] ☐ Decorate my house with Christmas lights
- [x] ☐ Dedicate a whole day to pampering another person
- [x] ☐ Dedicate a song to someone else on the radio
- [ ] ☐ Do a speech for my wedding
- [ ] ☐ Do everything by a magic eight ball for a day
- [x] ☐ Do everything with my left hand for a whole day
- [x] ☐ Do something in front of a large group of people
- [ ] ☐ Do stand-up comedy
- [x] ☐ Draw on a wall
- [ ] ☐ Drop a water balloon from a tall building
- [ ] ☐ Experience the Hookah, India
- [x] ☐ Fall asleep in someone's arms
- [x] ☐ Fall asleep on the phone
- [ ] ☐ Flash someone on the highway
- [x] ☐ Freeze a flower
- [ ] ☐ Freeze a water balloon
- [x] ☐ Get a hickey
- [ ] ☐ Get picked by kiss cam
- [x] ☐ Get rid all the negativity in my life
- [ ] ☐ Get shot with a bullet proof vest
- [x] ☐ Get stitches
- [ ] ☐ Give a eulogy
- [x] ☐ Give people a reason to remember my name
- [x] ☐ Go a month without the internet
- [ ] ☐ Go on a romantic picnic
- [ ] ☐ Go skinny dipping
- [ ] ☐ Go streaking
- [ ] ☐ Go to a strip-club
- [x] ☐ Go to middle of nowhere and scream at the top of your lungs
- [x] ☐ Grow a beard for at least a month
- [x] ☐ Grow a goatee for a month
- [x] ☐ Grow a mustache for a month
- [ ] ☐ Have a Buck's Party
- [ ] ☐ Have a romantic candlelit dinner
- [ ] ☐ Have a team jersey with my name on it
- [x] ☐ Have a wanted poster made up
- [x] ☐ Have an embarrassing moment
- [ ] ☐ Have my DNA analysis done
- [ ] ☐ Have my face painted
- [x] ☐ Have my name done as "name art"
- [x] ☐ Have my request played on the radio
- [x] ☐ Influence someone to start their bucket list adventure
- [ ] ☐ Jump in a taxi cab and scream "FOLLOW THAT CAR!"
- [ ] ☐ Jump into a pile of leaves
- [x] ☐ Kiss at the top of a Ferris wheel
- [x] ☐ Kiss in the rain
- [x] ☐ Kiss under a mistletoe
- [ ] ☐ Kiss under the Eiffel Tower
- [x] ☐ Kiss underwater

- ☑ Kiss someone
- ☑ Laugh until I cry
- ☐ Leave a letter in a library book
- ☑ Leave change in vending machine
- ☑ Letting the waves bury your feet at the beach
- ☐ Lie on a bed of nails
- ☑ Lift someone on my shoulders at a concert
- ☐ Light a candle until it burns out
- ☐ Light a dandelion on fire
- ☑ Make breakfast in bed for someone
- ☑ Make yourself physically sick from eating too many sweets
- ☑ Make someone realise there is more to life than technology
- ☑ Offer to look after a friend's or family's children
- ☑ One week's silence
- ☑ Overcome depression
- ☐ Pick a lock
- ☑ Picked from crowd for entertainment show
- ☑ Play an April fool's joke on someone
- ☐ Pose for a calendar
- ☑ Push all the buttons in an elevator
- ☐ Put dishwashing liquid in a fountain
- ☐ Put glow sticks in a pool and go swimming
- ☐ Put Mentos in a Diet Coke bottle
- ☑ Remember people's names
- ☐ Romantic picnic at night
- ☑ Run across a field of thistles
- ☑ Run across a field of bindis
- ☑ Run across a field of stinging nettles
- ☑ Say YES to everything for a day
- ☑ See an R Rated Movie
- ☑ See an X Rated Movie
- ☐ Send a message in a bottle
- ☐ Send a postcard to Post Secret
- ☑ Sleep in the nude
- ☐ Smash a guitar
- ☑ Smash a Pinata so all the lollies explode out of it first hit round
- ☑ Smash and break something
- ☐ Smoke a cigar
- ☑ Spend a whole day sleeping
- ☐ Start fire without matches/lighter
- ☑ Stay awake 24 hours
- ☑ Stay awake for seventy-two hours
- ☑ Stay in bed all day, cuddling
- ☑ Stop drinking soft drinks
- ☐ Successfully create an optical illusion
- ☐ Survive a disaster
- ☑ Swing on a clothes line
- ☐ Take my kids to see Santa
- ☐ Thank someone who has impacted my life with a letter
- ☐ Try all the positions in the Karma Sutra
- ☐ Try to walk in a straight line whilst blind folded
- ☑ Vote for Prime Minster of Australia
- ☐ Walk on a nude beach . . . nude
- ☑ Write a letter to Santa Claus
- ☑ Write a love poem
- ☐ Write my Will
- ☐ Write something in wet concrete

- ☐☐ Write with quill
- ☐☐ Write yourself a letter and read it 10 years later
- ☐☐ Your true age and insight into your health (Red Balloon)

Chapter 74:
Clocks and Lighthouses

"Don't watch the clock; do what it does. Keep going."

Sam Levenson

A lighthouse is a tower, building, or other type of structure designed to emit light from a system of lamps and lenses and used as a navigational aid for maritime pilots at sea or on inland waterways. Lighthouses mark dangerous coastlines, hazardous shoals, reefs, safe entries to harbours, and can also assist in aerial navigation. They help guide our way and have various beautiful designs of different shapes and sizes to make each and every one of them unique. Clocks help us live our daily lives; we all live by time and day by day our lives are run by the hours, minutes, even seconds. Our time is precious to us all and we try to use our time to the best of our abilities to ensure we don't waste our life away. Clocks are beautiful, in various designs, sizes and located all around the world, in every city. We wear them on our wrist, we have them on electrical appliances, we have them hanging on the walls around the house, we even use them on our mobile phones. Clocks are so important to our lifestyle; we use them all the time without fail.

- ☐☐ Abraj Al-Bait Clock Tower, Mecca, Saudi Arabia
- ☑☐ Barrenjoey Lighthouse
- ☐☐ Bass Harbour Head Station, Maine
- ☐☐ Belgium, Bruges, The Belfry
- ☐☐ Bell Rock Lighthouse
- ☑☐ Big Ben's Great Clock, London, England
- ☐☐ Boston Lighthouse
- ☐☐ Brant Point Lighthouse located on Nantucket Island
- ☐☐ Cape Bruny Lighthouse
- ☐☐ Cape Byron Lighthouse
- ☐☐ Cape Byron lighthouse first to see sunrise
- ☐☐ Cape Don Lighthouse
- ☐☐ Cape Hatteras Lighthouse, located on Hatteras Island in the town of Buxton, North Carolina
- ☐☐ Cape Neddick Lighthouse
- ☑☐ Cape Otway Lighthouse
- ☐☐ Cevahir Shopping and Entertainment Centre Clock, Istanbul, Turkey
- ☐☐ Chatuchak Clock Tower, Bangkok

- ☐☐ City Hall Clock Tower, Cardiff, Wales
- ☐☐ Clock Tower, Hong Kong
- ☐☐ Clock Tower, Waterford, Ireland
- ☐☐ Cosmo Clock 21, Yokohama, Japan
- ☐☐ Currituck Beach Lighthouse
- ☐☐ Diocletian's Palace, Split, Croatia
- ☐☐ Eddystone Lighthouse
- ☐☐ Evangelical Church Tower, Sibiu, Romania
- ☐☐ Fanad Lighthouse, Ireland
- ☐☐ Ferry Building Clock Tower, San Francisco
- ☐☐ Glockenspiel, Munich, Germany
- ☐☐ Green Cape Lighthouse
- ☑☐ Grotto Point Lighthouse
- ☐☐ Haymarket Memorial Clock Tower, Leicester, U.K.
- ☐☐ Hornby Lighthouse
- ☐☐ Independence Hall Clock Tower, Morris Arboretum Garden Railway, University of Pennsylvania
- ☐☐ Izmir Clock Tower, Turkey
- ☐☐ La Jument Lighthouse
- ☐☐ Les Eclaireurs Lighthouse
- ☐☐ Limoges Train Station Clock, France
- ☐☐ Lindau Lighthouse, Germany
- ☑☐ Macquarie Lighthouse
- ☐☐ Medieval Clock Tower, St. Albans, Hertfordshire, England
- ☐☐ Merewether Memorial Tower, Karachi, Pakistan
- ☐☐ Morris Island, Charleston, SC
- ☐☐ North Station Clock Tower, Brussels
- ☐☐ Peace Tower Clock, Ottawa, Canada
- ☐☐ Peggys Point Lighthouse
- ☐☐ Pigeon Point Lighthouse
- ☐☐ Point Lonsdale Lighthouse
- ☐☐ Portland Head, a historic lighthouse in Cape Elizabeth, Maine
- ☐☐ Prague Astronomical Clock, Prague, Czech Republic
- ☐☐ Rajabai Clock Tower, Mumbai, India
- ☐☐ Richmond River Lighthouse
- ☐☐ Robertson Point Lighthouse
- ☐☐ Sambro Island Lighthouse
- ☐☐ South Solitary Island Lighthouse
- ☐☐ Split Point Lighthouse
- ☐☐ Split Rock Lighthouse
- ☐☐ Start Point Lighthouse, England
- ☐☐ Steam Clock in Gastown, an ancient district of Vancouver
- ☐☐ Sugarloaf Point Lighthouse
- ☐☐ Sultan Abdul Samad Building Clock Tower, Kuala Lumpur, Malaysia
- ☐☐ Surin Circle Clock Tower, Phuket City
- ☐☐ Tacking Point Lighthouse
- ☐☐ The Clock Tower of St. Pancras Station, London
- ☐☐ The Floral Clock, Niagara Parks, Ontario, Canada
- ☐☐ The Grand Central Terminal Clock, New York, United States
- ☐☐ The Jubilee Clock Tower, Penang, Malaysia
- ☐☐ The Montauk Point Lighthouse
- ☐☐ The Oak Island Lighthouse

- ☐☐ The Portland Breakwater, small lighthouse in South Portland, Maine
- ☐☐ The Samrat Yantra, Jaipur, India
- ☐☐ The Saviour Tower, Moscow
- ☐☐ The Shepherd Gate Clock, Greenwich, London, England
- ☐☐ The St. Augustine Lighthouse in St. Augustine, Florida.
- ☐☐ Torre Del Reloj, Cartagena, Colombia
- ☐☐ Tower of Hercules, Spain
- ☐☐ Ulladulla Lighthouse
- ☐☐ West Dennis Lighthouse in West Dennis, Massachusetts
- ☐☐ White Shoal Lighthouse, Michigan
- ☐☐ Wilsons Promontory Lighthouse
- ☐☐ Wollongong Breakwater Lighthouse
- ☐☐ Wollongong Head Lighthouse
- ☐☐ Wrigley Building Clock Tower, Chicago
- ☐☐ Yaquina Bay Lighthouse, Oregon
- ☐☐ Zytglogge Tower, Bern, Switzerland

Chapter 75: Elevators and Steps

"There is always room at the top."

Daniel Webster

The daily question we ask ourselves: should we take the easy way up and take the elevator, or should we take the steps and do our daily exercise way of life. There are various great architecturally designed elevators and staircases that make each and every one unique in their own special way. Most times I would personally prefer to take the steps, but am sometimes convinced elevators and escalators get the better of us; they are easy to use and don't need to use our energy on walking. We need to change the way we think and, no matter how we feel, take the steps to help us feel like we have accomplished something.

- ☐☐ Anderton Boat Lift: Cheshire, England
- ☐☐ AquaDom, Berlin-Mitte, Germany
- ☐☐ Autostadt Silos: Wolfsburg, Germany
- ☐☐ Bailong Elevator, Zhangjiajie, China
- ☐☐ Burj Khalifa Elevator
- ☐☐ Canyon Steps, Pailon Del Diablo, Ecuador
- ☐☐ Climb the "Stairway to Heaven" in Oahu, Hawaii
- ☑☐ Colourful stairs at Collaroy, Northern Beaches
- ☐☐ Forgotten stairs, Croatia
- ☐☐ Gateway Arch Tram, St. Louis
- ☐☐ Gibsons Steps
- ☑☐ Go up/down a spiral staircase
- ☐☐ Hammetschwand Lift, Bürgenstock, Switzerland
- ☐☐ Hopscotch Stairs in Sydney, Australia that light up when walking up or down
- ☐☐ Lourve Elevator
- ☐☐ Luxor Hotel Inclined Elevator, Las Vegas
- ☐☐ Maritime Museum Birdcage Elevator, Victoria, British Columbia, Canada
- ☐☐ Oregon City Municipal Elevator
- ☐☐ Paternoster Elevator, Europe and Scandinavia
- ☐☐ Rising Tide Elevator, Oasis of the Seas ocean liner
- ☐☐ Santa Justa Lift, Lisbon, Portugal
- ☐☐ Sky Tower Elevator, Auckland, New Zealand

- ☐☐ Spiral Staircase in Mahabat Maqbara, India
- ☐☐ Stairs to Samrat Yantra, Jantar Mantar, India
- ☐☐ Stairway to Heaven, Iceland
- ☑☐ Steps to Barrenjoey Lighthouse
- ☐☐ Strepy-Theiu Boatlift, Le Roelux, Belgium
- ☐☐ The Bailong Elevator, also known as the Hundred Dragons Elevators, whisks tourists up the side of a massive sandstone column in a mountain range in China's Hunan Province
- ☐☐ The deepest step well in the world
- ☐☐ Trampe Bicycle Lift, Trondheim, Norway
- ☐☐ Umeda Hankyu Building Elevator, Osaka, Japan

My Inspirational Accomplishments

"One way to keep momentum going is to have constantly greater goals."

Michael Korda

Enjoy your lives. If someone has done it before it is achievable. If someone dreams of something take the leap of faith and give it a go. Anything life offers is an opportunity to discover yourself and learn new, interesting things. There are millions of steps you can take in your life but no matter where you look, where you're headed, or what path you choose, your journey will always start with one simple step. Put one foot in front of the next and never give up living your lives. Here are a few things that my journey has involved so far, and I look forward to doing many more things in the future. It's just a small taste of my lifestyle I wish to live. You would be amazed at how opportunity comes your way if you just open your eyes.

One of my biggest accomplishments was to be published in the *Sydney Morning Herald* and the local paper, *Blacktown Sun*, in the lead-up for The Sun Run in Manly. My story was told of weight loss, giving up the bad habits in life, enjoying my life as a bucket lister and completing some of my biggest challenges and goals in life, including a massive weight loss of over 60 kg thus far. *Sydney Morning Herald* - January 19th 2014 - Inspirational Article of Changing My Life.

Another memorable moment in my life was when I gave up the soft drinks – I saved the $200 a week that I used to spend on the 30-40 litres a week I was drinking. I saved the money up for two years towards a nice holiday to England, Scotland and France for myself. It was an amazing trip of a lifetime and one I will never forget. The first ever international trip for myself away from the comfort of my parents, out seeking the world for myself and I enjoyed every moment of it. I admit it was scary at first, taking that giant step into the big world, but we need to take the plunge to enjoy our lives and I am so glad I could enjoy this journey.

It started with landing in Scotland and doing a seven-day, six-night haunted castle self-drive tour. The castles were amazing and we got the chance to sleep in two of them, Airth Castle and Tullock Castle. We were also able to explore a few others: Linlithgow Palace, Edinburgh Castle, Glamis Castle, Cawdor Castle, Stirling Castle, Dunrobbin Castle and the Urquhart Castle with the view of Loch Ness. We even explored a few that weren't part of the tour, way up top of Scotland in the beautiful Isle of Skye, Armadale Castle Ruins, Eilean Donan Castle and Dunvegan Castle. There were also many marvellous mountain tops – one of the most famous being Ben Nevis. I also visited the famous tower of William Wallace monument where I climbed over 250 steps to the top for a wonderful view of Scotland's surroundings. I also got to view Falkirk Wheel and learn about its process of lowering boats from the canel. I challenged myself in Edinburgh and climbed up the top of the mountain to see Arthur's Chair – a stunning view of all Edinburgh. I even got to see a unique type of house built near Airth Castle: it's known as the Pineapple House and gardens.

I got the chance to meet my dad's sister in Scotland before going south to Yorkshire. In Yorkshire we stayed with Dad's brother and wife for four days. They showed me around to all my relatives who hadn't seen me since I was seven years old, so they noticed the change a lot. I was happy to meet them all and learn about my family history, for my family tree goes back as far as seven generations for our family now. We also got to view the wonderful stone walling work that my dad's brother does all through the Yorkshire dales. There was a great country feel as we went for a drive through the dales. On the way back we got to see the white house made from limestone many years ago, and the Abbey of Rivaelx, which was founded in 1132. It was built to be the first Cistercian outpost in the North – an abbey from which the White Monks could reform and colonise northern England and Scotland.

Leaving after a short time with family, we headed further south exploring things along the way. I got to the hotel in London where I dropped my bags at the Best Western at Earl's Court and I dropped the hire car at Victoria station. I had three big days, a very tiring experience, but I wanted to explore as much as I could while over there. Who knows next time you will get to go somewhere? A few things that I wanted to do, but didn't have time, were the Roman baths, the Lost Gardens of Heligan, St. Austell, Cornwall, and Windsor Castle. There was a lot I got the chance to see: I did the majestic London tour, an 11-hour tour of London which included royalty things, crown jewels, Tower of London. While at the Tower of London, we got a chance to see the spectacle of the bridge opening, Big Ben, Westminster Abbey, Trafalgar Square, a drive past Kensington Palace and even the Changing of the Guard and horse guards, then off to Canterbury Cathedral. After the long day, we went on a river cruise down the Thames River. The second day was a 10-hour tour of Stone Henge, Hampton Court Palace "Henry the 8th," and Oxford University. The third day was a 10-hour tour of Leeds Castle, White Cliffs of Dover and St. Paul's Cathedral. I also got the chance to see a few other things: there was a ride on the London Eye, the famous shard from a distance, the red doubl-decker buses and red telephone boxes known to be unique to England, even a drive past the parliament 10 Downing Street. I was busy and pretty much on the go every day to fit as much in as possible, but I don't regret one bit of anything we did see. I loved the experience.

After getting my luggage together, I had to make my way into the international terminal to the Eurostar, first class going to Paris, France. It was under the England channel in a tunnel and a unique experience with very comfortable seating and great service from staff on board the train always willing to help. When finally getting to the international terminal in Paris, I must admit, I felt lost a little bit for the first time. I did not not know much of the French language other than the basics to get me by. But knowing the basics helped out a lot, along with hand gestures, to get me where I needed to go. The things you can identify with other cultures I soon realised. I ended up finding a security guard who spoke English and he helped me understand how the train systems worked, and from then on I was fine working out where I had to go. It was even easier after we got our things to the motel and I went to pick up the Paris pass, which had our train tickets for the three days there. By this time I was becoming really tired and exhausted by my long journey, but one I will always remember: my first trip away together internationally.

The next day I woke up I had to make my way to my bus tours, where I noticed a wonderful statue. Reading the name of it I recognised straight away: Jeanne D Arc. It was my birthday, this day, and we had a lot of things to do. We did a tour around the Louvre and got to see the most known pieces of art in the world: the Mona Lisa and Venus de Milo, two of my most favourite art works. We then toured Versailles Palace, a massive mansion that could barely fit into my landscape lenses. Other tours I did while over in Paris was a Seine River cruise under all the bridges of Paris, and driving on the bus through the famous roundabout where no one stops and just powers through and hopes for the best. Crazy the way they drive with no fear over there, occasionally bumping into each other and bumping into one another to park vehicles. I got to see the Eiffel Tower and it had been lit up by night. There was a huge queue to see the catacombs, an ancient tomb beneath the city. It was a hard place to find, but finally got there with a map in hand after viewing the cathedral of Notre Dame and Archaelogical crypt of Notre Dame. During one of the bus tours I came across the mini Statue of Liberty close by the Eiffel Tower.

After visiting Scotland, England and France, I missed this journey and sought out ways I could take it with me, a part of the journey. Of course, there are plenty of pictures taken in my travels and many days of happiness to remember, but when I came home I did some research of the places I had visited. I found a way I could be a part of the places I had visited without being there all the time. The opportunity came up in a webpage where I could become A Lord of Glencoe in Scotland. So I bought a piece of land in Glencoe and bought an interesting shield – if you spend over a certain amount they plant a tree on your land in honour of restoring the land and forest areas. There is also an opportunity to become a Laird or Lady for anyone interested.

Just recently I have undergone a trip of self-discovery with a solo travel vacation to Melbourne, Australia. I had never been anywhere by myself and now I can say I have. It was definitely a struggle at first, because growing up with a sister and four brothers and Mum and Dad, I never personally had to deal with any organisation or accommodation, travelling car or public transport in the area. I am discovering a lot of new things. Yes, I travelled to England, France and Scotland, but I had my beautiful fiancé to help me realise it's not all that stressful. You get a little nervous at first discovering new things, but it develops you into a stronger person and you become more wiser in life's situations. I started out my journey travelling down from Sydney and stopped at Albury Quest Inn for the night. The next day I set out to visit Mansfield Zoo where I had a few animal encounters, bonding with them by feeding them pellets and ticked off my list the ostrich, deer and ducks. There were many others – kangaroos, bison and camels – but I was unable to feed those.

My second day was just as busy as the first. I got the chance to walk around the city of Melbourne with over 30kms walked in the day and many experiences that I gladly took away from this city with me. I started by paying my respects at the Shrine of Remembrance in St. Kilda, then continued with a beautiful walk through the Royal Botanical Gardens. I then went to Treasury Gardens and off to Fitzroy Gardens where I paid a visit to Cook's Cottage, the fairy tree and a model township. Then on to the MCG Museum and Tout – and this was just the beginning of my day. I then came across a tour group and decided to do a three-park tour where I had the chance to see Churchill Island and its farm with sheep shearing and sheep dog round up, amongst other farm activities. I then headed to Koala Conservation and got close up with koalas less than a metre from us, before heading for a night to Nobbies

Hill and penguin parade. It was incredible; in the short time there were over 13 groups of at least 200 little penguins. It was a wonderful experience that I would suggest to anyone. The next day I explored Sea Life Aquarium and Immigration Museum before heading on to my seminar.

While enjoying moments throughout Melbourne and discovering myself things I thought were unreachable, I finally realised I took the leap of faith into my new life and was enjoying it. I experienced Travis Bell's Seminar Experience, was able to abseil forward down a building of seven stories in height, known as Rap Jumping, while discovering what things I am grateful for in my life and the person I am developing myself into. With day one over, I was looking forward to the next three days of the bucket list experience. Day 2-4, we learned a lot about self-discovery and hopped outside our comfort zones. This included free hug signs in the busy station of Melbourne and myself doing public speaking in front of the class to overcome a fear. The following three days were to various zoos around Melbourne. At Healesville Sanctuary I had animal encounters with a few animals including the platypus and the dingo. I finished up the day with the edge experience on top of Eureka Tower overlooking a beautiful sunset and Werribee Zoo. During the next day, I was able to have a photo taken with an African Serval Cat. I took a safari tour and, in the evening, experienced the Melbourne Star. Next followed the third day of animal experience going to Moonlight Sanctuary where I experienced keeper for a day and a private night tour of the zoo. I experienced animal encounters with many animals, including a lot I needed to tick off my list: Tawny Frogmouth, Barn Owl, Sugar Glider, Spot-tailed Quoll, Lorikeets and many species of reptiles. The week in Melbourne had been a busy one still more with upcoming days of excitement. The following day I hopped on a tour bus to see Sovereign Hill Historic Town with Gold Discovery and Gold Museum.

I joined Raw Travels in an experience of a lifetime walking the Great Ocean Road and a unique experience of being able to sleep inside a light station. I had the chance to tour through a lighthouse and see it turn around and light up by night, truly amazing. The walk allowed many challenges for us all to face including soft sand, up hills, rock faces, steps, bush lands and much more. I would say I recommend anyone willing to give this experience a go to do so. The Great Ocean Road bypasses all the beauty and heritage areas of the walk, and you miss out a lot if you don't walk. It allows you to see the history behind the coast line, the unique landscapes and the view is sensational. Wherever you go on the walk there is another beautiful view just around the corner. Finishing off the walk is the most beautiful landscape of all: The Twelve Apostles.

I love to enjoy my life. From creative skills to learning new things every day, an adventurous lifestyle that I strive to achieve is to experience as many goals as I can and take on any opportunities that present themselves to me. I prefer to say yes to an opportunity than say no, I'm not interested in that. Just give anything a go, because you never know, you may just enjoy something if you just give it a chance. I have done many interesting things and every time I lose weight a bit, I can achieve certain goals that are weight restrictions. For example, when I got under 150kg, myself and one of my work colleagues gave Jet packing a go. It was an awesome experience where you fly over the water with water hydro jet packs attached to your back. We only did 15 minutes, but it was an experience worth giving a go as it will challenge your ability to coordinate controls at the same time as enjoying something not everyone in the world has had the opportunity to do. Just think to yourself while you're out there doing something with your life, there are millions of other people wasting their days away sitting down on the couch and doing nothing to change. It's never too late to start your own journey, anything in life is an experience. Just remember, the more we do in life the more you can tell others how much life can be fun if we just change negative habits and seek out bigger and brighter things. Anything in life is achievable. If someone else can do it, we can as well. If you know someone else who has done it, strive to do it better than they have. It's the human body's goal in life to be known, and to leave an inspirational message, a legacy, behind before they die. A lot of us live our life with no message left behind and no knowledge of any great achievements – just lived a life to a certain age. But people like myself aim to make a change not only for ourselves but for as many people out there in the world that we can help make an impact upon. Why don't you join us today in the message of enjoying your lives and try everything you can at least once?

If you would like to see more pictures and follow my experience, feel free to add me on any of my social media places. I like to hear people's stories and those who I inspire to change their lives for the better. Please feel free to leave me messages and I will respond to them the best I can. Remember, enjoy your lives and share it with others, it's the best way to get others to enjoy their life as well. Seeing you experience something makes people realise the journey you travel can be possible. I have been in the lowest places, but I have changed my life for the better. Anything is possible if you just change your mindset. Remember – never regret anything you do in your life because in the end, it makes you who you are. The story is endless and every adventure in life brings another thing to add to your list; one challenge opens your eyes to others,. Keep looking forward and trying new things every chance you get. Don't ever let your challenges get on top of you because you need to overcome the challenge – get on top of the challenges, overcome fears, conquer goals, enjoy life to the fullest so that in the end the top thing on your bucket list ticked completed will be LIFE. The Journey Continues . . .

Follow Me On My Journey

Facebook - Lance Garbutt

Facebook Fan Page - MY NEVER ENDING JOURNEY OF LIFE

Pinterest - http://www.pinterest.com/garb1985/

Twitter - @Lance_Garbutt

Youtube - https://plus.google.com/u/0/107244227601723501122/posts

My Webpage Thru Wix.com - http://lanceg6.wix.com/my-journey

My Personal Website – www.neverendingjourneyoflife.com.au

Acknowledgments

I would like to acknowledge and thank my publisher, Emily Gowor, and her team for all their hard work bringing my book to life – especially Rhi Butler for her ongoing support and helping with the understanding of how to develop my book.

I would like to thank all the people who have come into my life and been a part of my journey – from friends to workmates to everyone who has been even the smallest part. By hearing others' stories and developing my own journey, you have been my inspiration. I also would love to thank everyone behind each photo for allowing me to use such beautiful photos taken along my journey that have made my book complete – especially for one of the hardest things I have completed, my ultra-marathon photos by Stefica Key.

I would like to thank my family for all their support in helping me have my story told and being there for someone to ask questions when needed. I would like to thank the Manly Runners Group for the drive behind my running. The inspiration they gave me was amazing and helped me conquer some powerful goals – such as the 10km soft sand beach running I never knew I had in myself. Lastly, a big thank you to Sebastian Terry and Travis Bell for their inspiration behind my bucket list journey to enjoy life and live every moment of it.

About the Author

Lance Garbutt is the business owner of *Never Ending Journey of Life,* a professional speaker and first time author. Aiming to help millions of people around the world, Lance shares the powerful message of how important it is to overcome bad eating and drinking habits and create a better life. Lance has become an inspiration to many as he tells his story wherever he goes and leaves people in awe at what he has achieved so far, including an ultra-marathon status, being published in the Blacktown Sun and the Sydney Morning Herald, and writing his book, *My Never Ending Journey of Life* under the supervision of Emily Gowor, founder of Gowor International Publishing.

Lance's inspiration comes from the motto he lives by which is featured on his unique branded T-shirts – "Motivation, Inspiration, Believe, Leadership, Discover, Dream, and above all, Never Give UP!!" – an inspiration which has driven him to create an extraordinary bucket list with over 9000 items on it. A mentor and leader that other people can look to in order to achieve their dreams, Lance inspires people globally to overcome their fears, fulfill their dreams and live a better life. Lance's philosophy? Life is short, so make it count. Join Lance on his journey to be inspired and live a bucket list lifestyle.

To book Lance Garbutt for a public speaking engagement or book signing, email Lance on Lanceg6@bigpond.com or connect with him via the Facebook page "My Never Ending Journey of Life."

Your Bucket List

- [ ] _____
- [ ] _____
- [ ] _____
- [ ] _____
- [ ] _____
- [ ] _____
- [ ] _____
- [ ] _____
- [ ] _____
- [ ] _____
- [ ] _____
- [ ] _____
- [ ] _____
- [ ] _____
- [ ] _____
- [ ] _____
- [ ] _____
- [ ] _____
- [ ] _____

- ☐ _____
- ☐ _____
- ☐ _____
- ☐ _____
- ☐ _____
- ☐ _____
- ☐ _____
- ☐ _____
- ☐ _____
- ☐ _____
- ☐ _____
- ☐ _____
- ☐ _____
- ☐ _____
- ☐ _____
- ☐ _____
- ☐ _____
- ☐ _____
- ☐ _____
- ☐ _____
- ☐ _____
- ☐ _____

www.ingramcontent.com/pod-product-compliance
Lightning Source LLC
Chambersburg PA
CBHW070556300426
44113CB00010B/1275